THE GLOBAL POLITICAL ECONOMY
OF SEX

THE GLOBAL POLITICAL ECONOMY OF SEX: DESIRE, VIOLENCE, AND INSECURITY IN MEDITERRANEAN NATION STATES

Anna M. Agathangelou

First published in hardcover in 2004 by
PALGRAVE MACMILLAN™
175 Fifth Avenue, New York, N.Y. 10010 and
Houndmills, Basingstoke, Hampshire, England RG21 6XS
Companies and representatives throughout the world

PALGRAVE MACMILLAN is the global academic imprint of the Palgrave Macmillan division of St. Martin's Press, LLC and of Palgrave Macmillan Ltd. Macmillan® is a registered trademark in the United States, United Kingdom and other countries. Palgrave is a registered trademark in the European Union and other countries.

ISBN-13: 978–1–4039–7586–7 paperback
ISBN-10: 1–4039–7586–8 paperback
ISBN-13: 978–0–312–29466–3 hardcover
ISBN-10: 0–312–29466–2 hardcover

Library of Congress Cataloging-in-Publication Data

Agathangelou, Anna M.
    The global political economy of sex : desire, violence, and insecurity in Mediterranean nation states / Anna M. Agathangelou.
        p. cm.
    Includes bibliographical references and index.
    ISBN-13: 978–1–4039–7586–7 pbk; ISBN-10: 1–4039–7586–8 pbk
        1. Women immigrants—Mediterranean Region—Social conditions.
    2. Women immigrants—Mediterranean Region—Economic conditions.
    3. Minority women—Mediterranean Region—Economic conditions.
    4. Sex-oriented businesses—Mediterranean Region. 5. Sexual division of labor—Mediterranean Region. 6. Mediterranean Region—Economic conditions. I. Title.

HQ1725.7.A43 2004
305.48'96912—dc22   2003065562

A catalogue record for this book is available from the British Library.

Design by Newgen Imaging Systems (P) Ltd., Chennai, India.

First PALGRAVE MACMILLAN paperback edition: September 2006

10 9 8 7 6 5 4 3 2 1

Printed in the United States of America.

Transferred to digital printing in 2006.

To my cousin Margarita (1957–2004) a
comrade in struggle
and to
L.H.M. Ling
A friend, comrade, and mentor

CONTENTS

PREFACE

Reproduction is a productive economy. The desire industries substantiate this idea. While relegated to shadow economies they continually remind us that the agents of private property constitute mirages for us such as division of politics and economics, national and transnational borders, migrant and nonmigrant. Their interest is first and foremost profit and exploitation of surplus-value. This book also makes visible the complicity of the state in production relations and in the exploitation of migrant sex and domestic work. Its role is an integral part in the racialized gendered class struggles in the desire industries. The questions I ask include the following: How do peripheral economic states participate in the facilitation of the expropriation of racialized female labor in the desire industries? For what purpose? In examining various feminist and international political economy theories, I came to find that analyses of the peripheral economic state's role in the sale and purchase of labor, if done at all, often obscured the major connections between the expropriation of racialized reproductive labor, or sex and domestic work, and the relations to gender, sexuality, race, desire, and identity.

My work with non-governmental organizations (NGOs) in Cyprus and other countries such as the Hands Across the Divide, Global Change Institute and Coalition Against Human Trafficking, Houston, Texas has shown how some women and men are free to desire and exploit the labor of women and men as a sign of freedom whereas migrant women who sell it are just trying to survive in a world economy that depends on accumulation of profits and wealth. Through the many conversations with the women in these organizations as well as the women and men I interviewed in the desire industries, I came to develop my ideas, and I asked another question: How do our explanations obscure or make the transformation of our social relations possible? The many theories in International Political Economy (IPE) and feminism seem to obscure rather than shed light on the ways gender relations, sexuality, desire, constitution of people's personhoods are part and parcel of issues like labor, exploitation,

x PREFACE

and projection of hegemonic power. Moreover, my conversations with sex and domestic workers brought to light that globalization and the intensified desire industries are a process of rearticulating relations among personal, the local, the institutional, and the world economy. The struggles and contestations of working-class women and men, activist groups, NGOs and grassroots organizations are crucial in the rearticulation of an alternative vision to the one put forward to us by private powers, understood in terms of ownership, control and management of property, and command over the labor and the bodies of the majority of the world. At this historical moment, when "private" powers are not "democratically accountable," and draw extensively on sexist and racist institutions, policies, and practices to sustain themselves and limit possibilities for communal self-determination, it behooves feminist and international political economists to engage these local, national, and transnational phenomena from a Marxist-feminist historical materialist framework. Thus, I am writing this book to reclaim the critical knowledges of historical materialism for feminism and IPE and also to contribute toward reviving a method and a praxis for a feminism that contributes to building effective collective struggle for the emancipation of all people: working-class women and men, gays, lesbians, transgender, and non white peoples.

ACKNOWLEDGMENTS

This book would not have been possible without the participation of the many sex and domestic workers, their employers, immigration officers, and police officers in Cyprus, Greece, and Turkey. Many thanks to them.

I thank the publishers who have given me permission to publish part of my work: Anna M. Agathangelou and L. H. M. Ling "Power, Borders, Security, Wealth: Lessons of Violence and Desire from September 11," *International Studies Quarterly*, Vol. 48, no. 3 (September 2004): 517–538 (Blackwell Publishing).

Anna M. Agathangelou. "Sexing Democracy" in International Relations: Migrant Sex and Domestic Workers in Cyprus, Greece, and Turkey." In. G. Chowdhry and S. Nair (eds.), *Power, Postcolonialism and International Relations: Reading Race, Gender and Class* (New York: Routledge, 2002), pp. 142–169.

Deep appreciation is extended to those who have read this manuscript and provided me with excellent feedback: Delia Aguilar, Ann-Cooper Albright, Timothy Emmert, Kyle D. Killian, L.H.M. Ling, Tom Newlin, Laura Parisi, and Sonita Sarker, my editor David Pervin, Ian Steinberg, and Mukesh V.S. I may have not followed up on every suggestion, but their critiques have enriched this manuscript and my work more than they can imagine.

I am grateful to many in the community of feminists, activists, and scholars who have contributed to my development as a writer/scholar/teacher/person: Kristi Andersen, Apostolos Apostolou, Matt Bonham, Christine Chin, Geeta Chowdhry, Margot Clark, Constantina Constantinou, Gavan Duffy, Georgette Duncan, Teresa Ebert, Cynthia Enloe, Sue Gooden, Phyllis Gorfain, Maria Hajipavlou, Ben Joffe-Walte, Sarah Kaiksow, Mustapha Kamal, Marianne Marchard, Francesco Melfi, Chandra Talpade Mohanty, Donald Morton, Dianne Murphy, Sheila Nair, Nicos Peristianis, Randolph B. Persaud, Jindy Pettman, Shirin Rai, Marissa Ramirez, Mark Rupert, Simona Sharoni, V.S. Spike, Mari Spira, George Tolmas, Phryni Yiakoumetti, and a very very special thanks to the library staff at the University of Houston Clear-Lake and more specifically the Interlibrary loan staff, and Chris Cecot who very carefully prepared the index.

My family has sustained me and made it possible for me to write this text. My mother and father, whose own working class life-struggles inform the body of my research and teaching; my brother Christakis, my sisters Maria and Rita, nephews and nieces Sofronis, Artemis, Mikaella, Mihalis, Yiorgos, Angelos, Alexia, my cousin Chris and my aunt Christalla, sister-in-law Panayiota, and brother-in-law Haris, my cousins Maria, Omiros, Elli, Chryso, and Yiorgos who continue to challenge me to greater clarity and groundedness through their support; my second set of parents, David Lawrence Killian and Sallie Ann Killian for their unwavering affection and presence in my life.

To my partner in life, Kyle D. Killian, I give very special thanks. His unwavering comradeship, friendship, love, and support for the last 17 years has lifted me to greater heights and helped me express my thoughts, feelings, and experiences in the written word. In the roles of colleague and editor, he is there 24/7 and makes all the difference. My two sons, Mikael Lawrence and Aleksi Christos, bring joy and excitement to my life. I thank them for always being there to keep the struggle in perspective, and demonstrating that without collective solidarity and revolutionary internationalism, the feminist vision of emancipation remains only a dream.

CHAPTER 1

SEX AND DOMESTIC WORK IN THE
PERIPHERY: FENCED-OFF
ECONOMIES OF DESIRE

Vicky is a 35-year-old Filipina who works 10-hour days for Eleni, a 50-ish judge in Greece. Vicky serves as maid, confidante, and masseuse for Eleni who confides that her husband wants sex and massages all the time from other women. Marianne, a 28-year-old Russian, has worked in Greece's cabarets on and off for the last two years. Marianne could not support her ten-year-old child, living back in Russia, on $30 per month as a teacher. She migrated to Greece because "I thought I'd be working in a bar serving drinks, not selling sex." Svetlana echoed a similar sentiment: "I thought I'd be working in a bakery and here I am selling myself." A jobless Russian woman laments:

> I left school with distinction, went to a top-class institute, and this is what happens! I've been on six-month courses, I even did English for six months—technical translation—I've been to lots of institutes, and look at me! It's incredibly upsetting to me, and a catastrophe for the country. (Bridger et al., 1996: 161)

These women, and countless others, narrate similar stories. As this book demonstrates, migrant women are caught in a matrix of neoliberal global restructuring where they become targets of exploitation and violence and objects of desire for the facilitation of the status and power of the middle and upper classes (Anderson, 2000). Peripheral states, such as Sri Lanka, Myanmar, Rumania, Russia, and Belarus, facilitate the migration of female domestics and sex workers to Cyprus, Greece, and Turkey and mediate the expropriation of the surplus-value of their labor. The migrant female workers "are themselves means of production" (Aguilar, 2002: 11). They also participate in "the physical, cultural and ideological production of human beings" (Anderson, 2000: 13) in racialized, classed, and gendered ways. This production role of the state is important in that it produces the substance as well as an idea of gendered and raced underclass. In addition, these women are often targeted as one of the racialized, sexualized threats to nation-states' "security" and to a nationalist self. Typically, core economic states like Germany, France, and the United Kingdom in the European Union (EU) are able to shift the "dirty work" of capital and national (in)security onto their weaker, peripheral counterparts. Turkey now serves, for example, as a "security buffer zone" or ethnic gatekeeper for the EU. Herein lies the problem. The state's development/security double punch forecloses political space for female migrant workers' creating solidarity with the local working-class; it also disables the state from working toward substantive democracy. I define substantive democracy as: (1) the direct feminist public critique of the illegitimate use of the people's resources and the colonizing private power of the social relations of production and its contingent institutions such as the market and the state to sustain their right to own property, the right to exploit and exert undue influence on women, the working-class, gays, lesbians, transgender, and nonwhite peoples, (2) direct intervention to heighten the contradictions that emerge in a classed heterosexual, gendered and racialized order of social relations of production; through these public interventions, women, the working-class, gays, lesbians, and transgender and nonwhite peoples are able to fashion strong political bonds as they move to transform the structures that daily exploit them and subvert their self-determination and safety, and (3) simultaneously linking critique with cultural feminist production toward producing a political culture of self-determined people who enact a social movement with a social ontology free of necessity, fear, and lack of safety.

Conventional studies tend to depict migrant women as an issue that concerns the individual household, and, possibly, the local economy. Rarely do they focus on the complicity of the state, including those on the periphery of the world economy, in facilitating the exploitation of women's reproductive labor by its propertied class, specifically, and for transnational bourgeois capitalist interests, generally. This state intervention, despite being "strategic and necessary in the capitalist economy," is still directed by "the general coordinates of the reproduction of capital" (Poulatzas, 1973: 181). Through immigration laws and employment contracts, the peripheral economic state responds to capital's demands and requirements without capital's direct involvement, which, in turn, could endanger itself by deepening its contradictions (Bhattacharjee, 1997: 319). By reproductive labor, I mean an international sexual division of labor in which women's social and economic contributions are exploited, commodified, and sold for cheap wages. It involves the purchase and sale of labor power, and the very self of the worker as a commodity (e.g., sexual desire, nurturance/care-giving) and the employer's power to command this labor. Income-rich states—even those considered peripheral in the global economy—buy transnationally the reproductive labor of women "associated with a wife's traditional role—child care, homemaking, and sex" (Ehrenreich and Hochschild, 2002: 3).[1] The purchase and sale of this labor by upper and middle-class consumer-citizens requires no mutual obligations and no substantive relationships with the sex and domestic workers. It just requires cash (Anderson, 2000: 112). Because of their position in the international division of labor, Cyprus, Greece, and Turkey depend on services rather than heavy industry to generate their profits. For these states, remaining competitive requires the ability to access freely labor and markets that generate profits; hence, they closely follow the rules of the neoliberal capitalist restructuring economy. They reorganize their social relations in such a way that enables capital to position itself in an advantageous position in relation to labor, which in turn, sustains the asymmetries created by capital relations. On the one hand, the state reproduces the racialized class asymmetries while defining "the juridical conditions of private property, contract, and exchange" (Rupert, 1995: 22). It makes possible the constitution of the powers of the economic sphere and the power of the ruling and owning-class within it; on the other, such relations foment conflict and struggle between classes and citizens and noncitizens within and across its borders. Through the immigration policies, the state recreates a capitalist worldview in which some can and will exploit the surplus-value labor of the many because they have become the owners of the means of production either through colonization or other means. The state's design and implementation of employment contracts and laws, and its mediation and facilitation of labor markets become the means through which the propertied class extracts the surplus-value of labor of the migrant female workers as well as reconstitutes its power within the European regional capital regime. Similarly to the core economic state, the peripheral economic state "crafts its identity" according to the desires and demands of capital, and in turn, attempts to "privatize the nation" to respond to the interests of the very few owning-classes within its borders. However, the state is a site of racialized, gendered and class struggles, and once understood as such, the space opens for us to call into question the reproduction of the separation of politics and economics and the national–transnational boundaries. In turn, the state sustains the power in the hands of this class. The peripheral state may facilitate the "whitening" of this class by making possible the further capitalist control over the labor process through the import and exploitation of reproductive female migrant surplus value.

To ensure the economic and political power of its owning-classes and the multinational corporations, the peripheral economic state pushes to "whiten" itself or "rescue the [white] elements that it imagines itself to possess" (Bhattacharjee, 1997: 318) by actively facilitating the drawing and exploiting of the reproductive labor of sex and domestic workers from lower-income generating states. By obfuscating the social relations of economic and political power, the higher-income generating peripheral state draws upon the global circulating fantasies of having "white but not quite" servants for sex and domestic work as a method of enacting whiteness. Simultaneously, the owning-class can exploit the surplus-value of racialized female workers and reproduce itself as "white." "White but not quite" here refers to the peripheral economic states whose upper and middle-classes can never be "white" because race is also about class. Even when the upper and middle-classes can never occupy the same economic and political power position within the upper echelons of the world economy like their European counterparts, they still draw actively upon the strategies of capital to reap profits as well as reconstitute themselves as bourgeois subjects. In turn, these peripheral economic bourgeois subjects act as racialized economic and sexual bourgeoisie. They are, as Matsuda said, the "wannabes" of capitalism (Matsuda, 1996: 150) from the restructurings of the capitalist economy. Simultaneously, the term "white but not quite" reproductive workers refer to the sex workers who possess white skin and yet economically are not "white." These women may possess the bodies that upper and middle-classes in "white but not quite" peripheral states desire so that they may enact whiteness; however, their subordinate position economically as well as politically makes them "white but not quite" in terms of gendered class (i.e., they may be considered stateless in the sense that their states sell their labor and their bodies at fire prices in order to generate profits for its propertied and middle-class).

This process of "whitening" is racism and it is a strategy of exploitation and violence by capital: subordination of the sex and domestic workers' labor to production for profit. Turning the peripheral sites into sites of desire, capital justifies unequal wages within the working-class (i.e., migrant workers' wages are much lower than the local working-class). In a world of wage labor and capital culturalizing, social relations conceal the political economy of raced sex that depends on the exploitation of the majority (migrant and nonimmigrant) by those who own private property. It also conceals the idea that Greeks, Turks, and Cypriots can never become "white," that is, the hegemonic leadership of capital relations and, therefore, contradictions within the owning-class are also contained. They can become the racialized sexed bourgeoisie. As Matsuda (1996: 150) asks, "If white, as it has been historically, is the top of the racial hierarchy in (the world), and black, historically, is the bottom, will yellow assume the place of the racial middle?" Following Matsuda's logic I argue that the racialized sex middle-class subjects in Cyprus, Greece, and Turkey are the racial bourgeoisie and end up supporting an heterosexual white militaristic supremacy in the world in order to protect their interests. The position that the peripheral economic state and migrant female workers occupy in the social relations of production and global division of labor informs what positions they are economically compelled to take and hold within a restructured economy. For example, the peripheral economic state's position in the world economy compels it to participate extensively in the desire industries to generate profits. Similarly, sex and domestic migrant workers are forced to do reproductive labor for societies that are "white but not quite" because of their conditions. They find themselves working for male and female employers who may be well-paid professionals.

Domestic workers find themselves enabling their employers' middle-class desire of "having it all"—a full-time career, happy and healthy children and spouse, and a well-kept household. Sex workers make possible their clients' sexual and romantic desires. As Anderson (2004, 2000) argues, the labor of sex and domestic workers is expropriated for its surplus-value to generate profits for a social capitalist structure whose reproduction depends on the strategies of exploitation, violence, and accumulation of profits as well as the social reproduction of power relations within those structures. Historically, men comprised the vast majority of migrant laborers. Today, women comprise almost 50 percent of the world's 120 million migrants, seeking reproductive work in the nearest comparatively rich country.

Peripheral economic states like Cyprus, Greece, and Turkey increasingly orient their societies to the pleasures of the middle-class consumer as defined by nearby core economies like Germany, France, and the United Kingdom. They argue for a middle-class way of life where the freedom to consume "things" and "people" is central to the vision of the emerging, transnational neoliberal state, which is a mainstay for globalization.

As capital wants to assure its competitive self-expansion through the achievement of a higher rate of surplus-value, it moves to access cheap labor the world over. The state aids this process so that capital's search for competitive rates of profit through access to cheap labor becomes simpler. Globalization begins with the separation of the producers from the means of production, which estranges and alienates the worker from her "producing activity" (Marx, 1988: 73). These processes of estrangement and alienation make possible the subjection of the female worker to exploitation and violence by the owning-class. In turn, a new emerging state institution emerges as a result of the extension of the capital–wage labor relation on a transnational level to mediate the antagonisms and facilitate the interests of the owners of the means of production (Sahay, 2001: 6–7).

This freedom, or privilege, incites the middle-class consumer, both male and female, to buy cheap reproductive labor as a channel to becoming part of the white bourgeoise. "Whiteness" becomes associated with satiating one's sexual and other emotional pleasures anytime, anywhere, without the drudgery of household responsibilities: cleaning, cooking, taking care of children and the elderly and obscures the globalization racialized and gendered capital–wage relation. Indeed, desire industries constitute one of the fastest growing employment sectors for working-class migrant women. Donna Hughes (2000) estimates that a lucrative "shadow market" of desire industries generates between 7 and 12 billion dollars annually. The problem arises when peripheral economic states compound the exploitation of sex and domestic workers by drawing upon semantic regimes of violence and framing migrant women, like Marianne and Vicky, as an economic and cultural threat within their borders. The exploitation and domination of the female migrant worker by the peripheral state and those in the middle- and upper-class are dialectically linked. Middle- and upper-class propertied employers in an international division of labor privately appropriate the labor of female migrant working-classes, which, in turn, enables them to dominate them. These relations are ridden with struggle and subversions.

Both core and peripheral economic states traverse the same imperial capitalist geography that subordinates women and men's labor to private property. The context of world economy is characterized by the uneven process both spatially in different geopolitical locations and of divergent positions of various groups of people based on gender, race, class, and sexuality. The peripheral states draw from the same epistemic colonizing frameworks of exploitation, desire, and violence, albeit using different strategies, to exploit sex and domestic workers' labor, all in the name of restructuring their economies despite their peripheral location in the world economy and the international division of labor. Drawing upon the tropes of "national insecurity," global flexibility of gendered labor, and serviceability to invent and constitute their power in the new globalized context, the peripheral states obfuscate the politics of the exploited labor power, and more specifically, the exploitation of women as "collective producers" (Cotter, 2003: 3). In employing such strategies, the peripheral state colludes with capital's desire to accumulate profit and to control the supply of labor-power as well as their rate of exploitation. Moreover, its active participation in the desire industries colludes with capital to underdevelop social reproduction and commodify goods and services such as childcare, socialization, and sexual gratification.

What are the politics of exploitation, violence, and desire under conditions of increasing fragmentation between race, sexuality, gender, and class created by transnational structures of capital? What kinds of sexual cross-border solidarity movements are possible in a transnational context toward a transformative praxis? How is feminism going to be a transformative praxis toward the creation of movements that focus on women's need for material equality and freedom from necessity (Cotter, 2002: 1; Ebert, 1995)? How are these movements to embody sexual freedom, safety, and nonreified pleasures? I seek to address these questions in this book, and I begin with current analyses of the global political economy.

THEORIZING DESIRE IN IR/IPE

To date, no study in international relations (IR) or international political economy (IPE) has examined systematically the social organization and movement of reproductive labor within the world economy, let alone peripheral economic states. Studies of globalization typically focus on the "upper" circuits of capital relations such as increased levels of international trade, the transnationalization of production, financial markets, and commodity cultures. They tend to ignore "lower" circuits of global capital such as the migration of sex and domestic work for profit. In so doing, conventional studies of globalization miss the politics of economic development and accumulation as strategies of recolonization with the serviceability of working-class migrant women as a reserve pool of cheap labor. Specifically, these studies overlook the dialectical relationship of corporate globalization, the market, and the state in trading human beings through sex and domestic work. Put differently, these studies obscure the *global political economy of sex*, that is, the asymmetric sexual division of labor based on racialized sex and the institutionalization of desire with millions of women, primarily, paying the price of such exploitation and violence with their labor and their bodies. Sex here refers to a categorization between men's and women's labor, that is, male (human) and female (natural) (Mies, 1998: 45). My conceptualization of a global political economy of sex differs dramatically from Rubin's in the sense that I understand sex and sexuality as products of material conditions. Rubin, on the other hand, asserts

> the needs which are satisfied by economic activity even in the richest, Marxian sense, do not exhaust fundamental human requirements... [T]he needs of sexuality and procreation must be satisfied as much as the need to eat ...Sex as social product... [requires us] to understand the relations of its production... and forget, for awhile, about food, clothing automobiles, and transistor radios. (Rubin, 1984: 165–166)

Her collapsing of sexuality and nutrition and economic relations silences the materiality or the property relations of the production of sexuality and desire. Her theory seems to have played a leading role in the new theories of desire that substitute cultural and symbolic explanations for material social relations of production. Her theory informs newer theories on their equating needs of food, environmental safety, basic access to health resources with commodified consumer desires of sexuality and automobiles (Ebert, 1996: 47).

Critiquing an inherent masculinism in much of the IR/IPE literature (Pateman, 1996; Peterson, 1996; Enloe, 1989), feminist scholars have brought the role of sex industries to the forefront of policy and scholarly attention (Bulbeck, 1998; Pateman, 1996; Enloe, 1993). Nonetheless, there remains a need to theorize about the linkages of production and social reproduction and the "necessary," *praxis* reproductive labor makes possible (Peterson, 2003, 2002). For instance, how should we analyze prostitution, pornography, and women's trafficking for sex and domestic work, as part of the larger social relations of production and as industries constituted by private owners to generate profits, or as problems of morality? What about the intensification of the exploitation of reproductive labor as a process of corporate globalization? Too often, when considering matters of sexuality and gender, we ignore questions of material conditions within which a society produces its desires and political power. More specifically, we ignore that raced sexualities and gender are historical practices whose development and change are in accordance to the development of forces of production and the conflict with the relations of production (Cotter, 2002: 24). Mainstream analysts do not explain the intensification of "desire industries." Instead, they focus on how working-class migrant women, like Vicky and Marianne, could transfer their reproductive services from poor to peripheral rich-income sites. These analysts argue that labor movements result from transnational wage differentials, which encourage migration-for-employment. Market forces become translated into the social realm (Straubhaar, 1992). As Wood (1982) argues:

> In the neo-classical economic framework...labor moves from places where capital is scarce and where labor is plentiful (hence remuneration to the worker is low) to areas where capital is abundant and where labor is scarce (hence remuneration is high) (300).

According to these theorists, as *homo economicus*, the migrant follows market forces for a better allocation of resources around a given economic space. This "rational economic man" model is largely based on a masculinist, "white," and liberal ideal. Its subject—the professional masculine subject (man or woman)—erases from the view those who exploit female migrant workers' labor as well as other kinds of labor that generate the profits in servicing transnational capital's "rational economic man" through reproductive labor (Chang and Ling, 2000; Mohanty, 1997). The use of violence against sex and domestic workers by the state and other institutions, all in the name of maintaining public order and protecting national security and international interests, becomes invisible. The peripheral economic state uses policing and systematic violation of this labor's rights especially when the bodies of the owning-class are violated in some form. Transnational liberal legalistic theory explains violence as corporeal transgression, that is, the crossing of boundaries relating to personal space (e.g., the employer beats the domestic worker when she discovers jewelry is missing). The doctrine of liberal legalism constructs violence as the violation of the body of one person. Any invasion or physical incursion upon one body from another becomes a criminal offense especially within a context that legally privileges "the [propertied] body perimeters as the defining characteristic of personhood" (Hatty, 2000: 46). These analyses make invisible that violence is more than corporeal experience. It is also the systematic creation of conditions that threaten, neglect, or exploit people's lives and labor for the benefit of very few worldwide out of which these corporeal experiences emerge. The state deflects public attention from the real sources of violence in our societies, and the brutality of an economic system based on profit and inequality, by focusing on the social problems "created" by migrants' arrival (i.e., sex workers arriving in Turkey bring with them drugs and immorality). Moreover, these analyses further marginalize the reasons for this transnational migration-for-employment, that is, reproductive labor's role in the restructuring process of transnational capitalism, capital accumulation, and the social reproduction of inequality and violence.

Mainstream analysts typically exile this racialized feminization of labor to related domains of research, such as women's studies or area-studies. The result is an intellectual segregation of the racialized feminization of labor into a series of discrete, policy problems for "developing" economies "out there," effectively condoning the capitalist system's economic and political power in constituting this racialized feminization worldwide. The real power politics become invisible: the private ownership and control of the means of production provide the owning-class with its capacity to command the surplus labor of those who possess only their labor in the production processes. Moreover, this power depends on the social reproduction of identities along gender, race, sexuality, and class that are directly linked to global inequalities, often resulting in immigration (Agathangelou and Ling, 2003). Other studies explain this transnational phenomenon as a result of women from income-rich countries moving into paid work and therefore needing domestic workers to take over the household work and care-giving for both children and the elderly. According to the International Labor Organization, U.S. women in managerial and professional jobs work more hours than men. Simultaneously, these same states are cutting down on public services and are moving to privatize services such as social welfare. In the process of responding to these changes, income-rich states desire cheap labor from lower-income generating states to keep costs down, especially those of social reproduction, and respond to the demands to buy reproductive services made by their female (and male) citizens who have access to resources and money (Ehrenreich and Hochschild, 2002: 3). Thus, these studies' focus on the state's processing of the cost of social reproduction does not challenge the ways class, gender, race, sexuality, and nation are interwoven into the "desire industries." I take *desire industries* here to mean the neoliberal capitalist relations (e.g., legal and illegal trafficking; conditions of the sale/purchase of this labor; ideologies; products) organized to make possible the exploitation of the surplus-value of reproductive labor (sex and domestic).

The desire of women from lower-income generating states to migrate to escape relative and absolute poverty (Ehrenreich and Hochschild, 2002: 3) stems from this organization by private powers, not just individual motivation. These studies conceal the political economy of sex and desire and who benefits from its organization. States like Cyprus, Greece, and Turkey seek to cement their allegiance to multinational corporations and the global market by redirecting resources and reducing historical concerns for women in transnational capitalism such as exploitation of their labor and not expanding services to meet the needs of their rapidly expanding local female labor force. One way for the peripheral economic states and their propertied classes to "save" resources is through the exploitation of the migrant working-class, commodity production, and exchange with relatively poorer countries. Because of currency devaluation and cuts to health and food subsidy programs due to structural adjustment, poorer countries export women for sex and domestic work. Domestic and sex work promise quick infusions of cash into the household, the family, and the larger community. These feed into ideologies of desire such as: "I am very sexy and I know I can attract any male for cash," "Our fast working women are desired everywhere," "We are Russians and Russian women are queens of sex."[2]

It is not a coincidence that the desire industries are described in the global media mostly as economies staffed by men and women who infiltrate borders illegally to set up such illicit relations (*Economist*, May 8, 1999; *Economist*, February 14, 1998; *Economist*, May 8, 1999). Even documentaries (e.g., *No Experience Necessary*), whose goal is to expose the power relations of these industries, constitute the Eastern European woman as the victim who has to be "saved" by women of the First World both from the greedy pimps of her country and also the Western man of Europe. These constructions silence the close relationship between the formal economies whose organization and traveling occurs easily and legally and those informal economies whose activities are labeled illicit as well as the logic that guides both: "the secret of profit making," that is, the production "of surplus-value" (Marx, 1976).

The IR/IPE literature, in short, neglects a significant portion of the world political economy, that is, the exploitation of surplus labor and commodification of production and reproduction, the intimate social relations between men and women, formal and informal economies, licit and illicit development, hierarchies between states and within states, peripheral and core states. The state, the household, the cabaret, in addition to the market, play a key role in facilitating desire industries and their contingent social relations of production: exploitation of reproductive labor and the hierarchies between "public" and "shadow households," maids and madams, impresarios, sex and domestic workers, migrants and nonmigrants. This book contends that such structural intimacies are affected by, and reflect, larger changes in globalization at different levels: transnational, national, local, and personal. Seeing these connections allows us, in short, to rethink decolonization and produce transformative praxis. This book puts forward a materialist theory of global political economy of sex. This theory shows us the way to develop an emancipatory theory of sex and desire as an understanding of the inseparable dialectical relations of sex, desire, and the material relations of production. A global political economy of sex[3] theoretical approach is a practice for transforming the modern productive relations, which are based on economic exploitation, commodification of all relations, and a social division of labor, sex, and desire. It is the struggle to lay the foundations for a social formation that is not dominated by property relations as a form of substantive democratic freedom. Instead, a global political economy of sex is a struggle to create the conditions for the build-up of a social formation within which people are free and equal to love, have sex, and desire multiple connections that are not exclusive or merely sexual. These relations are built "on the principles of comradeship and solidarity" (Kollontai, 1977: 285) and are guided by love that entails multiple connections with others: an awareness of common interests, intellectual, emotional, sexual, as well as interrelations with others in the development and well-being of the work and the welfare of the collective (Kollontai, 1977: 285).

CONCEPTS AND METHODS

Global Political Economy of Sex: Productive and Reproductive Labor

I propose to analyze the flow of women's reproductive labor from lower-income to higher-income generating peripheries as a result of intensified globalization. A global political economy of sex[4] refers to the sexual division of labor in social relations of production perpetuated by particular practices and pedagogies of race, sex, sexuality, gender, and class (Ebert, 1996). Social relations of production here refers to the racialized and gendered class position of the subject of labor: some own the means of production and have command over the surplus labor of others, and many own only their labor power, and, thus, are exploited (Ebert, 2001; Cotter, 2001; Aguilar, 2002). Following those feminists who argue that domestic labor produces the major commodity central to capitalism, labor power itself (Anderson, 2000; Glenn, 1992; Brenner and Lasslett, 1989), I propose that sex and domestic work together constitute reproductive labor.[5] It is important to recognize that there are differences in the ways domestic and sex workers become hired and used by capital. The choice to group them together as reproductive labor is to show that the labor of female workers is utilized to socially produce other subjects and their lifestyles either through cooking, childcare, sexual pleasures and other kinds of intimacies. Exploited by property owners seeking to produce wealth, both sex and domestic workers do not escape being subordinated to the logic of profit despite reproductive's labor "private" nature (e.g., child care happens in the household and sexual gratification happens between two private self-contained bodies). In grouping them together we are also able to make apparent the ways spaces become declared public or private for exploitative and oppressive reasons. The "mirage-like quality" of these constructions is another strategy for capital to obfuscate its exploitation and commodification of labor "private" and otherwise. Despite imaginary constructions of public and private spaces within the borders of neoliberal nation-states, we see a parallel relation between a domestic and sex worker within desire industries. Whether working in a private household or across town in a public cabaret, hotel, or street, they are both exploited workers. In the case of the domestic worker the "private" space within which she works is considered both public and private. It is public in the sense that her employer has to acquire an employment migrant visa for her, through a public institution, which in turn makes her a "private slave." Simultaneously, the domestic worker live-in situation makes her public workplace her "home," that which is considered private. Similarly, the sex worker is employed in a public space to provide one with what is considered "private" sexual gratification. Thus, their conditions illustrate that these distinctions, albeit ridden with contradictions both in terms of spaces and work, are "largely imaginary." It is, as Bhattacharjee informs us in her chapter "The Public/Private Mirage," a method to obfuscate the ways all sites including home are public. I expand her point by arguing that all sites as well as different kinds of sexual relations such as sex and domestic work are social and are subordinated to the production for profit. Both sex and domestic labor are appropriated by "private" powers irrespective of the context within which the social relation takes place. In this sense, the labor of millions of women worldwide serves to create human beings (Engels, 1884: 4). Bridget Anderson (2000) states that reproductive activities perpetuate the generations through mental, manual, emotional, and sexual labor. Toward this end, I extend the Marxist foci on (1) exploitation and domination as they emerge from the production of things and (2) the ways in the which the social surplus gets appropriated, by arguing that reproduction of people at different sites (household, market, school, work) is also production and is subordinated to the logic of profit. Thus, the "production of things" is not the only material base for the oppression and exploitation of people; so is the production of people because it depends on the private appropriation of surplus labor of those who own nothing but their labor power to sell.

Global Political Economy of Desire: Discourses on and Social Relations of Gender, Sex, Sexuality, Class, and Race

Sex and desire are social and historical relations (Kollontai, 1977: 13). They are not private matters concerning only the persons involved in them. Despite definitions by poststructuralists, feminists, and queer theorists (Deleuze and Guattari, 1983; Kristeva, 1986; Gallop, 1988; Butler, 1987, 1994; Grosz, 1994) that desire is an individual circuit of pleasure and sex the relation between men and women for reproductive purposes, a global political economy of sex focuses on the gendered and racialized structures of sexual relations for pleasure and reproduction of human beings within the capitalist economic system.

   The desire industries are informed by the class positionality of raced and gendered subjects in the global division of labor, that is, the social relations under which the labor power of sex and domestic workers is produced as a commodity and exploited as such. They are also informed by the desires of gendered/raced/sexual classes. In this way, the global political economy of sex is also about the global political economy of desire. Here, desire itself represents a social product and takes on different forms and modes depending on the historical relations among sexual structures and "economic modes of production." For example, at this historical juncture, desire has been defined as a kind of *jouissance* or consumer satisfaction (Hennessy, 2000: 71). However, this definition centralizes desire and the desiring subject such that it silences the material conditions and economic structures that make possible the production of surplus-value and exploitation of labor that produce this desire (Cotter, 2003: 4; Hennessy, 2000; Ebert, 1996). Local and transnational institutions of power produce the desires and identities that are bought and sold worldwide. Simultaneously, these institutions depend on the logic of structural compartmentalization to enable this practical constitution of identities and desires: for example, sexual versus international division of labor, formal versus informal economies, public versus private, madam versus maid, madonna versus prostitute, security versus insecurity. Yet each is linked to the others in daily social relations of production. Madams exploit and oppress their maids, pimps violate their "prostitutes," the formal economies silence capital's power by focusing on the illegalities and corruption of the informal economies, the private is secured as a safe haven for the individual whereas the public is not, and so on. Ultimately, men and women of the upper and middle-classes benefit from these structures and institutions of capital (Anderson, 2000: 7) by securing their bourgeois subjectivity through the expropriation of surplus-value. According to Marx surplus-value is the surplus produced over and above what is required to survive which is translated into profit under capitalist production because it can be turned into a commodity that can be exchanged (e.g., sex). Accordingly, conflicts of interest, contradictions, and antagonisms inherent in the sexual division of labor as well as the larger sexual and economic structures become "contained" and managed (Anderson, 2000: 1).

The Complicit State

Within this context, state power is not neutral, but classed, sexualized, and racialized. In compliance with the neoliberal world order, the state hides the exploitation of the reproductive wage labor of women of color by constructing them as commodities or assets (a transnationalized class unto themselves), to be sold in service to the transnationalized upper- and middle-class profit-maker and consumer. These same women are also constructed as "foreigners" and simultaneously as "desirable" and "undesirable." The racialized feminization of reproductive labor and its contingent relations of desire and sexuality are subordinated to production for profit. These kinds of relations where women and men are buying the reproductive labor of others are indicative of shifts within the capitalist mode of production. Capitalist globalization has accentuated the commodification of this labor. Now, the disguise of the family romance is lost, in some cases so much so that it makes apparent the capitalist myth that labor power and the owners of commodities enter into relations on equal footing. Moreover, this accentuation unmasks what capitalism has historically been able to do: exploit the wage labor as well as the selling and buying of people's sexuality and their bodies. This relation, of course, is under the legal constraint that liberal democracy imposed on the buying and selling of people, unlike in slavery, so that it can legitimize the market. However, this legal sanction against slavery has not put an end to it. On the contrary, wage labor is a hidden form of slavery within a market within which exists a free reign of the trafficking of women and children for exploitation of their sexuality and bodies for profit all in the name of freedom and equal exchange.

OUTLINE OF BOOK

Serving as prime examples, Cyprus, Greece, and Turkey account for how the global political economy of sex constitutes this relationship of exploitation and commodity exchange with desire. I argue that these two processes pervade all sexual and racial relations of reproduction. Simultaneously, a global political economy of sex sheds light on the ways colonizing ideologies of racism and Aryan myths are used extensively by the market and political institutions to sustain the slave relations of wage labor in generating the demand for sex and desire within the desire industries. Globalization has intensified the possibility of exploiting female migrants' wage labor through an accentuation of the division of labor. Within these world structures the full expression of interpersonal relations and the birth and production of free citizens become an impossibility.

Chapter 2 focuses on how the state becomes the political structure that facilitates the movement of reproductive labor for profits through the sale and purchase of racialized bodies for self-centered sexual and racial consumption. More concretely, I examine how the peripheral economic state uses its migration policies and employment contracts to mediate the sale and purchase of racialized reproductive wage labor in the market, the household, the cabaret, and the club. In the process, it tries to constitute itself as a "white" state irrespective of a global racial politics whose sole purpose is the continued asymmetrical hierarchization and domination of people's lives. In this way, the peripheral economic state participates in neoliberal capitalism's recolonization of social relations of production by presenting the material relations between "the white but not quite" employer and the "white but not quite" and "black" worker as relations of equality and freedom of choice through the contract of employment. The state draws upon the Aryan myths to subjugate further the working-class to the regime of profit through the creation of the desire industries as gendered and racialized sites of exploitation. The desire industries are an instantiation of the larger social relations of production and its contingent inequalities that inform "personal" relations. Chapter 3 looks at the contradictions that lie at the core of the racialization, that is, that "white but not quite" bodies are for sex and sexual gratification and "black" bodies are for cleaning after one's self and family and the sexualization of the desire industries. Through interviews with migrant women workers, women employers, and impressarios (pimps), this chapter details the themes of a sexual, racial, and class division of labor, desire, reproductive services for cash and the fencing off of these desire industries as shadow or peripheral economies within what comes to be known as the formal white economy.

Chapter 4 examines the state's desire to constitute itself as a white power broker within the regional EU/transnational economy. It does so regardless of widening gaps between the rich and the poor within its borders and the state's further peripheralization within the EU through its economic marginalization/feminization resulting from its active participation in the desire industries. Moreover, its economic and political policies silence the fact that its attempt to rescue the white elements it imagines it possesses depends on the racialization and sexualization of wage labor for making possible the accumulation of profits for its owning "white but not quite" class.

Chapter 5 concentrates on the constitution of the desire industries by the peripheral economic state as sites of compromise of national security. It, in turn, constructs the working-class female migrant worker as a referent of transnationalized insecurity. This nationalist strategy enables the peripheral economic state to make invisible the exploitation and the transfer of the surplus-value of the working-class migrant woman into the hands of the owning "white but not quite" class while hiding its political power and role in constituting "national" insecurity by redirecting and privatizing large chunks of social resources, thereby transnationalizing insecurities by allying with multinational capital. Behind these strategies by both capital and its political institutions, such as neoliberal democracy, lie a whole world-view and a systematic approach to global politics. Thus, in our efforts to think beyond this global capitalist neoliberal project to envision the fundamentals of an egalitarian, nonexploitative, and post-gender and postracial future, we need to move beyond the historical limitations of current knowledge production and praxis about social change. We need to examine historically unexamined sites, social relations, and methods for they may contain the seeds of an alternative movement to the capitalist society whose whole understanding of social relations is property ownership and exploitation. A comradeship and solidarity that articulate a new theory and praxis for the creation of a collective society guide the writing of the next chapter.

Chapter 6 concludes with possibilities for fundamentally transforming the material conditions of necessity for reproductive laborers, that is, the transformation of the social relations of production that are based on private ownership of production. Within the neoliberal capitalist economy, a reorientation of IR/IPE toward sex and desire while critiquing feminist understandings of desire and sex as dialectically linked to material and institutional power may inspire a feminist materialist project that grasps the "totality of relations of production" and works toward forging a collective solidarity for a feminist IR/IPE that participates in the racialized and gendered class struggle to abolish capitalism's regime of profit and wage labor and also creates the material conditions in order to emancipate all people from exploitation (Cotter, 2001: 8). This chapter sees violence and exploitation as the lynchpins to the global political economy of sex and desire, and how the class struggle of sex and domestic workers of all sexes and races challenge these processes. Finally, I look at possibilities for a transborder solidarity politics among workers toward emancipation and revolutionary work that makes substantive democracy a reality instead of an unfulfilled promise.

MYTHS, LURES, AND OTHER CONSEQUENCES

Desire industries constitute people as spectacles. Sometimes the relations between employers and domestic workers, impresarios and sex workers, clients and sex workers lead to more long-term relations that can take a romantic or nurturing form that seem to contradict the exploitative and commercial form of the parties' initial exchanges. In this second form of employer–worker, client–worker relations, cash exchange plays an ambivalent role in the "contract." This is significant because men and women who desire sex and domestic workers are able to escape facing the larger context within which their desires and needs are produced. It is not enough to focus on the legal and moral conditions that impact individual's personhoods (such as their desires and their agency) but also the conditions that produce them (Marx, 1976: 42). The privilege of these subjects secures them a safe haven within which they can lull themselves to bliss, and thus, avoid the contradictions and antagonisms of their social relations.

Commodity exchange in the desire industries comes home, literally. The meaning or value of commodities at home for laborers reflects those in the household for employers and clients. The migration and trafficking of women from lower-income countries to rich-income countries derives, I argue, from the private ownership and control of the means of production and social reproduction. This form of power makes it possible to command the surplus labor of others and its value within a global economy. Moreover, the desire to consume the "other's" labor and body as a form of pleasure is becoming a crucial aspect in reclaiming the owning middle- and upper-class' identities and personhood. In turn, this relates to the new emerging "white but not quite" and "black" subjects' position as employers in a changing economy who purchase and sell the labor power and bodies of working-class "white but not quite" and "black" woman's as commodities.

Desire for reproductive labor (mental, productive, physical, sexual, and emotional) stems from another social product: social reproduction itself as a commodity product for exchange. The peripheral economic state shapes and constitutes its power within the restructured global economic institutions, practices, and social relations by mediating and controlling the privatization of social reproduction. It actively participates in constructing working-class women's labor, sexualities, and bodies as natural and private commodities that can be exploited to their fullest. The state, the market, the household, the cabaret, the strip clubs, and other institutions work with each other to privatize social reproductive labor.

> Production and social reproduction in this broad sense are bound up with one another. It is not just that reproduction is a necessary prerequisite to production, but that much of what is produced has labour added and is used/consumed in the home. (Anderson, 2000: 13)

This privatized reproduction is as much about domestic as sexual labor.

Anderson does not discuss sexuality as being one of the relations of social reproduction. I want to extend her idea to include sexuality as a social relation of reproduction that produces labor that is used and consumed publicly and privately in the home. For example, Marianne talked about the way men approached her when they came to the cabaret in which she worked: "They expect you to be gracious, smiling, praising, and gentle and sometimes they act like they have never seen a woman before in their lives...[H]e approaches you for drinks and then he expects you to stir milk into his glass of white Russian, caress his arm, ask if he is comfortable...[H]e pays for an hour and he expects you to be attentive to him for hours before you tell him his time is up."

This sex work is not piecework but all-inclusive, more seemingly human and less commodified even though it is obtained through the same means of commodity production and exchange. The woman's services constitute a new kind of "romantic relations" than the ones the client is already familiar with and which can later be used as a point of reference in the home or other relations.[6] In interviews, Greek and Turkish women whose partners at one time or another have been with a sex worker expressed the idea that their husbands and partners are becoming better lovers: "I find my husband more attractive and more sexy now than ever before. I know this is crazy, but it is the way I feel" (28-year-old Greek woman).

In this situation, the sexual relation of exploitation of the sex worker has produced value for those who sell as well as those who buy reproductive labor. The consumption of sensuality, sexuality, and the satiation of desire via the exchange between the sex worker and the client in the public "illicit economy" is reproduced in the private "family hearth and home." The client and his spouse can now enhance their sexual relationship, and, in the process, fetishize pleasure and sensuality on the back, literally, of the immigrant woman. These processes are all part of social production that occurs within the politico-economic arrangements of an emerging neoliberal world order, and, in turn, affect and shape subjectivities. A postcolonial feminist historical materialist approach to sexuality and desire reclaims the attention to women's sexuality and agency in relation to the neoliberal capitalist conditions that produce them and moves beyond understanding desire as a private, natural, homogeneous experience to which all men and women have a right. By rethinking sexuality and desire for others as part of larger structures of sexual division of labor and exploitation on which capitalist production depends, we make visible that the politico-economic arrangements affect the production of hierarchical sexual and racial relations among different subjects as well as their desires. Social reproduction's organization depends on the sexual division of labor within the capitalist desire industries: immigrant women end up doing most of this labor, if not all of it. This sexual division of labor is raced. Women of "color" and "white but not quite" are now imported to peripheral-rich economies to produce bourgeois subjects and their life styles and its contingent identities through cleaning, provision of pleasures, intimacies, and sexual acts.

Desiring to constitute its power within the neoliberal world order, the state actively participates in "feminizing" (redirecting social resources from the majority of its population to secure the freedom of capital and its exploitation of surplus-value) aspects of its economy through the intensification of the desire industries. However, this desire for recognition and acceptance within the regional power of the EU, and the desire for generating profits by exploiting women's bodies and their labor, result from its elites' recognition of their incapacity to totally secure national capital (a sense of national insecurity): a peripheral economic state may not achieve the status of the EU's core economies (Germany, France, Britain). It lags behind and displaces its insecurity on the working-class migrant women. This is a violent strategy that links the peripheral economic state's participation in the sex and desire industries to desire for power and for securing a certain *kind of whiteness*.

This violence (Fanon, 1963: 37)[7] is committed on the body of the working-class migrant woman daily while she and the local working-class hold the peripheral economic state's economy on their shoulders. A colonizing logic guides the use of sustained violence, the same logic that guides the global political economy of sex and desire: the exploitative structure of neoliberal capital. Facilitated by the hiring of a domestic worker, local professional and working-class women can move into the public and what is considered formal economy and acquire employment with its "masculinized patterns" (such as intense competition, violence, exploitation) (Anderson, 2000: 5). For example, the professional woman is now able to move into the market and earn a high salary while hiring a domestic worker who cleans and sustains her household. Simultaneously, the professional woman manages the domestic worker at home. This ability to move between the two imagined domains of the public and the private makes it possible for her to contain and make manageable the contradictions arising from the organization of the neoliberal capitalist-patriarchal structure and its relations.

While as a woman she is subject to a sexual division of labor in relation to her male partner and children, she now as a white bourgeois subject is able to hire a domestic worker without herself having to experience the domestic drudgery. The employment of the domestic worker enables the white but not quite woman of middle and upper class to avert the gender and racial contradictions within the larger social relations of capitalist-patriarchy: the household, state, and the market. The female employer is complicit in sustaining a gendered racialized order when she does not challenge her partner or children over sharing domestic chores. Instead, she hires a domestic worker, and in the process transfers this conflict on the relations between herself and her domestic worker. Within the household she is now participating in a vertical sexual division of labor. She is subordinated to her partner and children and property relations. The domestic worker is subordinated to her. Within the market she participates in a similar vertical division of labor. She is subordinated to the privatized economy and men while the non white women are subordinated to both her and privatized economy. By not challenging this order of things and reproductive privatized relations, she sustains in place, albeit with the sustained use of force and violence, her own exploitation by capital as well as the exploitation of reproductive workers. Her complicity is further seen in her use of the splitting of women and their roles in the market and household into "mutually dependent but antagonistic stereotypes: pure/dirty, emotional/physical, madonna/whore/"black/white, clean/dirty (Anderson, 2000: 19).

In this transnationalized context, the female employer emerges as an agent with sovereignty and "equal power" to men by having a job outside the household and also having the opportunity to consolidate much of her power by managing her domestic worker: "the worker may be treated as 'part of the family' (governed by customary relations) when it is a matter of hours and flexibility, and as a worker (governed by civic relations) if she becomes too sick to work" (Anderson, 2000: 5). At the same time, she is "different" and thus, unequal to the professional man because the social contract is and remains a sexual contract (Pateman, 1988: 194).[8] Thus, the professional woman herself participates in her own colonization because the conflicts with men and the capitalist-patriarchal order are displaced on the working-class migrant woman through exploitation and violence on her personhood and body.

The same colonizing logic applies in the case of relations with the sex worker. The prostitute provides intimacies and pleasures because the client is paying. The pimp or employer sells the prostitute and her services in the public space for profits, even though her sexual intimacies with her client are considered something of a private nature. Moreover, when both sex and domestic workers are paid for their services, their social relations in the desire industries are characterized by personal dependency on the employer, a dependency mediated by the state's regulation.

These private relations are crucially linked to public capitalist production. And the peripheral economic state, both sending and importing, plays a mediating and active role in this process. Thus, slave and colonial relations (madam and maid, master and slave) are part and parcel of capitalism even when they are fenced-off as marginal and illicit economies. These industries, with their contingent slavery relations, produce and are produced by people whose agency in the public and the private sphere "appropriate and devour...value" (Firat and Dholakia, 1998: 138). Yet, this agency is not necessarily "productive" and "creative" especially in a world context within which economies' major logic is exploitation through colonization of people's surplus-value and violence against their personhood. In this way, public as well as private sites are turning into major loci of exploitation and consumption (Anderson, 2000: 4).

It is no wonder that many migrant workers of reproductive labor are considered "women and prostitutes of color" and "white but not quite" prostitutes (including ethnics from Russia and Eastern Europe) coming from poor economies. The clients and employers of these women are simply identified as "rich"—implying at least a middle-class background for men and women from the North, Japan, and other wealthy economies in Asia, Latin America, and the Middle East (Agathangelou and Ling, 2003). Moreover, since most of this work is done by both "women of color" and "white but not quite" women in private homes, hotels, and cabarets, these workers are pushed into the informal or shadow economies and societies, and their employers, both male and female, paradoxically conceal them and sell them in the process of producing their own power and status through accumulation of cash and profits.

Within the "new Europe," the desire industries are fenced-off to the margins of the formal capitalist economy, and yet, these economies are growing at an unprecedented rate (Lazos, 2002; Lazaridis, 2001; Psimmenos, 2000; Campani, 2001). Peripheralized states are actively participating in producing aspects of their socioeconomic and political power through these economies even when they argue that migration as a phenomenon endangers their "national security" (Perni, 2001; Hyde-Price and Reiter, 2001; Moller, 2000; Ergüvenç, 2000, 1999, 1998; İlhan, 2000; Manisali, 2001, 2002; Ugur, 2003; see also National Security Policy Document, 1997; Karadayi, OSCE, 1998). Some authors place these industries (such as sex tourism) in the context of exploitation of developing countries (e.g., O'Grady, 1992; Reinhardt, 1989; Latza, 1987), arguing that

> At a psychological level these nations are forced into the "female" role of servitude, of being "penetrated" for money, often against their will; whereas the outgoing, pleasure seeking, "penetrating"...[buyers] of powerful nations are cast in the "male" role. (Graburn, 1983: 441)

Others have argued that developing countries are participating in a new kind of colonialism through the commodification of women from the peripheries.

a new wave of colonialism appears to overrun the developing countries.... The women in the periphery become the last "unspoilt
resource"—a good that can be traded unscrupulously. (Reinhardt,
1989: 90)

These studies raise important issues about the imperial capital relations
but remain focused on only the traveling of tourists from developed to
developing countries (Kempadoo, 1999). This represents but one
important piece of the desire industries. Within the newer restructurings in the world economy, more and more peripheral economic states
are demanding sex and domestic workers (Oppermann, 1997) as
cheap labor. Why are peripheralized states in general, and peripheralized states in Europe in particular, participating in the import of sex
and domestic workers? What is this desire to consume and exploit the
labor of migrant females about? Anderson (2000) partially explains the
reasons behind the "new" migration policies in Europe and the politics of importing sex and domestic workers below:

Racism dubs black people natural slaves, immigration legislation makes
of them "legal slaves" in the Aristotelian sense... conquest in global
economic terms makes contemporary legal slaves of the poor of the
Third World, giving the middle class of the First World materialistic
forms of power over them. Racism also continues to make of certain
people "natural slaves," however, regarding them as suited by nature to
subjugation and labour. (148)

Anderson talks of the First World in her book and the reasons it
imports reproductive labor. She includes Greece as part of the First
World. This same colonizing process is prevalent in peripheral
economies as well, which find themselves fantasizing being like the
First World and its upper and middle-classes. They are "there but not
quite." She explains that the flow of reproductive labor from lower-
income generating states to higher-income generating ones is, in
effect, a result of international power relations and the racialization
and class status of the migrants involved. This explanation segues to
the next point about the context within which migration and welfare
policies take place. The mere fact that a household is now able to hire
a female migrant worker and compensate her for aspects of her reproductive work does not mean the wages are nonexploitative or that
they are independent of an asymmetrical sexual division of labor
between men and women. The asymmetrical racial division of labor
between men and women is an integral part of the dominant production relations, that is, the class relations, and of the sexual national

and transnational divisions of labour (Mies, 1998: 49). More specifically, the labor of workers serves the development of the status of
their employers at their expense and against their own interests
(Aguilar, 2002: 5 citing Anderson, 2000). Thus, when peripheral
economic states participate in the import of sex and domestic workers, they both facilitate the production of their own socioeconomic
and political power and that of their upper- and middle-class citizens,
whose status is reproduced through the exploitation of the labor and
personhoods of women from elsewhere in the peripheries. They
actively participate in sustaining a social order that depends on the
gendered, racialized, and sexualized exploitation of wage labor, that
of migrant women, mostly from countries of the Third World, in
addition to the exploitation of the local working-class. Thus, this
study examines closely the state's role in producing social relations of
genders, sexualities, races, and class through its policies as well as its
role in processing the cost of social reproduction. What constitutes
the female migrant worker/employer relationship, the female migrant
worker/client relationship, and what is the buying/selling relationship between female migrant worker/employer, female migrant
worker/client? These relationships shed light on class, gender, race,
nation, reproduction of community, sexuality, family relations, and
the politics of the body.

   Moreover, a close examination of the peripheral economic state
and its role in the import of reproductive labor for the staffing of the
lucrative desire industries sheds light on the hidden connections that
exist between desire and violence. The connections are the insecurities that are generated at different levels in the reproduction of this
"unnatural" order. The wars of power are waged locally and globally
amid different historically situated agents. The peripheral economic
state relies heavily on the desire industries to boost its allegiance to
the global market and multinational corporations and institutions. To
silence and perhaps obfuscate the insecurities generated structurally
by the neoliberal capital relations and to make them appear as "integral to the 'natural' order of things" (Alexander, 1998: 280), this
state machine (i.e., the educational system, the police force, the labor
department, and the media) occludes contradictions within the
restructuring of the world economy and generates violence against
many, including the migrant working-class woman by claiming that
she is a threat and a danger to its "national security," a code for
masking capital's ability to exploit at the most competitive rate.
Simultaneously, the working-class migrant women's desire to escape
violence and exploitation at home, to seek opportunities and to

search for fast cash pushes them to migrate and work for women and men of rich-peripheral economic states who end up consuming, naturalizing, and exploiting the reproductive labor of women of lower-economic states. Moreover, the rich-peripheral economic state facilitates and mediates this exploitation and socially reproduces it through its policies, practices, and discourses. In sum, all these different struggles and contestations lead to a "containment" of the insecurities and compromises of national, social, communal, and personal sovereignties with their contingent emotions, practices, and self-understandings that are generated as a result of a social organization of a transnational economy that is based on "private" powers.

Marxist Feminists and an Alternative Method Toward Transformative Praxis

The present study seeks to shed light and provide answers that move beyond "blaming the female migrants" and calls for a transformative feminist agenda (Aguilar, 2002; Ebert, 2001; Cotter, 2001, 2002; Mies, 1998). This study uses the method of historical materialism to analyze and critique the desire industries as they are constituted in the peripheral economic states of Cyprus, Greece, and Turkey. It argues that this method makes it possible for us to open our eyes to alternative possibilities and see windows to a substantive democracy that is inclusive of all its peoples, migrants and nonmigrants.

Taking seriously the operative logic of capitalism and the Marxist critique of exploitation and its attendant processes of violence (e.g., militarization and policing of borders), alienation, and inequality, materialist feminists argue that understanding production and reproduction of social life are crucial in the movement to transform asymmetrical social relations. Historical materialist feminists acknowledge that class, racial, and gender politics inform the struggles over the construction of hegemony (Mies, 1998; O'Brien, 1988). Marx's focus on production as a form of wage labor contributes to the naturalization of women's productive and reproductive labor and the naturalization of men as universal productive beings and women as nature.[9]

Mies (1986) and Mies et al. (1988) theorize the relations of production and sexual inequality, contesting the "narrow, capitalist concept of 'productive labor' " and arguing instead for a more general concept of the productivity of labor. In addition, they argue that the production of life is not simply the reproduction of human beings, but also "the production of all forms of subsistence goods and use values necessary to meet the basic human needs" (Ebert, 1996: 79). Mies states:

> It is my thesis that this general production of life, or subsistence production-mainly performed through the non-wage labour of women and other non-wage labourers as slaves, contract workers, and peasants in the colonies—constitutes the perennial basis upon which "capitalist productive labour" can be built and exploited. Without the ongoing subsistence production of non-wage labourers (mainly women), wage labour would not be "productive." (1986: 48)

Building on this broad concept of productive labor and Marx's theory of primitive accumulation, their work sheds light on the production of surplus values and the accumulation of wealth as a result of the appropriation and exploitation of subsistence labor. Mies et al's explanation sheds light on the construction of social differences in relation to colonization and the development of asymmetrical divisions and appropriation of both reproductive and surplus labor as part of a capitalist system.

This analysis allows for us to avoid separating sexual and racial differences from the economic sphere. On the contrary, these different forms of productivity (wage, subsistence, colonization, reproductive labor) are all imbricated and the subject occupies multiple and contradictory places within them. Their work is important for a global political economy of sex and desire because they theorize the relations of production with reproduction. As Ebert accurately assesses, they

> move beyond the binary of public/private and [do] not simply equate the production of life with domestic labor; yet [they] still account for household work. ... the gender division of labor is, for Mies, the precondition of all appropriation of surplus value and accumulation, and thus of class differences, in any economic system. Materialist feminists can use this theory to explain the importance of the division and exploitation of labor around race with the development of capitalism, first through slavery, one of the primary means of capitalizing the industrial revolution, and then through colonization and systematic economic racism. ... th[is] work ... provides a basis for explaining the collective exploitation of women—in different ways—around the gender division of labor. (1996: 81)

This dynamic theorization of gender and relations of production is very important in the debates among feminists and international political economists around the issues of production, reproduction, and the patriarchal neoliberal world order. Conceptualizing the production of life as an aspect of production for wages and profit makes possible the recognition of racialized patriarchy as a material force, "a feature of class societies." It is a system that naturalizes gender, sexuality, and race in such a way that makes possible the selling of women's labor, sexual and otherwise, cheaply (Ebert, 1996: 90). It is a strategy that naturalizes women's exploitation. Capitalism is the effect of wage labor, the surplus extracted from workers. I argue that this capitalist logic operates in the production of the desire economies as well.

Clearly, feminists who posit these two modes as semiautonomous "in the name of overcoming the flaws of Marxist notions of family, sexuality, and gender" argue that "desire—the reproduction of life—determines capitalism, and the agency of the subject is the most important part of social transformation" (Ebert, 1996: 82, 98). Moreover, along the same lines, debates about domestic labor often adopt the position that women are oppressed because their productive work in the household is not paid for by the state, arguing that women should protest labor if the state does not compensate them for their work. This strategy prioritizes the state as the agent of social change and seems to be a common variable shared by world systems theorists. Wallerstein held that "actors in the market" try to "avoid the normal operation of the market whenever it does not maximize their profit" by deploying state power (1979). Imperialism is the logic of the relation among states, and the powerful core systematically develops underdevelopment in the periphery. It is, in short, the state that is the dynamic force of social and economic relations. Within the state relations, the "white" working-class woman is the leading agent of class and gender struggle, an analysis that marginalizes the agency of working-class women in the peripheries and the possibilities of solidarity with those working-class peoples in the core economies. In sum, these theories silence class, the position of racialized and gendered subjects in the structures of exploitation (Ebert, 1991: 406).

In addition, exploitation, power, and ideologies in the desire industries must be understood in social relations that do not "just happen" and are ineluctable. For example, discourses about the bodies of Eastern European female workers in Cyprus, Greece, and Turkey revolve around how "the blonds of Russia and Rumania" come to these countries because their own nation-states are poor. They are the women who "lead astray" indigenous men. A Turkish Cypriot woman said the following to Scott about Rumanian croupiers in Northern Cyprus: "Imagine you are a man, single. Of course you look at women, and try to talk to them. If you are a terbiyeli [decent] woman, you look away, you don't talk back, or you just return their merhaba [hello]. But if you say: [in English] 'hello you are very nice,' and invite them to your house, of course the young man will go" (Scott, 1995: 399). Naturalizing male and female sexuality, this story affirms a liberal capitalist order that is sustained by racialized and gendered hierarchies. This narrative privileges the "good" Cypriot men and their women over the "bad" women of other ethnic backgrounds who "tempt" Cypriot men. Men are susceptible to "other" women's charms because it is their nature to be sexual, and, thus, it is natural for them to desire them and accept their invitations. In contrast, there is a corresponding vigilance about the presence of Rumanian women in Cyprus because these women threaten to "modernize," and, thus, destroy traditional values. Such understandings about women and men's sexuality are rooted in transnationalized, racialized, and sexualized discourses, confirming that men can involve themselves sexually anytime they want without any social consequences whereas women cannot. Emphasizing the commodification of women and men's sexuality, these discourses are not fully explained by the politics of nationalism and state policies. They are structurally produced, share similarities to parallel narratives produced in other social contexts, and take a very local and nationalized form. What informs the production and circulation of these discourses?

Both the social context and these discourses impact the asymmetrical reproduction of power for men and women. For example, circulating discourses by institutions such as the state and the market about the Rumanian woman's morality in relation to the Cypriot woman's suggest that Rumanian women should not be protected by the state or the authorities in Cyprus if they are sexually harassed or assaulted. Their indecency leads to the problems they experience. Similar discourses are available transnationally in other local contexts. Questions about the politics of an invitation in a Rumanian woman to a Cypriot man become reduced to questions of culture. For example, sex workers are conceptualized as "international whores" (*Sun-Star Daily*, August 26, 1993) for the consumption of men who desire and fantasize of enacting "whiteness."

This study moves beyond this discursive analysis and provides suggestions toward a praxis, which fights against sex, racial, and class ruling (Ebert, 1996: 96). The social relations of men and women within the desire industries are not merely abstract and ahistorical man–woman relations (patriarchy) but are historically produced within the social relations of capitalist production in which all the discourses of domestic maids and sex workers are articulated. When hearing stories about sex and domestic workers many times, it seems that sexuality and domestic labor are experienced as private and personal. However, when using a materialist theory that argues for an accounting of the global structures and globalization practices (so that one can act on them and transform them), it becomes apparent that domestic and sexual labor done in the home or the cabaret are effects of capitalism and not sheer personal experiences of pleasure and leisure. This labor is the process through which human beings make not only their world but also themselves (Capital, chapter 6). Feminists traditionally silenced the fact that the subject's desires and sexuality are not independent from class. The subject and his/her contingent feelings, emotions, and experience of personal desires are "formed historically in the social relations of production" (Ebert, 1996: 97).

An emphasis by postcolonial theorists on representation, agency, and cultural practices needs to be located in material structures to enable praxis toward transforming the asymmetrical gendered, raced, and classed power relations between the peripheries and metropoles. Asymmetrical power relations cannot be simply wished away because these are part of the "material realities of the subject's circumstance, realities that have become intensified in the local/global intersection of globalization" (Paolini, 1999: 153). Thus, a postcolonial historical materialist feminist framework is concerned with the reasons the social and systemic reside in the subjective (expressed as gendered, racialized, and classed agency and cultural practice). Each feeds off the other.

This imbrication is a fundamental aspect of capitalist relations, bringing into being the preconditions for capitalism's transformation and change. For example, the current restructurings of the world economy and the drastic changes in the mode of production demand production of new subjectivities to reproduce the capitalist mode of production through their practices. The flexibilization of production, the development of "lean management," the development of autonomous, globalizing financial markets and institutions, and the further segmentation of markets are the changes in the mode of production. In turn, these changes in a dialectical manner inform institutional changes as well as changes in identities.

To understand what is really at stake in globalization and the production of desire economies, one can go beyond culturalist and IPE theories and focus on materialist factors such as exploitation, labor, inequality, class, sexual and racial relations, the relation of production and reproduction as well as the rate of profit within capitalism. Theorists who have focused on these issues argue from a number of contesting points of view. Globalization, I argue, is a struggle over the structured inequality in the world economy and its manifestations in the desire economy to unfold the fundamental mirage in capitalism: the separation of the worker from the product of her labor, which is appropriated by the capitalist. It is the exploitation of labor by capital that produces the structured inequality under capitalism, old or new. This is perhaps another way of saying that globalization begins with the commodification of labor power itself and comes to commodify the body of the laborer as well through the purchase of her sexuality and reproductive labor. The commodification of labor and the subject herself is the necessary condition for profit. In chapter six of volume one of Capital, Marx gives a sustained analysis of this historical-economic matter and writes that labor power is the only commodity "whose use-value possesses the peculiar property of being a source of value, whose actual consumption, therefore, is itself an embodiment of labor and consequently a creation of value" (1954, 164).

This process of the globalization of exploitation through the ready access to surplus labor and surplus bodies sets in motion a highly complex set of secondary processes that require, for example, changes in the status of the sovereignty of the state and its transformation into a poststate and the development of global underground banking system and investment laws. Among other things, Marx and Engels offer the first sustained theorization of globalization, discussing these cultural and political changes at length:

> The bourgeoisie cannot exist without constantly revolutionizing the instruments of production, and thereby the relations of production, and with them the whole relations of society. Conservation of the old modes of production in unaltered form was, on the contrary, the first condition of existence for all earlier industrial classes. Constant revolutionizing of production, uninterrupted disturbance of all social conditions, everlasting uncertainty and agitation distinguish the bourgeois epoch from all earlier ones.

The market's need for constant expansion for its products chases the bourgeoisie over the whole surface of the globe. It must nestle everywhere, settle everywhere, and establish connection everywhere. The bourgeoisie through its exploitation of the world market has given a cosmopolitan character to production and consumption in every country. In place of the old wants, satisfied by the productions of the country, we find new wants, requiring for their satisfaction the products of distant lands and climes. We have intercourse in every direction in an universal interdependence of nations and peoples.

It is within this context that the explanation of the production of desire industries and the contestations around the issue of sex and domestic workers can be better explained. It is within this context that we can start thinking about a global political economy of sex. As suggested in this chapter several theorists through critiques of IPE such as Marx (1972), Marx and Engels (1976), Lenin (1939), Amin (1989), Mies (1986), Mies, Bennholdt-Thomsen, and von Werlhof (1988), Fuentes and Ehrenreich (1998), Enloe (1989), Miliband and Panitch (1992), and Agathangelou (2002) put forward a materialist critique of coloniality and postcoloniality by arguing that all social practices need to be studied in relation to the history of capitalist production and exchange as the capitalist system is founded on profit (Ebert, 1996: 85). For them, materialist critique is a practice that is operating on the logic of "total transformation," that is, the change of all the structures of the global context instead of "practical, reformist, and local ameliorations" (Ebert, 1996: 85). This difference in expectation regarding social change is what differentiates this feminist study from other IPE and feminist studies of sex and domestic work (Kempadoo and Doezema, 1998; Murray, 1998). If change is theorized as the reform of current practices within the existing socioeconomic structure, we get one kind of social theory, and if change is understood as transformation—overthrowing existing structures and not simply amending and repairing them—we end up with a completely different form of social theory (Ebert, 1996: 85). Through a careful examination of the desire economies I want to put forward an understanding of freedom different from the one preferred by transnational feminists who theorize about sex and domestic workers: having the freedom and control to choose to sell one's labor and body (Kempadoo, 1999; Murray, 1998) but rather freedom from necessity.

COMPARATIVE RESEARCH METHOD

The foundation of this book is formed from several sources of data—historical interpretation of state documents such as employment policies, employment contracts, and analyses on sex and domestic work, analysis of media documents; analysis of EU documents on migration and female import of sex and domestic workers; and field data, including in-depth interviews with state officers, migration officers, policemen, pimps, women working in the industries, clients, as well as focus groups. The absence of previous research on the political economy of domestic and sex work and the structure of these industries in Cyprus, Greece, and Turkey influenced the choice of my investigative methods. Interviews with sex and domestic workers provide a significant amount of information regarding their employment contracts (such as work schedules, earnings, recruitment patterns, the organization of household and sex work spaces, and the dynamics between the sex and domestic workers, their employers and their clients). In addition to exploring the relationship with the state through the employment contracts and citizenship status, I also sought to explore the women's own understandings of these relationships, thereby enabling a comparative analysis of the same relationship from different angles and perspectives. Thus, I decided to interview the employers of these workers in the desire industries. Since the whole purpose of historical materialism as a method is to show the contradictions present in particular social relations, this collection of empirical data opened up the space for us to explore and identify the contradictions. I sought to explore how the migration of these women to peripheralized states and their working for middle- and upper-class women and men affected the ways they understand and explain themselves. I also wanted to examine the ways in which gendered, racialized, and economic relations embedded in household and sex workspaces regulate the operation of the desire industries.

Interviews, Participant Observation, and Focus Groups

Interviewing the employers of the domestic workers in the three countries began with an introductory phone call from a friend who had a friend who employed domestic workers. Interview opportunities came from colleagues who knew women who had domestic workers. Meeting with the employers, I prefaced the collection of data by briefly describing the purpose of the research and emphasizing confidentiality. More often than not (44 out of 60 times), I was able to interview the domestic worker of the same employer. However, eight employees reticent to share details about their relationship to their employers were willing to outline their schedule and some of their concerns. One Sri Lankan employee kept saying that she could not understand English, and thus, our interview finished within half an hour instead of the usual one to three hours with the rest of the employees.

While interviewing the employees, the question of how much time I needed for the interview emerged. Ninety percent of the employers expressed concern that they needed their employee for preparing dinners, or lunches, or being present for any eventuality in the house. Most employers explained that they "already told me all I needed to know about their maid," and so, I should not take as much time with their employees. However, 85 percent of the employees really wanted to share their own version of the story. Some of them were really happy that their employer had an event to attend, and thus, would not be at home to "demand all their time." Rarely did employers express interest in what their employees had to say.

In contrast, interviews with sex workers were more complicated. Even though many people knew women in the sex industry and suggested that they could help me interview them, most early attempts failed. In the beginning, I was able to interview sex workers through their employers, the pimps who were willing to let them speak to me. However, the interviews with sex workers were more difficult on several levels. Many of the women were scared to be tape-recorded and wanted to meet more than once before they could really begin "unfolding their lives." Many young women who had just arrived in these countries did not want to say "as much" and often used the phrase "you know what I mean" when they described their sexual experiences or the desires of their clients. However, some who had been in the "profession" longer (at least a decade) were less reticent.

I came to interview several women (60 percent) through suggestions of local "friends" who suggested that I pay them for their time (approximately $20). Some of these women asked for the money and others refused it. Typically, interviews with the sex workers ranged from one to three hours, except for three interviews that lasted four hours.

Additionally, I took part in many Sunday gatherings of domestic workers in the social center in Cyprus and Greece and in gatherings (domestics renting their own flats and coming together on Sundays for chatting and meals) in all three countries. In these spaces, issues such as who is dating whom, who is going out to bars, who is having another job such as sex work, who is wearing what, and who is a good cook were discussed. All these interactions added to the larger picture of domestics in these countries and provided me a deeper understanding of the fabric of their lives away from home as well as the establishment and maintenance of informal social networks among themselves.

In the case of sex workers, such gatherings happened only in cafes. In these gatherings, visions about their lives and possibilities for change were presented as well as jokes about their employees and their clients. Their strategies of confronting their daily injuries were also described in a humorous fashion.

Nine focus group interviews were conducted (three in each country, one with domestic workers, one with sex workers, one with employers of domestic workers), four persons in each group, to explore how women share their stories and how such a space opens up possibilities for social change. There were some major differences in the way the domestic workers spoke and the way the sex workers spoke about their experiences. Domestic workers seemed to describe their labor relations, their contracts, and their recruitment more directly than the sex workers. The sex workers giggled and looked at each other when they spoke about their sexuality and its sale. The employers focused mostly on the "violations" of the domestic workers in their household and their own "goodness" toward their employees. Very few of them admitted that they "exploit" or are "demanding" of their domestic worker.

These interviews shed light on the many contradictions that exist within the relations of production. These interviews also provide us with insights about the social organization of capitalism within the desire industries and push us to move beyond individual experiences and cultural differences to a global political economy of sex and desire. This economy of sex and desire is a project that critiques the current social relations and also articulates basic principles for an emancipatory feminist theory of sexuality and desire that does not separate sex and household/domestic work from the material relations of production and reproduction. An emancipatory theory of sex and desire is a commitment to ending the economic exploitation and commodification of social relations and the sexual/racial/class divisions of labor and desire. It is a struggle that reorients us toward building a different kind of freedom and equality from the one advocated by neoliberal capitalism. It is a project that argues and works for equal relations of love, sexuality, and comradeship in which desire is not merely sexual or exclusive. This comradeship involves solidarity of several connections with and interest for the collective including work, welfare, and its well-being. As long as property relations dominate the social formation, the possibility of freedom of all from necessity remains unrealized (Ebert, 2001: 19).

Let us now turn to the state's role in mediating capital's and labor's social relation by facilitating the flow of reproductive labor and processing the cost of social production of the economy (formal and informal) and household.

CHAPTER 2

PERIPHERAL ECONOMIES WORKING AND PLAYING HARD: SOCIAL REPRODUCTION AND RACIAL AND SEXUAL DESIRE IN THE MEDITERRANEAN

> What makes labor a different commodity is in fact its process of reproduction, which is necessarily material and social and follows historically established norms.
>
> (Picchio, 1992: 2)

Some feminists and IR/IPE scholars centralize the power of the state in their analyses of the flow of reproductive labor, and rightly so, since it plays an important role in the restructured world economy (Kempadoo and Doezema, 1998; Enloe, 1993, 1989). However, the state cannot produce exchange value, nor can it fundamentally alter social asymmetries (e.g., sexual, class, and racial relations) by redistributing wealth and status. The state mediates the relation between racialized and gendered capital and labor through immigration policies and laws, and controls labor markets and the cost of reproducing labor. As Picchio states here, labor is different from other commodities because of the conditions of its reproduction (http://www.marxists.org/archive/marx/works/1861/economic/ch15.htm).

The position of the neoclassical analytical framework is that the "labor market is just like other markets" (Solow, 1990: 3). Nevertheless, in a capitalist economy, production is predicated upon the underdevelopment of social reproduction in the interest of reducing costs. For example, the desire industries are a site where women's reproductive labor is commodified and being sold for cheap wages. The state mediates the relation between capital and reproductive labor and facilitates its flow within its borders. Reproductive labor is another commodity circulating in the market for sale and purchase. The term *commodity* conjures up images of women as machines, the service providers, and goods for sale that embody and represent commodity exchange itself. Focusing on reproductive labor of sex and domestic workers as a commodity may broaden "definitions of work to include the unwaged work of reproduction" (Picchio, 1992; Gershuny and Jones, 1986; Pahl, 1984), but this process silences the larger social and politico-economic relations that commodify labor power and make its supply/demand and sale/purchase possible. It also silences the production fantasies that circulate regarding accessing "white but not quite" and black women's bodies through the sale/purchase of that labor to enact a bourgeois "white" identity. The fantasy of the impresarios who sell (and sample) sex work by "white but not quite" women is to emulate that pinnacle of patriarchal masculinity, James Bond. Cypriot, Greek, or Turkish women who employ "black" domestics see their freedom to hire a Filipina or Sri Lankan as a way of enacting feminine bourgeois whiteness, permitting a respite from their own "white but not quite" status.

Social reproduction represents the bridge among the "political, the economic, and the domestic" sectors (Elson, 1998; Picchio, 1998)[1] and it is the process through which the next generation of labor becomes reproduced within the capitalist mode of production. In understanding the role of the state in this process, I look at the migration policies and labor laws of Cyprus, Greece, and Turkey. In focusing on migrant labor policies we come to see the state's role in social reproduction and more specifically, the reproduction of the unequal racialized and gendered relations between capital and labor. What are the terms on which the state intervenes at moments of crisis (Connell, 1988: 158)?;[2] how are its interventions shifting under globalization? How does the state use its institutional regulatory framework to deprive the working female migrant class of any citizenship and human rights in order to enforce the interests of the middle and upper classes? How does the state facilitate the reproduction of sexualized and racialized boundaries between the licit and illicit aspects of the market economies and for what purpose? How does it produce its own power by securing the material interests of the owning-class such as the agents of the employment agencies, the employers, and the impresarios?

THE MATERIAL PROCESS OF SOCIAL REPRODUCTION: PERIPHERAL ECONOMIES' DESIRE INDUSTRIES

> If no body did want, no body would work; but the greatest Hardships are look'd upon as solid Pleasures, when they keep a Man from Starving.... it is manifest, that in a free Nation where Slaves are not allow'd of, the surest Wealth consists in a Multitude of laborious Poor; for besides that they are the never-failing Nursery of Fleets and Armies, without them there could be no Enjoyment, and no Product of any Country could be valuable.
>
> (Manderville, *Fable of the Bees*, 1970)

Manderville's quote raises several issues regarding peoples' desires in the world economy. The question of desire and the production of wealth by "the laborious Poor" are two major issues in the desire industries. Who desires whom, what, and for what purpose, and who ends up doing what, for whom, and at what cost are hotly contested issues across a variety of sites. A complex series of social and political forces, embodied in a variety of institutions, such as the media, the state, and the family, are expressed through a variety of social norms and interact and contribute to the commodification of labor power, which in turn, makes possible the privatization of the ownership of the means of production setting the stage for accumulation of profits. Among all these one also finds the capitalists fighting each other to lower the cost of labor. The wages of sex and domestic workers as reproductive laborers are designed to make possible the reproduction of labor while also accumulating enough wealth and generating enough profits from their labor. Picchio (1992: 29) expresses very succinctly this idea when she speaks of the wages of the workers in a free modern nation-state. The wages, she states, are set "within the bounds necessary for a viable relationship between social reproduction and accumulation" (Picchio, 1992: 29).

In all three peripheral economies, the state plays a crucial role in social reproduction and in the production of capital (Ricardo, 1951: 95). Migration policies, employment contracts, as well as the practices of the immigration officers who interpret the state's laws and policies, the media, which circulates particular stories, jokes, and songs, are not simple "dry quota numbers." They are institutions that simultaneously, albeit in a contradictory manner, control the methods and pedagogies that circulate about migrant working-class communities within its boundaries to support the fight to lower the cost of labor power. More specifically, all these institutions work together to sustain the unequal class relations between "white" and "white but not quite" and "black" nation-states as well as to secure the "white but not quite or bourgeoisie" capitalist character of these peripheral economic nation-states. It is not surprising to see how in controlling the labor market and, more specifically, the labor market of the desire industries through the use of immigration policies, labor policies, and employment contracts, the state deports those who attempt to assert their human rights. Before discussing the role these different institutions play in the social production of people and their subjectivities, it will be useful to provide some historical background about migration in these states. Understanding this background is crucial because it helps us connect past social practices with present ones and connect local and national practices, which seem to be autonomous, to the global economic situation. It is only then that we can produce a "historical knowledge of social totality" (Ebert, 1996: 7). Drawing upon historical materialist critique we can pinpoint possibilities for social transformation within the current structures (e.g., the sexual division of labor), which are suppressed because of the existing dominant relations of production and racialized class relations (Marx, 1973: 140). A feminist historical materialist critique produces knowledges that indicate that current structures are changeable and points to the possibility of a new social organization that is free of exploitation and oppression. A historical materialist critique

> disrupts "what is" to explain how social differences—specifically gender, race, sexuality, and class—have been systematically produced and continue to operate within regimes of exploitation, so that we can change them. It is the means for producing transformative knowledges. (Ebert, 1996: 7)

International migration worldwide is intensified with world restructuring or globalization. The international economic and political power relations create the conditions that make possible the flow of and the controls over migrant female reproductive labor within Cyprus, Greece, and Turkey. As migration movements expand, both regular and irregular, more countries are actively participating in the import and export of cheap labor for the generation of remittances and profits. Countries (Cyprus, Greece, Turkey) that historically exported labor are now becoming importers of labor, specifically cheap labor. With migration, regular and irregular, the issues of the day is human trafficking activity driven by internationally organized networks intertwined with violence. In this intensified current phase of globalization in which capital depends on productive wage labor,

Cyprus, Greece, and Turkey are now destination countries of such labor, and more specifically, reproductive labor. Beginning in the 1960s, all three countries followed official policies to attract tourism and enhance their foreign currency reserves (Lazaridis, 2001; Erder and Kaska, 2003; Erder, 2000; Agathangelou, 2002). In the 1990s all three countries began actively recruiting cheap wage labor from other peripheral economic states such as the Philippines, Sri Lanka, Myanmar, the Balkans, Azerbaijan, Georgia, Moldova, Romania, Russian Federation, and the Ukraine. Migrants from different neighboring countries arrived in these countries before the 1990s. Subsequently, however, all three states changed their liberal border policies to respond to intensified globalization by designing more restrictive labor migration policies to control the labor market.

One way that the global capital controls the labor market is through dividing the process of migration under the rubrics of *regular* and *irregular*. Regular migration refers to the process through which the state officially involves itself to control the movement of the worker. Irregular migration refers to a process involving violations of the national laws of the state. However, this division and mirage between regular and irregular migration is a method that historically privatizes the space of the nation-state in such a way that it allows "some people to walk some of the time" (Bhattacharjee, 1997: 317) through the use of law. However, the division of regular and irregular migration is an arbitrary dichotomy for public consumption. The EU designs policies and implements laws to control irregular migration, arguing that it is intertwined with drug and human trafficking (Ghosh, 1998; Erder and Kaska, 2003; Lazaridis, 2001; Lazos, 2000; Country report on trafficking in human beings: Turkey, 2002; Global Survival Network, 1997; Erder and Kaska, 2003), but these policies do not stop the exploitation of working-class migrant women. The sale of women's labor and women's bodies is inseparable in regular and irregular migration. This dichotomy becomes a tool to control the flows of profit and is not intended to change the exploitative and violent relations in the desire industries.

The EU is moving to design a comprehensive policy on human trafficking so that it can allow for trafficked women to have public recourse. When these comprehensive laws and judicial process are implemented in the EU, it will be possible to reduce human trafficking (Ucarer, 1999; IOM, 1996, 1995; Democratic Women's Movement, Greece; Women Against Violence, Europe, Austria; Research Centre of Women's Affairs, Athens; Emke-Papadopoulou, 2001). In these discussions, the migration of sex and domestic workers (almost always women) in the household, cabaret, or hotel is significant in the sense that one can see that irregular migration is state controlled and regulated. However, this regulation does not change the fact that these working-class women are not citizens of the state, and thus, do not officially have access to the state apparatus. The condition of sex and domestic workers in peripheral economic states exposes the mirage of regular/irregular migration and reminds us that capitalism depends on buying and selling women's labor power as a commodity to generate profits in all sites. Regulating migration and with it human trafficking is really a way to keep in place the founding myth of capitalism and its political system of liberal democracy: that the "owner of money" and the female working-class laborer enter the market on equal footing in the eyes of the law, and, therefore, regulation of migration will succeed in managing abuses in capitalism, such as human trafficking.

Sex and domestic workers in Cyprus, Greece, and Turkey are drawn mostly from Eastern Europe, such as Russia, Rumania, and Albania, and also the Philippines, Sri Lanka, and mainland Turkey. In Cyprus, these women workers constitute one among several groups entering the northern part of the country. Most of these women are associated with prostitution and the state has special regulations that govern their entry into the country (Scott, 1995: 387). Some of these women travel to Turkey to engage in prostitution, and from there, travel to northern Cyprus. The women who come to Cyprus depend on their employer to deal with entry visa requirements and health and blood tests. Since the work permits and permissions are agreed upon by the employer rather than the employee, changing jobs requires permission from the state through the new employer. If women are brought to the country as a group, some formalities are waived (e.g., health exams). In Northern Cyprus, if a woman is traveling alone to find a job, she must produce a visa and health certificates upon embarking on a plane from Istanbul to Kyrenia. The southern Greek Cypriot state and states like the Philippines work with each other and design laws for cheap wage labor import and export. These laws facilitate the transfer of female labor to Cyprus and into homes and businesses that can afford it through the issuance of visas, training lessons about domestic work, and production of ideologies about a "sexy" and productive labor force.

In Greece the migration of domestic and sex workers began in the late 1970s (Kontis, 2000; Cavounidis, 2002; Droukas, 1998; Demetriou, 2000; Karasavvoglou, 1998; Lazos, 1997; Katsoridas, 1994; Lazaridis, 1995; Ventura, 1993; Zographos, 1991). Part of a larger migration phenomenon in Southern and Southeastern Europe, many people migrated from places nearby such as Albania, Bulgaria, Poland, Rumania, Russia, the Ukraine, Moldavia, and Georgia. Many others arrived from the Philippines, India, Ethiopia, Pakistan, and India (Kethi, Human Resources Information, 2002; Ministry of National Economy, 1998; 1999). The migrant population of Greece is primarily from 20 different countries (including Albania, Bulgaria, Rumania, Pakistan, Ukraine, Poland, Syria, Moldavia, Egypt, India, Georgia, Poland, the Ukraine, Pakistan, Rumania, Bulgaria, and Russia). According to the data based on the 372,000 migrants who applied for permanent residence (Organization of the Development of Human Resources, 1998), 56.3 percent of female migrants were employed in sex and domestic services.

Against the backdrop of the political contestations swirling around its quest for full membership in the EU, Turkey actively participates in the importing of reproductive labor as well. Gender and race play a crucial role in the division of labor within Turkey. The new migration flows in Turkey exhibit dramatically different patterns (Erder and Kaska, 2003; Gülçür and İlkkaracan, 2002; Narli, 2002: 2; Günçikan, 1995). Some of the new migrants, both males and females, participate in the "suitcase industry" (Günçikan, 1995; interviews with sex and domestic workers). They enter Turkey carrying suitcases that contain small commodities and plastic bags from their country of origin so that they can sell and buy goods to take back to their home countries (Gülçür and İlkkaracan, 2002: 3 citing Morokvasic and de Tinguy, 1993; Narli, 2002). Most migrants who participate in this industry are Russians, Ukrainians, Bosnians, Bulgarians, Romanians, Tunisians, and Algerians. Simultaneously, many women who participate in the "suitcase industry" work in the sex industry to "supplement their incomes" (IMO 2003; Gülçür and İlkkaracan, 2002: 3 citing Beller-Hann, 1995; interviews with women in the sex industry). Women from Russia, the Ukraine, Georgia, and Moldavia work as sex workers, bar girls, and dancers. Many women from Moldova and Azerbaijan are now replacing the young women from the Philippines as domestic workers (Narli, 2002; interviews with female Turkish employers, 2000).

Turkey draws most of its workers from Albania, Azerbaijan, Bulgaria, Moldova, Rumania, Russian Federation, and the Ukraine. African and Asian women use the country as a transit point to Western European countries. Even though the state officially claims that there is no trafficking in Turkey, in 1998 there were arrests, and in most cases, deportations, of 6,700 women from Rumania, Moldova, and the Ukraine. In 1997, 7,000 Rumanian women were deported. In 1999, 11,000 women from Eastern European countries were deported. Between the years 1996 and 2001 the deportation figures for prostitution reached a total of 22,000 (see tables 2.1 and 2.2).

Table 2.1 Causes for deportation of foreigners in Turkey (2001)

	Prostitution and STD	%	Visa expired	%	Illegal entry	%	Illegal work	%	Other	%	Total	%
Azerbaijan	695	—	549	—	26	—	188	—	628	—	2,086	—
Georgia	813	—	768	—	114	—	70	—	762	—	2,527	—
Moldovia	938	—	2215	—	9	—	138	—	551	—	3,851	—
Rumania	274	—	511	—	34	—	259	—	358	—	1,436	—
Russian Federation	615	—	296	—	14	—	33	—	296	—	1,254	—
Ukraine	872	—	489	—	3	—	28	—	349	—	1,741	—
Subtotal	4,207	88.4	4,828	80.5	200	0.8	716	78.4	2,944	48.0	12,895	29.1
%	32.6	—	37.4	—	1.6	—	5.6	—	22.8	—	100.0	—
Other	554	11.6	1,171	19.5	26,300	99.2	197	21.6	3,190	52.0	31,412	70.9
%	1.8	—	3.7	—	83.7	—	0.6	—	10.2	—	100.0	—
Total	4,761	100	5,999	100	26,500	100	913	100	6,134	100	44,307	100
%	10.8	—	13.5	—	59.8	—	2.1	—	13.8	—	100.0	—

Source: General Directorate for Foreigners, Ministry of Interior.

Table 2.2   Deportation of foreigners for prostitution (1996–2001)

	1996	1997	1998	1999	2000	2001	Total	%
Azerbaijan	207	271	234	286	422	530	1,950	8.6
Georgia	559	522	743	544	575	663	3,606	15.9
Moldovia	187	602	849	708	975	729	4,050	17.9
Rumania	1,385	1,339	1,949	1,254	449	178	6,554	28.8
Russian Federation	317	417	332	206	231	495	1,998	8.8
Ukraine	214	726	650	530	642	662	3,424	15.1
Subtotal	2,869	3,877	4,757	3,528	3,294	3,257	21,582	94.90
Other	200	206	163	115	235	251	1,170	5.1
Total	3,069	4,083	4,920	3,643	3,529	3,508	2,2752	100
% ST	93.5	95.0	96.7	96.8	93.3	92.8	94.9	—
% Other	6.5	5.0	3.3	3.2	6.7	7.2	5.1	—
% Total	100	100	100	100	100	100	100	—

Source: General Directorate for Foreigners, Ministry of Interior.

The changes in the migration patterns in these three peripheries are a result of globalization and political reorganizations. Capital's move to locate, commodify and exploit cheap labor wherever it can be found pushes it to create markets and achieve competitive rates through the cheapest labor available internationally. The existence of asymmetries and desire for imperial power among nation-states pushes them to compete for profit by accessing cheap labor. This move as well as offering to an heterosexualized citizenry access to more capital by peripheral economic states like Cyprus, Greece, and Turkey extends capitalist relations of exploitation to every corner of the globe. Each peripheral state accesses cheap labor by using racist and gendered policies and practices to socially reproduce its power and its owning-class identity.

MIGRATION POLICIES, EMPLOYMENT CONTRACTS, AND DISCOURSES OF PERIPHERAL ECONOMIC STATES

What do the migration policies and employment contracts embody and constitute simultaneously? All three states' migration policies and employment contracts are written in a way that enforces the interests of the employers of the sex and domestic workers as well as depriving reproductive labor's basic social and human rights. Simultaneously, these national policies constitute particular gendered, racialized, and classed identities by following and conforming to certain norms of behavior, always within the constraints of the changes taking place in the European context. The "notion of production of human beings" (Engels, 1884: 4) goes beyond the production of labor power and seems to draw on reproductive labor to socially maintain existing life as well as reproduce the next generation (Brenner and Laslett, 1989: 383). Reproductive labor (both domestic and sex work) is necessary for social reproduction and is not confined within the household. On the contrary, the immigration policies of peripheral economic states demonstrate that reproduction is taking place in both the "private" household and the public arenas where sexual gratification and affection is being sold. The political economy of sex and desire is directly linked to a racialized and heterosexual gendered division of labor in social production and reproduction (Anderson, 2000: 13).

DESIRE FOR REPRODUCTIVE LABOR AS A CLASS/STATE ACT TO PRODUCE SOCIAL POWER

Commodifying Women's Reproductive Labor

All three economic peripheries focus on women's reproductive labor as a commodity. Commodity here refers to a social relation in which the value of one's labor and personhood is gauged solely by the use value of that labor by those who pay for her services. For example, the Greek Cypriot state designed a law that allows the import of sex and domestic workers (Aliens and Immigration Laws of 1952–1989; Regulations of 1972–1988). This law structures the relationship between employer and employee and as a tool sets forth who has what "rights" within the national boundaries of Cyprus. In the official contract of employment from the Ministry of Interior Civil Registration and Migration, we read:

> The employer shall pay to the employee as remuneration for her services a fixed annual salary of _____ Cyprus Pounds payable in (12) equal monthly payments of _____ each on the last day of each consecutive month.

Migrant women's services are to be remunerated through a fixed salary. This document by itself does not seem different from any other employment contract. However, upon closer examination, the role of the state in facilitating the flow of the female migrant, reproductive wage labor as well as its enforcement of the interests of the owning-class becomes apparent in this contract. This contract is a tool for guiding/mystifying the social reproduction of classed subjects within the borders of the state. The state mediates the relation between the worker and the employer by presenting the laborer (from lower-income generating peripheral economies) and the employer (from higher-generating income peripheral economies) as equal because they are both "owners of commodities" (Marx, 1976). However, this notion of the free exchange of wages for labor power is fraudulent and obfuscates the exploitative racialized and gendered relation between the domestic worker and her employer. It further obfuscates that these services are specifically domestic and sexual in nature (housemaid, homehelp, nanny, governess, artist) and are compensated by cheap wages. Moreover, the women and men who are employers and managers of these services are the Greek and Turkish Cypriot ones whereas the women who perform these services are the women of Sri Lanka, India, Myanmar, the women of Eastern European and of the former Soviet Union countries. The state's involvement in the mediation of capital and labor ensures that the exploitation of sex and domestic labor is a necessary violence. It is this violence that can secure the production of bourgeois hegemony and subjectivity (Razack, 1998: 355–356). These commodified relations between employee and employer are further managed by the state through the following clause of the employment contract that enables the middle- and upper-class Cypriot woman to both produce herself as a putative manager of the bourgeois heterosexual family and manager of the relationship between herself and her employee:

> The Employer shall employ the Employee and the Employee shall work exclusively for the Employer as nanny/governess/housemaid/home-help (strike out what is not applicable) at her residence situated at.... The term of the employment in Cyprus shall not in any way exceed the period of two years... The employer shall deposit with the Migration Department of Cyprus a bank Guarantee of 500 pounds [about 1,000 dollars] as security for travel expenses of possible repatriation of the Employee. (Immigration Office, 2002, Republic of Cyprus, Contract of Employment)

Contracts for sex workers are the same. The state regulates the relation between capital and wage labor as well as the costs of social reproduction. The employer has to deposit about 1,000 dollars with the state in case the employee (always female from lower-generating income peripheral economies) dies or is fired, and, thus, resources become necessary for repatriation. Employees tied to their employers in a master–slave relation must perform their duties according to their employers' requirement.

> The employee's entry, residence, and employment shall be subject to the provisions of the Aliens and Immigration Laws and its relevant Regulations and the period of employment in Cyprus shall not in any way exceed the maximum period of four years. [In the case of sex workers—3 months per time]. The temporary work permit and residence will be issued every year to the maximum of four years. The employee shall undergo a medical test, at the time of his/her arrival in order to provide a certificate that he/she is free from contagious diseases....The employee shall not be allowed to change Employer and place of employment during the validity of this contract in his Temporary Residence/Work Permit...shall work 6 days per week, for 7 hours per day, either during the day or the night and shall perform his duties or any other duties relevant to his employment according to the requirements of the Employer....and contribute to the utmost of his abilities in promoting the interests of the Employer, protect his property from loss, damage, etc....shall obey and comply with all orders and instructions of the Employer and faithfully observe the rules, regulations and arrangements for the time being in force for the protection of the Employer's property and in general the good execution of work...shall produce work of the highest standards and in no way inferior in quality and quantity to the work produced by skilled or unskilled workers of the same specialization/occupation in Cyprus. (Republic of Cyprus, Contract of Employment)

These property contracts and policies put in place to manage the employment relationship, outline the duties and responsibilities of the employee as well as the exclusive expectations towards the employer. This contract not only indicates the state's securing of the interests of its middle- and upper-class citizens but also outlines what needs to be protected (e.g., property and reputation) by the employees. Thus, the employees are more than workers; they are the guardians ensuring the protection of the private property and the reputation of the Cypriot employers. Additionally, the employees are expected to follow particular rules if they are to be considered legitimate objects of desire (temporary, healthy, noncontagious).

The black (Sri Lankan, Myanmaran, Filipina) female working-class domestic worker is temporary, flexible, and, in some ways, the "property" of her bourgeois "white but not quite" (Greek Cypriot) employer as outlined by the state. The employee's labor power is a commodity, and the person herself becomes a commodity and object of desire for the peripheral economy and the employer. The employee "shall not at any time be guilty of any act or conduct which may cause damage, according to the judgment of the Employer, to his property/ interest or reputation.... shall not engage, contribute or in anyway, directly or indirectly take part in any political action or activity during the course of his stay in Cyprus, and shall observe faithfully the laws governing the conduct and behavior of aliens" (Immigration Office, 2002; Republic of Cyprus, Contract of Employment, 3). This "liberal" contract outlines (1) the role the state chooses to play in the mediation of the relation between capital and female migrant wage labor; (2) its role in processing the cost of social reproduction; (3) the "agency" and "freedom" of the employer and the worker; and (4) the spaces and bodies where "violence can happen with impunity" (Razack, 1998: 358).

The state pushes for the contract to be signed both by the employer and employee and also to be notarized. This liberal democratic labor law/contract is a relationship of exploitation, despite the mirage that the relationship between the wage laborer and the employer are taking place on equal footing and that it is a relationship of commodity product and exchanges. The contract ensures the enforcement of the interests of the Greek Cypriot owning and middle-class and the social reproduction of a racialized and gendered class relation between the employer as a citizen and the employee. The employer possesses the political rights and agency, whereas the female migrant working-class Sri Lankan, Filipina, or Myanmaran does not possess the right to approach the state to hold accountable her employer or even involve herself in political organizing. The contract moves beyond the exchange to outlining that the employee is also responsible for securing the material interests of the employer. Thus, this contract outlines how the social relation between the employer and the employee should be organized and managed for a particular time period. Yet, the severity of the contract does not seem to deter female migrants from migrating to Cyprus for dependent employment and even being paid by the hour in homes/cabarets/taverns/clubs (Interviews with domestic workers, 2002). Despite claims that the worker is "equal" and "free" to choose her own conditions of labor, it becomes apparent through this contract that the owning and middle-class who commands her labor has the power and the freedom to do as s/he chooses depending on the situation. S/he has the power to dispose of her on the spot and without explanation. Even when an immigrant woman possesses the opportunity to become an economic actor in the transnational service economy and society, she still cannot command her own labor. She provides her labor/services to her employer, but is not a political agent who can challenge the violence she faces daily since she lacks citizenship and, therefore, the full rights of the social contract (Mills, 1997; Pateman, 1988).

Domestic and sex workers' reproductive labor and bodies are positioned in servitude spaces in a recent bill for immigration policy in Greece (Baldwin-Edwards, 2002, 1998). The bill's wording shows the ways the state and market mediate the social relations between the Greek subject/employer with the "other" object/employee or wage laborer. Race, for example, is almost always the first sorting mechanism in reproductive labor services. Domestic workers are collapsed under the general category of foreigners/Third country nationals entitled "for the allocation of 'dependent employment' " (Article 19). In Article 34 we read the following about sex workers: "It might be possible with the decision of the Minister of Interior to define as entertainment centers other places outside the definition provided in the textual provisions." The employer of "entertainment centers" can request the entrance of particular artists provided that these artists are "owned" by the employer while working for them. Of course, the "artist-lover" has to prove to the state that he:

- Possesses four times more income from that of his unskilled [artist] worker
- Has supporting documents in which he states that he possesses no criminal record in the past five years and that as an employer he possesses a shop with at least 50 seats and that he employs no more than 20 foreigners
- Possesses a certificate from the general hospital of the artist's country of origin stating that the artist has no "sickness that can constitute a risk for the public health in conjunction with the conditions set in WHO" (paragraph 2)
- Has a bank guarantee note that covers the expenses of (re) promotion (*epanaproothisi*) or deportation expenses to the country of origin (paragraph 2).

Moreover, within the same bill, paragraph 4 of Article 34 states that the artist is "given a permit of six months that she cannot renew. A change of employer or employment is not allowed."[3] Sex workers whom I interviewed regarding their work related the following:

> My impresario in Belarus told me that I was to work in a bar. I was just to serve drinks to the clients. When I arrived in Greece I found that my boss wanted me to do something else. He wanted me to go out with clients (have sex with them). I did not want to have sex with anybody.

When I asked him to let me go, he said, "Find another employer who can pay me $1,000 and I will let you go." Where was I to find another employer? I did not know anybody else except my boss. I am from Belarus. My impresario knew my boss in Greece and sent me to him. The Greek impresario picked me up at the airport. He took me to his house telling me that I had to stay over at his place till the next day when my employer will be ready to meet me at his nightclub. He offered me several drinks and then wanted to sleep with me. He said: "Before I sell you to _____ I want to try you out...I am your first and foremost boss in this fucking country."

More specifically, the sex work of migrant working-class women in Greece is often times collapsed under the rubric of "entertainment" and it is often times undocumented (Lazaridis, 2001: 81; Lazos, 2002).

When I arrived here I thought I would be just serving drinks to customers. After a few hours at the job, I came to a realization when my boss prodded me to go and sit with customers at different tables that I was to offer more than just drinks. I was to make conversation even when I did not know Greek, and I was to smile and nod my head stupidly and agree to whatever the customer was saying. (Interview with 22-year-old woman from Russia)

I knew that I was to sleep with customers. I had to close my eyes and be with even the most disgusting guy, always thinking that I can make some money to send back to my sister who was taking care of my 3-year-old daughter. (Interview with 25-year-old woman from Belarus)

Many women who come to Greece come to work as dancers or waitresses, but, upon arrival, come up against an expectation to perform sexual services as part of their job as artists, a euphemism for prostitute. Other political and social forces affect the commodification of women's labor power and bodies within Greece. For example, the import of sex workers takes place in a country where prostitution is legal and is seen by citizens as a "necessary evil" serving a "necessary function." The political practices and policies of the state (Kandaraki, 1997 cited in Lazaridis, 2001: 96) run parallel to the proclivities of public clientele: their approach to sex workers reflects the same assumption of necessity (Magganas, 1994). When I asked men and women to explain the reasons behind the increased levels of prostitution (Interviews with Greeks, 2001), they expressed views similar to those found by Kandaraki. Greek men and women seem to assume that men's sexual drives are "natural" (Loizos and Papataxiarchis, 1991: 222). Loizos and Papataxiarchis identify two forms of male heterosexuality, one that argues that men have sex to produce the next generation and another in which men's natural sexual desires are informed by *kefi*. Kefi is "a state of pleasure wherein men transcend the pettiness of a life of calculation" (Loizos and Papataxiarchis, 1991: 17) or "the spirit of desire that derives from the heart" (Loizos and Papataxiarchis, 1991: 226). "Such desire is spontaneous, ephemeral and individualistic" (Lazaridis, 2001: 76) and women who participate in fulfilling these desires are condemned as "women of the road" (Magganas, 1994).

The 1981 Greek Law (1193) conveys the expectation that all women who work in the sex industry must be registered, and while it does not define prostitution as "employment," it does accept it as "work" (Lazaridis, 2001: 78). The Greek state's informal condoning of prostitution is reflected in the parliament's discussions over public health care. Following the reports by Roumeliotou and Kornarou (1996, 1997), one of the prime ministers, Mr. Gialoumatos, focused on the fact that many prostitutes need to gain access to public health care because they are the ones that suffer from contagious diseases and yet cannot afford private health care. In the past few years, the state faced pressures from public opinion, feminists, and Europap/Tampep members to change the law on prostitution. Because of the violence and exploitation that these women suffer from both Greek impresarios and impresarios of the same national background (Russia, Albania, Balkan, and the Ukrainians), the state was forced to pass new legislation, 2734/5-8-1999. While this law is not yet enforced, it accords some rights to sex workers, both males and females. It

> recognizes male prostitution; female and male sex workers, registered and non-registered, can be tested for STDs and AIDS in Public STD Clinics; registered prostitutes are obliged to be tested every 15 days, (in the past registered sex workers have been checked twice a week); migrant sex workers can work legally as long as they have a visa and they are registered; sex workers must pay for social insurance in order to have health care and pension rights; municipality is in charge of sex workers. (2734/5-8-1999)

Similarly, domestic workers have to follow several procedures as stated in the "Entry and stay of foreigners for the allocation of dependent employment" (Article 19 both in the draft bill and the official bill in the government newspaper of May, 2001: 1696–1697). With this Article, employers interested in hiring a domestic worker are allowed to apply for a permit for her. In paragraph 2 of this Article, we find that employment is dependent on a specific employer and whether the national economy "needs" this particular employee (paragraph 2). The employer has to confirm that s/he wants to hire the "specific foreigners" as well as accept responsibility for their own living expenses till they receive permission to work, and if they are not issued a permit, till they leave the country (paragraph 6). In addition, the employer has to present to the state a guarantee bank note and the permit signed by the monarch. The guarantee, is equal to the tri-monthly wages of the unskilled worker while in Greece plus an amount that covers the repromotion (selling of the worker's labor) to somebody else or till she is deported to the country of origin (paragraph 6). The permit is provided once the local police clears the way by stating that the migrant could not endanger the public order and security of the country (paragraph 6).

The entry and hiring of domestic and sex workers (see Article 19)[4] are tied to the employer, and this raises issues regarding the freedom of movement of racialized and feminized non-EU labor even when the state opens up its borders to the flow of workers. The idea that a non-EU worker's employment is tied to the employer's demands justifies and sustains a servitude power relation between what are considered economically independent European states versus economically "dependent" non-EU states, and, also, between what are considered legitimate and well-off subjects who can afford to buy the labour power and bodies of working-class migrant women within their national boundaries. The state intervenes to mediate this relation in such a way that it obfuscates the class/gendered/racialized relations between those who are "white but not quite" and "black" working-class women whose labor power is commodified and those "white but not quite" subjects within the new emerging transnational owning-class who command not only the labor power but also the whole person, by exploiting and using different methods of violence such as exploitation, name calling, beating, sexual assault, and rape.

Reproductive labor (both domestic and sexual) is defined by naturalist notions (e.g., kefi, or protection of one's employer's property), camouflaging the political and economic processes that organize and reproduce these relations. This process of social reproduction commodifies migrant women's labor and bodies and produces sexualities and domestic services as a personal essence. These politics, which focus on the imaginary of an heterosexually married, two-parent family as the norm, displace and marginalize households that do not fit into that model. Thus, class, race, and gender with the upper-class and middle-class accessing high-income levels and expensive spaces of living condition the social reproduction of Greek and Turkish bourgeoisie in Cyprus, Greece, and Turkey. The female migrant worker as well as the local working-class ends up accessing lower wages as well as becoming ghettoized within these peripheral economic states' borders and spaces. The working-class, migrant and local, becomes relegated to the margins, by the state and those enterpreneurs who hire their labor. This spatial moral ordering premised on the idea of consent of liberal democratic states makes possible the further domination of the working-class and more specifically the sex and domestic workers. Sherene Razack brilliantly articulates how the marginalization of and the violence against the prostitute secures property and home for men. This is what she argues.

> Actual spaces express relations of domination—relations mapped as degrees of belonging to the nation state...the idea of how much we can care. We care less about the bodies in degenerate spaces and often define out of existence the violence enacted on those bodies. The spatial system of moral ordering is enabled by the notion in liberal democratic states that we are all free individuals entitled to pursue our own interests. The idea of consent as it operates in prostitution bolsters the hierarchy of bodies and spaces. Further, the consent framework effectively dissolves a consideration of the production of spaces. We do not ask what the spaces of prostitution enable nor what happens in them. There are simply designated bodies and spaces where so called contractual violence can happen with impunity. (Razack, 1998: 358)

These conditions, for example, create higher employment rates for the upper and upper-middle-classes and lower wages, higher stress, and increased violence for the female migrants and the local working-class. Simultaneously, these practices make possible the heterosexual white bourgeoisie production of masculinity and femininity as well as the securing of property, the surplus-value of the labor from the working-class, and the treatment of their bodies as places where violence can occur with impunity (Razack, 1998: 358). Moreover, the labor of the "white but not quite" and "black" female worker, that is, their life-activity, appears as a "means to life" (Marx, 1988: 76). The female worker is thus both estranged from her life-activity and from those she works for. This social reproduction of asymmetrical racialized, gender, and class identities is constituted through the social practices (e.g., valorization and commodification of social reproduction, buying one's labor, signing an employment contract) within an international division of labor. The peripheral economic state facilitates this social reproduction through its mediation and support of the sale and purchase of reproductive labor and its exploitation. The upper and middle-class of Cyprus, Greece, and Turkey is constituted as "white but not quite" (economically powerful but not as powerful as their EU core country counterparts) through the labor of women of color (or black) and "white but not quite" sex workers.

While migration flows have not accelerated over the past three decades at a pace comparable to those of capital flows and trade, the state-sponsored migration and immigration of sex and domestic workers for the desire industries do indicate the "globalization of [female] migration flows" (Lisbon Conference November 2 and 3, 1998). The increasing diversity of migrants' nationalities and the migration channels used, as well as the growing proportion of movements of temporary and skilled workers in total migration flows, show that migration today is taking place in the context of economic globalization. Peripherally economic sending and host countries' owning-classes collusion and dependence on each other for generation of profits and surplus-value becomes apparent and it has intensified due to changing politico-economic and social (e.g., human rights violations) practices to respond to corporate welfare and other market pressures: the political and economic pressures on the country of origin and the receiving country to respond to transnational capital's demands, the contestations over the national cohesion and future of the welfare state in both countries, the human rights of people (Tapinos and Delaunay, Lisbon Conference 1998), and the ways we understand social and sexual relations.

The new migration bill of Greece as a political document reflects the participation of the Greek state, like other EU states, in the in-migration of foreign workers for political and economic reasons. Foreign workers, especially non-EU citizens, serve as boundary-markers ("white" European class as opposed to "black" migrants) for the expanding of the Greek middle-classes (Ministry of National Economy, July 2002: 5; Menegou, 2000: 23) in a time when Greece is trying to reach the economic and political levels of other countries in the EU and legitimize its power by showing its capability to reach the political, economic, and social levels that exist in the European context which create the conditions for capital's free and secure movement.

REPRODUCTIVE AUTONOMY OR MARKET IMPERATIVE?

All three peripheral economies and the state mediate the sale and purchase of the reproductive labor of migrant women and in the process encourage prospective employers to specify racial and other social characteristics/contradictions for the reproductive labor and the bodies they wish to buy. This "encouragement" and "mediation" support a particular kind of economic exchange of reproductive labor. When a migrant woman decides to pursue paid reproductive labor, it may seem like a totally individual choice, but she ends up being hired to sell her labor power and perform tasks/sexual favors for men and women who belong to the owning and middle-class and as Razack calls them, in degenerate spaces. In addition, they sell their labor power by offering tasks/sexual services that a working-class Greek or Turkish woman would not want to undertake. For many within these peripheral economies/states this "choice" is explained as the reproductive autonomy of the woman and at the same time, as the transnational market's demand.[5] However, a different picture unfolds when we take a closer look at the state's intervention and the people who sell/buy these services.

> Two of my friends were working with families in Turkey. They came here ten years back. Their Madame had a friend who needed a maid. They applied for a visa for me, bought the ticket and sent it to me and that's the reason I came. (50-year-old Filipina domestic worker)
>
> In my own case, it is a bit different. I found an agency and they told me that I could get a visa for Turkey in a few days. My husband just lost his job and I lost mine in Dubai where I was working as a floor manager in a warehouse. [She shows her ID, which she is still wearing.] I was in Dubai for 6 years and I really enjoyed it. (Tricia, 49-year-old Filipina domestic worker)
>
> I entered Turkey along with 13 other women. We came here with a Russian guy who knew where to take us through the port of Trabzon. Once we arrived at the border, two Turkish guys took us to a cabaret where guys walked in and picked us up for...you-know-what. (Miriam, 27-year-old Russian sex worker)

The 50-year-old Filipina woman who decided to go to Turkey and work as a domestic worker made it there because of personal connections with other Filipinas who traveled there before her. After her husband loses his job and she finds herself without a job in the Middle East, Tricia uses an employment agency to facilitate her finding a job in Turkey. Miriam, through the help of a Russian impresario, is trafficked to Turkey along with other 13 women. Despite the different routes these women followed to traverse the borders into Turkey, they are all considered unskilled labor and end up working in the desire industries. Many female migrant workers explain their "choice" via social and economic motivations. For example, many of the sex and domestic workers that migrated to Turkey explained that they had migrated for economic reasons. Most women interviewed said that they wanted to travel to Greece, Italy, or other Western European countries and chose Turkey as a transit country because the visa requirements were not as stringent. Moreover, migrant women from the former Soviet Union and Eastern European countries added that the proximate borders to Turkey made travel between countries easy. Other women explained that the "mafia" facilitated entrance into Turkey:

> Several of us from Russia, Georgia, and the Ukraine were told that if we wanted to go to Turkey we could make a lot of money. We just had to pay $2,500 to this Chechen guy and he can get us visas. That's what we did. And I ended up in Laleli with 20 other women forced to work in a hotel without any freedom. I worked there for 2 months and then I escaped. I made enough money, but I hated my boss who charged the clients so much money because I was Russian, and he gave me one-third of what I was making. (Anna, 25-year-old Russian sex worker)

> I went to an agency in Moldavia. I talked to an employer there who told me that I could have a visa to Turkey in two days if I wanted to work there. What could I do? I just separated from my husband who was beating me all the time and was left with a child to take care of. My mother could take care of my son but I had to make money for their food, clothes, and other necessities. I said "yes" and I found myself in Istanbul. (Maria, 28-year-old Moldavian sex worker interviewed in Greece)

Anna and Maria find themselves using the mafia and businessmen to seek employment in the desire industries of Greece and Turkey. In addition to different motivations for leaving their countries, they use different networks to make their migration a reality. A restructuring world economy throws unskilled labor into the owning exploitative class either Greek, Turkish, Cypriot, or alternatively, the Russian mafia.

> Since the height of the Brezhnev era[6] with its official concern over the birth rate, the media have produced a deluge of images and language portraying women as "different" and "special," their thoughts and actions irrevocably determined by their reproductive function. For the best part of a decade before the advent even of perestroika, women's characters were being habitually portrayed as inextricably bound up with their sexuality. By the time the process of liberalization began, therefore, the "otherness" of women had been emphasized to such a degree that to objectify them further in an overtly sexual way was but a small step to take. As the pronatalist discourse contrived to ease women off the workforce, it became much easier to depict them not as

skilled or intellectual but as domestic, decorative, and sexual. In effect, the representation of women was being restricted to either wife and mother or mistress and whore. (Bridger et al., 1996: 166)

In the Russian Federation and other Eastern and Western countries, an expansion of the commodification and exploitation of "white but not quite" and "black" sexualities and bodies for profit began in the Brezhnev era. The growing number of women from ex-socialist states who end up working as sex workers is a part of that Soviet legacy. The pronatalist discourses during the Brezhnev era focused on women's reproductive functions and depicted them as unskilled workers whose major goal is sexuality for reproduction of the nation. The multinational corporations draw upon these discourses and identify ex-socialist countries' women's sexuality as a commodity to be sold for profits in the desire industries.

However, these discourses conceal the exploitation of women's labor and the violence on their bodies in a global market whose sole interest is accumulation of profits and exploitation of surplus-value. Women from the Philippines, India, and Sri Lanka are forced to seek employment that could provide them with subsistence income since many of their states do not provide them even basic social welfare because of their high debts to the International Monetary Fund (IMF) and the World Bank (WB). The patriarchal political economy of social relations within these countries already defines the position of women in the national market, which, in turn, makes it possible for the "new enterpreneurs" such as sex traffickers to draw upon them as the "new" transnational flexible and ephemeral labor force. In the countries of the former Soviet Union and Eastern Europe, women have lost their employment and social benefits, and the gender segregation of a number of occupations has led to the massive "redundancy" of women. The major sectors dominated by women such as textiles and health services have been drastically cut down and now women constitute around 70 percent of the unemployed. In Russia, for example, the feminization of unemployment and poverty as well as the revival of semi-feudal patriarchal relations under the "free-market" reforms have created the conditions for "sexual terror" and harassment as well as women losing their jobs if they resist sexual advances (Ebert, 2001: 10; Bridger et al., 1996). With the return to a system of commodity exchange and the private ownership of the means of production, women within ex-socialist countries are turned into a source of cheap labor in certain areas of production, and discarded again when not needed (Munoz and Woods, 2000: 1).

Similarly, we see three phenomena in many of these countries. First, a pushing of women "back to the home" as a way of reducing and eliminating costly payments to women for child care and maternity benefits, which reinforces gender asymmetries, and also promotes men as the sole breadwinner and authority in the family. Second, a pushing of women into the roles of mistress and whore stifles the working-class women's search for freedom from necessity. Women who are pushed to stay home and are materially dependent on their husbands become disempowered and alienated:

> women won't go rushing off to petition for divorce so easily.... Centuries of human experience show us that materially dependent women don't leave their husbands, like serfs don't leave the village. (Galina Iakusheva cited in Bridger et al., 1996: 36–37)

Third, within these social contexts, sexual cultures of terror emerge to keep women in their place (e.g., you made the choice now enjoy the consequences). Women who find themselves being prostitutes or mistresses face similar alienation, disempowerment, and violence.

Contrary to the Turkish state's public discourse that "skin trade" should be managed and controlled in the Genelevs (brothels), sex trade has absorbed a large number of women from ex-socialist European countries to work as prostitutes. The Genelev structure employs about 100,000 women and is part of a larger industry: the desire industry (*The Guardian*, April 17, 1992; *Sunday Telegraph*, July 5, 1992). Many of the women who work in the genelevs are local; however, the number of women from ex-socialist countries has increased through the work of "organizations of white-slave traders" (Turkey, Country Report, 2002: 458). Genelevs are

> walled complexes in which legal prostitution takes place, consisting of a number of houses where prostitutes work. By law, the high wall surrounding each complex has only one door, to allow strict control over the movement of the prostitutes and their clients either by the police or by the brothels' own security staff. These licensed brothel complexes are all privately owned. (457)

Metaphorically and materially, these "public houses" become sites of social reproduction of masculine and feminine racialized identities. The men's temporary excursions into the Genelevs to buy sex secures them an heterosexual (e.g., bought a woman and had sex with her), and a portion of hegemonic (white) masculinity.[7] Moreover, it makes it possible for these men to renter the "nondegenerated" national public spaces as men who possess respectable bodies and resume their relations to nonprostitutes. Immigration as well as labor laws around prostitution privatize the nation, and in turn, the national public spaces. Sex workers are not considered subjects that are or could become bourgeois (Poulatzas, 1980: 90) and therefore their presence within the national borders/spaces has to be controlled and managed, including the acknowledgement of her as a member of what constitutes the public. Despite her intensely exploited labor and contributions through production the state will not open its "public" space to her since this space is really "private" power understood in terms of ownership and control of property and not democratically accountable. Their spatial architectural structure is such that allows close control and surveillance over the sex workers and clients by the security of the brothel as well as the state. Law regulates the brothel. The Istanbul brothels are controlled by men who are the "city's top taxpayers," that is, private powers. The state does not control these private powers, on the contrary, it supports them even when the state may appear as a class-neutral public space. This example clearly challenges the work of many transnational feminists who centralize the state and its power when analyzing sex work (Kempadoo and Doezema, 1998; Murray, 1998). Sex work is not just a power relation in a neoliberal capitalist economy; it is more importantly, an economic relation that informs dialectically that power relation as well as the production of subjects. In addition to the exploitation, prostitutes also suffer violence, which makes it possible for many of us to live lives of lesser violence and be constituted as respectable. Clearly, in the Genelevs of Turkey, women's sexuality and its exploitation are increasingly subordinated to both the state and the logic of transnational capital (Cotter, 2001: 7).

The idea that women have reproductive labor autonomy when they become involved in the sex industries is a contradictory one. Many of the sex workers interviewed for this book talked of a search for quick money that led them to employment in the desire industries. But any "get-rich-quick" schemes lose their luster when migrant women experience the harsh realities of debt bondages to the men and ex-sex workers who trafficked them to Cyprus, Greece, or Turkey and their relations with particular members of the networks such as the Russian, the Bulgarian, the Greek, or the Turkish. Yet, even when their earnings are minimal, they still arrive daily in the hope that they can fulfill their "fantasies" and be free to escape the abject conditions in their own countries. However, the sex workers are not free to choose their work. On the contrary, in a transnational capitalist society where work presupposes class society, women are restricted to a formal freedom, that is, the sale of their labor power, and thus, are accorded the freedom to be exploited. The contract obscures the historical constraints on the freedom to choose. "In short, it is the 'freedom' to be exploited in the way one 'chooses' but not the freedom from exploitation" (Cotter, 2001: 7).

Some women view paid reproductive labor as one option among a series of economic choices. For example, many of the women explained their choice to seek employment in Cyprus, Greece, and Turkey as being a result of restricted economic opportunities in their countries and a lower standard of living experienced under communism. The desire industries advertise opportunities to earn comparatively good wages, but women's decisions to seek such opportunities occur against a restrictive backdrop of structural sexism and racism. While the decision to sell one's reproductive labor is not an expression of pure free will, neither is it simply a matter of false consciousness. Feminists (Kempadoo and Doezema, 1998; Murray, 1998) argue that until the overall social structure is transformed, women should have the "choice" to sell their services and bodies if they so choose. Otherwise, women's sense of reproductive autonomy is violated. What is meant by reproductive autonomy within a transnational market economy? It connotes some degree of choice, albeit from a very limited set of options and within a particular social and political environment. For many women it means the possibility of saving some money for a small house back "home" or for transnational ties with a man or woman who can accord them security. Even when a small house "represents security" it does not catapult her out of poverty. As Marianne and Galena told me in an interview:

> When we leave here [Turkey] to go back to Russia and Moldavia we want to be able to sit in our homes with our daughters and mothers and drink our vodka without any impresarios around sucking your blood [they both laugh].

RACIAL SOCIAL RELATIONS AND PRACTICES: COLONIALISM REDUX WITH A POSTMODERN FACE?

"Sucking your blood" is a reference to the exploitation that they experience in the desire industries, and yet, their knowing that a structure of exploitative relations exists does not stop them from migrating to make quick cash or from selling their bodies or reproductive labor "as a strategy of subsistence survival" (Ebert, 2001: 14). Kollontai would not have been surprised to see the increase in the desire industries under the neoliberal capitalist system and the state's role in facilitating the sexual, racial, and class relations. Discussing prostitution, she stated: "the trade in women's flesh . . . is not surprising when you consider that the whole bourgeois way of life is based on buying and selling" (264). The economic exchanges, the commodification of women's bodies and labor, the profits that accumulate in selling women's flesh and labor under neoliberal capitalism result from the social production of families as units of consumption, and in the case of the owning-class, units of capital accumulation (Ebert, 2001: 16).

Despite the commodification, the fetishization of pleasure, sensuality, and other kinds of reproductive labor, many theories of sexuality and reproductive work (Lascamana, 2004; Aguilar, 2004; Anderson, 2004; Ebert, 2001: 16; Aguilar, 2002; Cotter, 2001) obscure the social relations[8] of desire and the class/sexual interests embedded in their current forms. The theorists that address the commodification of women's labor in the desire industries (Kempadoo and Doezema, 1998; Miles, 2003; Rohatynsky, 2003; Trepanier, 2003) focus on women's rights, identity, self-determination, free expression, reproductive autonomy, women's choice, and free expression independent of the socioeconomic and political questions such as labor exploitation. Moreover, many of these studies make invisible the political economy of colonial desire for reproductive labor. When the peripheral economies of the Mediterranean seek domestic and sex workers for the middle and upper classes to keep their households clean and also to satiate their desires, they use racial images of potential employees. This racial image is conveyed through the use of briefly worded descriptions depending on whether somebody desires a sex or domestic worker. For example, men's demand for Eastern European or women from the former Soviet Union has proved to be an important factor in causing, generating, and shaping the current sex industry.

> Immigration Police Officer in Cyprus (IPO): The liberalization of Russia and other Eastern European countries has led to the increase of women from there. The import of women from Thailand and other Asian countries has decreased.
>
> Author: Why do you think there is such a change?

IPO: It is a change of product. It is a change of commodity. It is a change in people's desires. The women from the former Soviet Union and Eastern European countries possess bodily skills: long legs, they are tall and beautiful and can work in the top cabarets. Of course, the prices vary too! If you arrive from Africa or Asia your price is much lower than if you are from Central Europe or Eastern Europe. The women from Asia are like small monkeys with flat faces. The desire of the man has changed, he is hungry.... The Filipinas are more educated and possess a better approach towards nurturing kids; they possess muscular power and nursing skills. In sum, the skills of each are different from the other.

The racialization of women and the naturalization of their labor as skills and sexy bodies are prevalent tropes in both the discourses of immigration officers and the practices of the state. The IPO is talking about a distinction in the specific services (e.g., nurturance and muscular power versus beauty and offering of pleasure) of immigrant women and frames his narrative by suggesting that culture shapes desire in the form of demand for erotic leisure or domestic work. What becomes apparent also from his narrative is that such racial distinctions expressed in these commercial services are economic issues (whose labor is cheaper) in social reproduction. The national distinctions identify whose reproductive labor and flesh will end up in a domestic household or in cabarets, clubs, and hotels. Using a global political economy framework, we see that these relations are all affected by politico-economic influences shaping the demands for various forms of commercial reproductive labor. For example, women from Eastern Europe and the former Soviet Union have a higher market demand in the sex industry than women from the Philippines or Sri Lanka. The employment agencies, impresarios, and ex-sex workers from the former Soviet Union and Eastern European countries strategically place solicitations for sex workers in newspapers. Such solicitations are based on particular colonialist racialized assumptions: women from these countries are more "sexy" and more beautiful and women from these countries would be interested in that aspect of the desire industry, that is, sex rather than domestic work. These women may see sex work as an easy way to make money quickly. Simultaneously, the colonialist logic that emphasizes that women of Asian countries are "less sexy" and naturally better caregivers makes invisible the political economies of desire and its historical constitution. Nevertheless, "sexy" or "non-sexy" women are both subject to exploitation in the process of reproducing a world order that perpetuates the idea that women and women's reproductive labor is a personal possession of men and women in peripheral economies. The "contemporary psyche" is characterized by an "extreme individuality, egoism that has become a cult" that demands possession and experience of all married partners and employees (remember the impresario that wanted to taste all his sex workers before he sold them to their employers?) and is guided by the colonialist belief "that the two sexes are unequal, that they are of unequal worth in every way, in every sphere, including the sexual sphere" (Kollontai, 1977: 242). These colonialist and racialized aspects are intensely being revived in the peripheral economies as local strategies of difference, as if difference is not power, constituted in turn by those who own property and control social wealth within a neoliberal capitalist-patriarchy. The strategy of difference is one of capital's tools for exploitation.

CONTRADICTIONS AND CONFLICTS AVERTED IN SOCIAL REPRODUCTION?

Various feminist and IR analyses that tend to centralize the state and its power conceal the colonialist and exploitative logics that inform the social organization of the desire industries and the interventions of the different institutions such as the market, the state, and the media to socially reproduce sexual and other subjectivities out of particular class interests and economic relations of the neoliberal capitalist structure. Racialized and sexualized discourses inform social relations within these peripheral economies and affect the sale and distinction of migrant reproductive labor. In a focus group conducted with eight, well-educated Cypriot women, I asked what they thought about the issue of migration in Cyprus. An older woman, in her fifties, said:

> For everything ... the Russian women are responsible. [They burst out laughing]. Their presence alone "excites" (*erethizei*) the young, resulting in the kinds of behaviors they currently exhibit.[9]

A similar feeling was expressed in *Zaman* of October 11, 2000: Karadeniz'de sorun "Natasa" [The Problem is Natasha in the Black Sea].

Such racial discourses and practices promote an economic racial hierarchy in the transnational sale and purchase of reproductive labor. Moreover, such practices and discourses contribute to the social reproduction of racial, sexual, and gender transnational relations: men and women of rich-income peripheral economies and their families are units of consumption, the owning-class, units of capital accumulation

through the exploitation of reproductive labor. Commodifying sexualities and bodies for profit is a norm and is presented as a liberating
force (e.g., Irigaray, 1985a, 1985b; Cixous, 1998). Thus, colonizing
reproductive labor is also a guilty pleasure and a sensuous excess irrespective of socioeconomic and political relations of desire and the
racialized class interests that it upholds. The mostly private social relations of family formation and personal intimacies that we typically
ignore as private social relations are still guided by the logic of
exploitation and violence: "relations of sexuality, love and desiring are
all grounded on property relations" (Ebert, 2001: 17).

Contracting a sexual partner or a domestic worker, the owning-
class gains access to the emotional, physical, and spiritual world of the
working-class. This strategy

> Foster[s] . . . the ideal of absolute possession of emotional as well as
> physical 'I', thus extending the concept of property rights to include
> the right to the other person's whole spiritual and emotional world.
> (Kollontai, 1977: 242)

Socially reproducing classes and their contingent subjectivities
become the vision of the neoliberal capitalist project all over the world
and in the peripheral economies. For example, different forms of sex
services coexist: the low-cost cabarets for working-class men and the
high-cost hotels/clubs for the middle and upper class men, which
emphasize the refinement of the women in distinction from a "go-go"
style. Some of these cabarets and clubs cater to men who are interested
in consuming women's bodies by providing more explicit sex shows.
Naked women dance around poles (or phallic symbols) and display
their bodies and sexuality on one end while other women engage in
identifying clients for the evening (Interviews with Greek Immigration
Officers, and clients of sex workers in Cyprus and Greece, 2002).

The purchasers of reproductive labor are typically oblivious to the
racial practices and discourses they bring to economic transactions
because racist, sexist, and class violences function on structural levels.
We may be all participating in these racist and sexist practices, but the
emotional and economic costs of racism fall disproportionately on the
shoulders of migrant women (positive and negative racist stereotyping)
from lower-income generating nation-states. The imperial class/racist/
sexist practices and discourses circulating in the desire industries as
strategies to socially produce consumers who fetishize women's bodies
and labor may result from patriarchy. Yet the use of such labor enables
men and women of middle and upper classes to avoid the conflicts and

contradictions inherent in the sexual and racial division of labor transnationally as well as the challenges (national, social, and personal) that the social organization of the desire industries poses for the peripheral economic state, the family, and the person (Anderson, 2000: 1). As long as the peripheral economic state actively participates in colonizing immigrant women's reproductive labor and their flesh, always in the name of supply and demand or market imperative, it participates in reviving the colonizing of its own people:

> In a society where the division of labor becomes more accentuated, where the vast majority of people are deliberately deprived of creativity, where work has no other value than its explicit monetary one, sexuality becomes...a means of escaping from society through self-centered sexual consumption, rather than the full expression of interpersonal relations. (Broyelle, 1998: 2)

In socially producing itself as the profiteer from the sale/purchase of reproductive labor and some of its people as consumers of women's bodies and their reproductive labor, the peripheral economic state participates in averting the conflicts and contradictions of a global/regional European structure that is intensely interested in hiding exploitation of desire and sex in the desire industries. The peripheral economy/state finds itself colluding in a process parallel to that of the hired reproductive worker, producing social beings and sets of relationships that do not enable their own development, but also are deeply antagonistic to their own interests. As Rupert argues, drawing from Wood (1995: 29–30), the state is not class-neutral. The state may appear as class-neutral public sphere in which abstract individuals may interact as formally equal citizens pursuing an instrumental politics of self-interest (Rupert, 2000: 3). Its practices and ideologies in facilitating the migration of reproductive labor prove that the state is a classed, raced, and gendered institution whose powers are drawn upon to mystify contradictions and to sustain in place the hegemonic, heterosexual, and white "private" powers.

The domestic and sex worker's presence serves to emphasize and reinforce her employer's identity: a competent household, of "white but not quite" middle-class, and her own identity as the opposite. The same occurs for the peripheral economic state: its labor and participation falls short of becoming equal to the economically core transnational/European state. "Buying and selling of caresses" destroys the sense of equality among the states and reinforces the need for the peripheral economic state to "fit" at any cost, desiring economic and financial security even at the expense of reinforcing its own role in the constitution of the illicit economies of reproductive labor.

In chapter 3 I focus on the specific strategies of difference, that is, mystifications of class, race, and gender contradictions employed by capital within the peripheries to exploit and dominate this labor, as well as to reproduce itself and its contingent logics.

CHAPTER 3

REPRODUCTIVE LABOR: SEX
AND DOMESTIC WORK IN
CYPRUS, GREECE, AND TURKEY

Why should IPE and feminism be concerned with the sale and
purchase of reproductive labor under globalization and the strategies
capitalism uses to exploit female working-class migrants' labor?
Female sex and domestic workers migrate not merely to survive but
also to advance their positions in the fringe economies of desire. Put
differently, the working-class migrant woman tries to navigate the terrain that simultaneously makes it possible for her to seek opportunity
while making possible the expropriation of her labor. Within this
transnational economy, gender, sexuality, and desire cannot be separated from the political and economic conditions that shape them
(Altman, 2001: 2), and, more specifically, labor exploitation and production (Ebert, 1996: 129). And yet, many IPE theorists (Cox,
1987; Scholte, 2001) and feminists (Ehrenreich and Hochschild,
2002; Lutz, 2002; Irek, 1998; Hochschild, 2000; Parrenas, 2001)
ignore these issues in their analyses. The intensified restructurings of
the transnational world economy (e.g., privatization of social
resources, high rates of unemployment, poverty, militarization of
everyday life) are further separating the producers from their own
production which, in turn, subjects them to exploitation by "private"
powers, that is, those owning and controlling private property, that is
upper and middle-classes within the peripheries.

In the desire industries, profits are generated through four
processes: (a) commodifying, or turning everything, including reproductive labor power, into things for the production of profit (Cotter,

2001: 7); (b) colonizing the labor power of migrant "white but not quite" and "black" working-class women and their bodies (e.g., socially subordinating women to private property by naturalizing working-class women's labor and bodies sexually and racially); (c) organizing and perpetuating particular kinds of masculine and feminine desire as informed by the dialectic relation of the domestic and neoliberal global social relations, including the sex and domestic workers' fantasies for opportunity, security, and success as well as their employers' fantasies about them; and (d) criminalizing the local/non-local working-class by identifying both sex and domestic workers as "threats" to the society, the sex workers as "dirty," immoral, and/or "deviant," and the domestic workers as "polluters" who "black" the society. The upper owning-class draws upon racist and sexist mythologies that "white but not quite" and also "black" women's labor is natural so that it can be sold cheaply. Sexual reproduction becomes the terrain on which struggles and conflicts are fought around the dialectic of material relations of production, global capital, and ideas about sex and desire.

The next section focuses on the dialectics among the construction of desires for consumption, identity, and needs, the ways individuals fulfill their desires, and how their position in the international racialized and sexed division of labor affects the fulfillment of such needs and desires. For example, a woman's position in the international division of labor (e.g., a sex worker) compels her to take up a strictly heterosexual position in this sexual and economic service to a pimp, or a client, in order to make ends meet. The material conditions of domestic (and sex workers) are quite stringent when compared to those of a woman who is a well-paid professional in a bank and is able to hire a domestic worker (Cotter, 2001: 8). In the next section, I examine the ways "private" powers through the market control the circuits of capital, labor, and production of ideas in the peripheries through the desire economies to increase profits.

SEXING AND RACIALIZING DESIRE AS A COMMODITY

[S]exualized, gendered, cross-cultural bodies...have histories of production in the United States at the nexus of academic and nonacademic discourses. These histories are histories of tourism and exploitation. They are histories that simultaneously seek and produce commodities as queered fetishes, feminized fetishes and nativized fetishes.

(Alexander, 1998: citing Patel, 1996)

Patel foregrounds the imperial, which allows us to see the interdependence, competition, and cooperation between the "peripheral" and "metropole" capital. While both the media and IR theorists employ pervasive discourses in which the peripheral is captured as a spectacle (i.e., a social relationship between people mediated by images of each other), the migration of reproductive labor within peripheries cuts through this construction, challenging its premises (Debord, 1988). This imperial discourse represents women in the desire industries of the Third World as: (1) victims of backward peripheral economic patriarchies struggling to survive against all odds, and (2) flexible, ephemeral servants without attachments and loyalties that may impede their transfer anytime within the world economy for wage-labor. The Third World woman's body is the " 'site of experimentation and mass production'.... once production dissolves human agency, it finds the human body a fertile site for production" (http://www.emory.edu/ENGLISH/Bahri/transnationalism.html). These sets of discourses universalize the peripheries as regions where violence and abuse of women is commonplace. They replace the tangible experiences in peripheries with a selection of images of violence (Debord, 1988: 35) and against the backdrop of these images, we read the presence of working-class migrant women in those peripheries.

Feminists such as Shrage (1994) and Kempadoo (1994) argue that a large percentage of sex customers seek workers with a racial, national, or class identity that differs from their own. "Sex industries depend upon the eroticization of the ethnic and cultural Other [which] suggests that we are witnessing a contemporary form of exoticism which sustains postcolonial and post-cold war relations of power and domination" (Kempadoo, 1994: 75–76). Shrage explains that Western men demand women "different from their own" (142). Similarly, the logic that operates for the Western men operates for the "white but not quite" men of the peripheries. Being able to buy a "white but not quite" sex worker and have her in their arms becomes a sign of status both for the man himself, and his state.

> [C]ulturally produced fantasies regarding the sexuality of these women.... [are connected] to socially formed perceptions regarding the sexual and moral purity of white women. (1994: 48–50)[1]

These fantasies that "white but not quite" men have about "white but not quite" women work hand in hand with fantasies that sex workers have about the economic power of these men. However, a focus on this "hypermasculine hegemony" and its abstraction from the basic processes of capitalist exploitation, including the exploitation of sex workers, hides that the discursive logics circulating in the desire industries work hand in hand to sustain the asymmetrical social relations between labor and capital in the peripheries. Such racialized and gendered exclusions and "otherings" are strategies that conceal the methods that the "private" powers of capitalism utilize to justify commodifying women and their labor power, which in turn, make possible the exploitation of their waged labor.

To generate profits for the owning-class and, more generally, to increase the national Gross National Product and the incomes of many in these countries (Sitaropoulos, 2003: 75–76), all three countries import women in a direct or indirect promotion of the desire industries. To restructure itself and remain a viable power in the world economy, the importing peripheral economic state moves toward reorganizing itself so that more and more of the surplus labor of the working-class (local and otherwise) is privately appropriated. Its new emerging professional middle-class and those men and women desiring "exotic" foreign bodies for reproductive labor are free to buy this surplus-value legally through the employment contracts that the state deploys; they are accorded this freedom because of their classed in its racial and gender configuration position in the material relations of production and the international division of labor. The exporting state follows the same colonialist/profit-making logic despite the fact that it does not produce exchange value. Many of its women who come to these countries are either (1) directly promoted by their governments that face economic crises and desire to attract a flow of remittances, or (2) indirectly enticed with the unique cash potential of the desire industries from the sale of their bodies. The sending countries are as diverse as the Philippines, India, Myanmar, and those of Eastern Europe and the former Soviet Union. All are beset with acute financial crises while becoming market economies in varying degrees or are restructuring to meet the neoliberal demands of generating profits for the owning-classes. They export their citizens to generate remittances to cover the loans they owe to financial institutions such as the IMF and the WB (Aguilar, 2002; Rosca, 1995).

Neoliberal corporate globalization intensifies the social relations between the working-class and the owning-class. First, the restructuring of the world economy greatly relies on a global division of labor, which depends upon racism and sexism to expropriate the labor of the working-class, at very low costs and fewer tax revenues are going into state coffers. Second, even though there is probably more of a need for government responsibility in trying to make up for these shortfalls in wages in other ways, governments have become less responsive to their populations and more responsive to markets in order to remain competitive globally and attract investment FDI (Mittleman, 2000). Third, because of these changes, social welfare policies have been gutted, so states rely on legal and illegal immigration of women to other countries as a subsidy for social welfare in two ways: through not having to provide unemployment benefits, and through the money that gets sent back to the home country. While the individual women's migration may be "benefiting" in the short-term, the exporting country's ability to export labor for the desire industries becomes greatly dependent on the importing country's economy. In other words, a dependence/subordinate relationship develops among the elites of the peripheries. In the end, the potential for domination of the social process of production by "private" power, one of the major implicit principles of the neoliberal form of the state, becomes fulfilled. The social organization of production in the desire industries draws upon unskilled labor and reduces its self-direction (Rupert, 1995: 102) and transforms the migrant female working-class into "objects of desire" that can be controlled by pimps, the larger trafficking networks, the employers, and the official machine of the state. If they have not become married in the importing society, they might have to return home, which the state explains as increasing its costs regarding social welfare. In addition, the desire industries, which must continually adjust to changing "tastes," constantly search for younger, docile women.

What kind of reproductive practices, relations, and discourses sustain "desire economies" in the peripheral context? For what purpose and for whose benefit? In interviewing women and men involved in reproductive work in the peripheral economies, we see that the desire industries' formation and sustenance of "privatized" power draws upon women's reproductive labor as a natural commodity, their bodies as sexual objects, discourses that constitute and are constituted through the racialized commodification of black and "white but not quite" women's bodies, the policing and criminalizing of the working-class, and the myths of opportunity, femininity, masculinity, and racism.

THE MARKET AND THE PERIPHERAL ECONOMIES AS OPPORTUNITY: MYTHS AND REALITIES OF SECURITY?

Cyprus, Greece, and Turkey have come to be seen as transnational opportunity sites because of their desire industries. Many sex and domestic workers are drawn into the tentacles of these industries in their search for fast-track economic success. Many narratives of violence, death, exploitation, and opportunity circulate in the desire industries, and yet many sex and domestic workers choose to focus on the success stories of women living out a fantasy: sex workers having clients who continually entertain them with fancy dinners, take them out to nightclubs, and buy them jewelry and clothing, and, if very lucky, rent them a house to live in, and domestic workers have employers who treat them as one of the family. These myths of opportunity and creation of security as well as the racialized and gendered pecking order become the currency that circulates among pimps, employers, sex and domestic workers, and clients in justifying the exploitation of labor of the "white but not quite" and "black" migrant working-class.

In order to understand how the desire industries become constituted and staffed by "particular populations," I asked the men and women I interviewed about the economic, social, political, and cultural factors that shaped their decisions to choose work in the desire industries over other kinds of employment and labor. Many women suggested that they choose to migrate from Eastern Europe, countries of the former Soviet Union, and Asia because of the consequences of local economic and social transformations and larger, external forces such as structural adjustment programs in their countries. Just as international investors seek their countries as sites of cheap labor for multinational corporations, peripheral economic states perceive these sites as sources of cheap reproductive labor that they import for the promotion of the desire industries to bring money into the country.[2]

In addition, the constitution of the desire industries requires more than just the peripheral economic states as sites of opportunity, and the countries from which to import sex and domestic workers as sources of cheap labor. It requires the labor power itself, and also requires the fantasies and imagination of the working female migrant class. Many times these fantasies are mystification tools for continuing the separation and estrangement of the producers from the means of production, an estrangement of the female workers from those who exploit their labor power and violate their bodies, a separation that prevents them from realizing the product of their own life-activity and thus, subjects them to exploitation transnationally. Moreover, it is necessary to gain an understanding of their local realities that act as obstacles to women's better life gain.

NATURALIZING USE VALUE/EXCHANGE VALUE OF WOMEN'S LABOR AND BODIES

Impresario: My job is to identify shops, cabarets, taverns that want women. The owners of these places ask me how much do I charge for each woman. And I tell them the following: if she is a commercial woman I charge 1,700 dollars, if she is not, I charge 1,500 dollars. Author: What do you mean by "commercial woman?" Impresario: Commercial woman refers to a woman that can be sold for sex. Noncommercial refers to women who just serve drinks to the client. Also, my job is to fill all the appropriate immigration forms...and make sure that the woman who is going to arrive to the country is healthy and meets the basic health requirements (without HIV or hepatitis).

(John, a fifty-year-old impresario in Cyprus)

John talks about how he came from a working-class background and continues to be on welfare ($400 per month) due to an almost fatal accident. He became an impresario in pursuit of work that would provide him more than a subsistence income. He drives a Mercedes-Benz and spends hours every day on the phone finding women for the different shops, taverns, and clubs in Cyprus. He reports that he is "happily married" to a 43-year-old Cypriot woman (who was quite affectionate toward him during the interactions I observed) and spends most of his time with the sex workers that he assists in bringing to Cyprus.

There is a lot of poverty in the Ukraine. With $60 per month you cannot survive. Here each woman can make around $1,300, plus extras, and the drinks. And, of course, men, both locals and tourists, enjoy having sex with them. They receive a change of sex routine. They can do anything they want with the women from Russia and the Ukraine....oral and other kinds of sex. Cypriot women do not want to offer this variety of sexual regimen. Usually, when I walk into the shop, into the tavern or the cabaret, the bosses ask me: "Did you bring 'a good one?'" They are really interested in a woman who can do the whole program...[he lists a variety of sexual acts that they can perform]. Of course, the Filipinas are warm and passionate in bed as well but they do not have the face. The women of cabarets are models. I know because I test them out. I want to make sure that the women I bring are the best.

This impresario presents himself as a nice guy who really cares for these women because of their impoverished conditions back home. He is somebody who has their best interest in mind despite the fact that he talks about them like sexual objects and as his property. Simultaneously, he draws on the mirage/division of commercial/

noncommercial to decide the price of the sex worker. In discussing trade in the *Outline of a Critique* (1988: 176–177), Marx argues that the relation between the purchasers and the sellers is fraudulent even when it appears as moral and legal.

> In every purchase and sale, therefore, two men with diametrically opposed interests confront each other. The confrontation is decidedly antagonistic, for each knows the intentions of the other—knows that they are opposed to his own. Therefore, the first consequence is mutual mistrust, on the one hand, and the justification of this mistrust—the application of moral means to attain an immoral end—on the other. Thus, the first maxim in trade is "discretion"-the concealment of everything which might reduce the value of the article in question.... In a word, trade is legalized fraud. ... A nation therefore acts very imprudently if it fosters feelings of animosity in its suppliers and customers. The more friendly, the more profitable. Such is the humanity of trade. And this hypocritical way of misusing morality for immoral purposes is the pride of the free trade system.

In the case of domestic workers' employers we hear additional discourses that support legalized fraud:

> .... My decision to bring in a foreign domestic worker was a need. I married very early and I always wanted to work. I decided to hire a domestic worker in my adult life. I was one of the lucky ones because 'til five years ago I had a local woman helping me out with the housework. Unfortunately, the market has changed, and, thus, I cannot have a Greek woman any longer. Nobody from Greece wants to be in-house all the time. They see it as an issue of shame.... I demand honesty and respect, and will not tolerate a thief. I had three foreign workers before I found Delia. I had three Sri Lankan women before who proved to be thieves. The domestic I have now I trust 100%. I love her as a person, I respect her as a person...I chose a Filipina...they have their own culture, they are cultivated. They are closer to our ways of life. They are cleaner and they are sensitive. They are very good with their hands. Not that it is important, but they can make good packages and good things by hand...things that interest me. (Ino, a 55-year-old Greek judge and employer of a Filipina domestic worker)

This Greek female employer of a domestic worker naturalizes women's labor from other Third World countries. The narratives of both employers are juxtaposed in relation to other women: the Cypriot, the Greek, and the Sri Lankan. In the impresario's interview, we learn about commercial women versus the women who are there to serve drinks, and the women who offer a buffet of sexual intimacies versus those who do not. In the case of the employer of the domestic

worker, we find a similar dichotomization of the reproductive labor
of women: those who are "good" and natural about being servants
because they produce value for their employers, and those who are
not. The domestic worker who focuses all her energy on sustaining
the household of an upper-class professional Greek woman and the
sex worker who can provide "the whole program" of sexual intimacy
to her clients are commercial in an industry that possesses profit
potential from the reuse and resale of women. Compared to the
woman who does not offer the "whole regimen," she is in an advantageous position to earn more cash through her labor. Regardless of
the hierarchical discourse around the hiring of domestic and sex
workers (e.g., commercial versus noncommercial; women from
Eastern European countries have "the face"; the Sri Lankan domestic
worker is a thief whereas the Filipina domestic worker can be trusted),
all working-class migrant women are being exploited. Drawing upon
the logic of racialized and sexualized patriarchal and hypermasculine-
hegemonic heterosexual order to make such decisions, employers pay
some women more wages than others. The social organization of the
desire industries is founded upon property relations and expropriation of the value of female migrant working-class labor. The material
differences between female migrant reproductive labor and their
employers as well as the circulation of discourses which allow the
"choice" to exploit and/or compensate some more than others
become tools in the appropriation of their surplus labor. Power over
sex and domestic workers cuts through the interrelated spheres of
work, sexuality, love, and violence and are underpinned by the ideology of exchange and the use value of women's labor and bodies.
These relationships are explained and justified by focusing on the
earning/productive potential of a woman described as "commercial"
and "noncommercial," "good with hands," and a "house-in" as if she
is equal and free to make the choices that her employers make.

   In these industries, sex and domestic workers become second-class
citizens dependent on the possessing classes of rich-income generating
countries. Lack of access to local institutional resources reinforces the
feminization of poverty and violence. The interrelation of material
inequality and the ideology of exchange (women's labor and bodies are
for sale, use, and abuse) serve to reify sexual, racial, and class inequalities and the owning and controlling of women's bodies and labor.

REPRODUCTIVE LABOR AS A NATURAL RESOURCE

In the racialized and sexed neoliberal world order many peripheral
economic states under the direction of the IMF, the WB, and now the

WTO are pushed to participate in export-led models of development and the export/import of human labor (Aguilar, 2002). These peripheral economic programs are capital's strategies to further bring social processes of production under private power ownership and control (Rupert, 1995: 102; Chang, 2004). According to Chang (2004), in the Philippines "the peasant women under SAPs, have had to relinquish all the profits of their labor to landlords and that lands once used to grow rice, corn, and coffee have been converted to growing orchids and 'Other' exotic flowers that you can't eat for export. Lands not used for growing export commodities are "developed" instead into golf courses and luxury hotels, strictly for tourists' enjoyment" (Chang, 2004: 235). Furthermore, Chang citing Cenen Bagon, who works with Filipino and other immigrant women workers in Canada through the Vancouver Committee for Domestic Workers and Caregivers Rights, argues that WTO leaders like Michael Moore are hypocritical and have to look at women's forced migration as the true indicators of the impact of global restructuring.

> The experiences of immigrant women workers can serve not only as a measure of the effects but also as true indicators of the intentions of SAPs and other neoliberal economic policies. The sheer magnitude of women's migration—with millions of Third World women leaving their homes each year to work as servants, service workers, and sex workers in the United States, Canada, Europe, the Middle East, and Japan—urges us to examine this phenomenon and view it not merely as an effect of globalization but as a calculated feature of global economic restructuring... These economic interventions in Third World nations, embodied in SAPs and free trade policies... [are] deliberate. They facilitate the extraction of resources, especially labor or people. (Chang, 2004: 241 quoting Cenen Bagon)

These financial institutions are effectively actualizing this potential by reorganizing the social organization of production within these peripheries through the peripheral state's facilitation. Through the export/import of reproductive labor by the peripheral economic state, the migrant worker is transformed into a commodified object of desire and controlled by being subordinated to the desires of the possessing class, both male and female, of the periphery. Interviews with sex and domestic workers, their employers, and immigration officials in Cyprus, Greece, and Turkey suggest that the hiring for reproductive labor of domestic and sex workers by middle- and upper-class employers makes possible their gendered and racialized power within the world economy. Nirmala discusses her employment in Southern Cyprus:

> Loulla brought me here for a year to help with the children. Life in Sri-Lanka was very difficult. My husband and I divorced a while back. She paid me $325 monthly before taxes and I was left with $290 after taxes. She will wake me up everyday at 6:00 a.m. and ask me to clean the house, wash the clothes, help her with cooking, and then take me to the family restaurant. I would have to work there till 1:00 a.m. (Nirmala, 40-year-old Sri Lankan domestic worker)

Nirmala's arrival in Cyprus is a result of several forces: (1) a global restructuring of economies so that they can generate more profits for less costs; (2) a market that seizes opportunities for the production and sale of new commodities including sexuality and desire; (3) states that mediate the relations between the global and local markets in order to facilitate the movement of cheap labor; and (4) the desire of the upper and middle-classes to hire reproductive labor cheaply as well as the structural circumstances within which the female migrant worker finds herself. Despite her labor in production, she is unable to buy the products produced by her and other workers, and thus, she has to seek other ways to earn a living, which further subordinate her to the owning-class for exploitation and control.

Loulla, a Greek Cypriot woman, is buying these services from another Third World country. She argues that Nirmala can make much more money in Cyprus than she would at home, and thus, Loulla is committed to extracting as much value as possible for her 180 Cypriot pounds a month. As we shall soon see, the abject conditions to which Nirmala is subjected would be unacceptable under any other circumstances, and Loulla would have a difficult time hiring a Cypriot working-class woman to do all this work for $325.00 per month. Since Nirmala is a woman of color and, within sexual narratives of consumption, possesses no agency in relation to the Cypriot woman, she is naturalized as the poor and despondent woman who is provided for by the emerging upper- and middle-class women of Cyprus through a job, housing, and food (Alexander, 1998: 295). In this way, the working conditions of degradation and humiliation are obscured through the colonial myths that supplant the racial subjectivity and labor of the employee with the sexualized "native" who can endure all in trying to ensure the reproduction of the next generation.

Similarly, the wages and working conditions of sex workers from Bulgaria, Rumania, Russia, and the Ukraine compare unfavorably with those of the British croupiers who previously dominated the profession. The British women were less subject to the controls and restrictions on their social life than are Eastern European women today. Julie Scott (1995) cited a British former croupier whose words validate the racism that is prevalent in the desire industries: "There would have been a strike if they'd tried to do that to us."[3] Additionally, British women could terminate their contracts any time and still be hired anywhere in the world without much difficulty. It is different today because the antagonism between capital and labor has intensified. Restructuring worldwide has intensified the conditions of the political economy of sex and desire and the racialized sexed class struggles. Peripheral states work closely with the global and local markets and each other to facilitate the sale/purchase of reproductive labor to generate remittances and profits for the owning-classes. For example, unemployment in Albania has hovered at 30 percent. According to a study done by an Albanian women's organization, this unemployment leads Albanians to sell "girls usually to the mob in Italy or Greece for up to $10,000" (*KR Herald*, May 30, 1999). In interviews I conducted on a cruise ship, two women who worked cleaning the ship in the morning and entertaining the tourists through dance shows at night told me that they did not like their job but it helped them to earn enough money to send home to their families. They both had children staying with their parents and had to make enough money to bring them to Greece. Another woman was sending money to her sister to go to school.

Greek and Turkish Cypriot women of the upper and middle-class seem to equate true femininity with unbridled control over women's labor from other peripheral economies. When women like Loulla argue that domestic workers should be grateful to have the opportunity to do so much work for so little compensation, their class, racial, and sexual power over the migrant worker is reaffirmed. Additionally, this social relation of exploitation and power sustains in place a class sexual division between women in its raced configuration. Domestic workers' labor enables bourgeois households to be maintained as clean and ordered. Domestic workers, in addition, are always under the risk of sexual violence from the husbands and sons of the bourgeoisie. Many domestic workers I talked with brought up the issue of sexual violence and violation. Many of the husbands and sons spent hours in the domestic workers quarters. "Every midnight after the madame went to sleep he will knock at my door. I'll ask: 'What do

you want, sir? I am trying to sleep.' 'I will like you to prepare me a
nescafe.' I'll dress up very quickly always with fear and anxiety that he
wanted something else. And every time I was right" (Chandra, 27-
year-old domestic worker in Cyprus from Sri Lanka)."

The exploitation and violence of domestic workers is facilitated by
the way spaces are divided and imagined as well as by the ways "white
but not quite" imagination constitutes racialized bodies. The household space is divided between the lady's quarters and the "back pas-
sages" where the domestic workers sleep. Simultaneously, racialized
bodies, albeit hierarchically, "can seldom leave the space of prostitution in the white imagination; it is a space worn on the body"
(Razack, 1998: 356). Within the peripheral economic spaces we see
the same logic at work. Men and women of the peripheral economic
states who are themselves racialized in the world economy can non-
theless secure power through racial and sexual domination and control of the migrant working-class woman. The female employer of the
domestic worker secures her heterosexual femininity and citizen
rights by racially and sexually exploiting her labor.

Similarly, the pimp secures his masculinity and profits by selling
"white but not quite" sex workers and the client secures a little bourgeois prestige when he pays for sex.[4]

Domestic work provides women (and men) with opportunities to
manage and control both themselves and others. The challenge is to
begin to see domestic labor as a form of reproductive labor power and
to recognize that the subordination of women based on color or economic power and the feminization of the Third World (Kempadoo
and Jo Doezema, 1998: 27) are all about racialized class politics and
maintaining property relations.

Eleni, a 30-year-old working-class Greek Cypriot woman who
befriended Nirmala, talked to me about the abject conditions that
Loulla put her under:

> I used to visit her when Loulla was not home. In the beginning she
> would cry and show me her dry and bloody hands. She will tell me
> about her headaches and her hurting teeth. Finally, it seemed that she
> became accustomed to her pain. I do not think you can really get used
> to it, but if you have family back home to feed and no job, what can
> you do? I asked Loulla a couple of times about her mistreating
> Nirmala. She responded that the money they make here can buy them
> the world back home. Loulla "killed" the poor woman [sarcastically
> saying "she was so generous"]. (Eleni, 1995)

When Eleni finds out that Nirmala is being mistreated, she
proceeds to question Loulla about her relationship with her domestic

worker. Loulla's response reveals her class politics as they are gendered and racialized. For her, Nirmala makes enough money to "buy the world" back in Sri Lanka. Domestic work as a relation of sexual power and as productive and reproductive labor, is integral to the local and global economy. It is a sexual and racialized global division of labor through which the core and peripheral economies and the new emerging transnational class reconstitute their power. In hiring a migrant domestic worker, not only does she receive services at harshly exploitative rates, she also reconstitutes herself as a more powerful "white but not quite" bourgeois woman in relation to both Eleni and Nirmala. Race is class. Gender is class. Her position as well as her practices in sustaining it in the international division of labor makes that possible.

The subordination of the working-class woman of color and the local working-class woman are critical in reconstituting new forms of socioeconomic and political power, and all is done in the name of formal freedom and exchange of capital relations. The domestic worker is free to sell her labor power and the freedom to be exploited in the way she chooses (Kempadoo and Doezema, 1998; Murray, 1998) within the desire industries, and the employer is free to exploit in the way s/he chooses (Cotter, 2001, 2003). For example, the emerging professional woman is free to purchase the reproductive labor power of women of color, and of the working-class, to do the domestic chores she detests for little compensation because as "women of color" they are expected to nurture and sustain the household. Accordingly, the professional woman in Cyprus, Greece, and Turkey does not challenge why women from Sri Lanka, the Philippines, or Cyprus should be doing this reproductive labor privately for so very little compensation. In this way, the economies of reproductive labor remain intact, and the owning as well as the middle-class of the periphery do not challenge the ways the market and the state pushes the costs onto the worker herself as well as her manager. Her class power is sustained through this sexual, gendered, racial, and class "othering." In these peripheral sites, an emerging middle-class is co-implicated in the very processes of exploitation, violence, and recolonization that originated in heterosexual "Western" capital.[5]

Desire industries exist in both peripheries and metropoles. The difference between these two kinds of "desire" economies is that cash inflows and a large chunk of profits in the peripheries are largely generated from this kind of production because of their structural position in the world economy, a parallel position to that occupied by their workers in the international division of labor. However, this is changing. As long as new consumer markets are created and can be colonized, capitalist development in its globalized form does not distinguish among sites to the extent it once did. Consuming the labor of women of particular races, the owning-class of the peripheries is also complicit in recirculating earlier colonial myths about reproductive labor as being "natural," rendering invisible the exploitation of women's labor and personhood.

Relations among Loulla, Nirmala, and Eleni are anchored further in gendered ideologies of protectionism, property, and individual opportunity and success. These ideologies are heterosexist in their restrictive definitions of women as sex objects for men, producers, and care takers of children. The explanation given to Eleni by Loulla about her domestic laborer was one of protectionism as well as support: protectionism because she is providing employment for her, and support because she is providing her with the opportunity to make enough money to be able to buy the products of the market.

These interactions mystify the structural conditions that enable this relationship. These asymmetric social relations, as well as the movement of labor and the appearance of certain types of economies, are explained as being the result of the "invisible hand" (see Smith's *Wealth of Nations*) and not the result of the practices of the agents and proponents of a free global market and its embodied local formations. The idea of women as servants is based on the assumption that women's labor is a "natural resource" (or not really labor at all). It is perceived as just a "natural" extension of femininity, a "natural" extension of race (i.e., the perception that these women are naturally docile, etc.), thereby not costing the same as men's labor. For example, Greek Cypriot women of middle and upper-middle-classes, who are upwardly mobile via professionalization, hire women from the Philippines, Sri Lanka, and Eastern Europe to do their household chores as well as take care of their children and their elderly. In this relation, patriarchal and capitalist understandings of production (in this case, the middle-class and its professionalization) and reproduction are sustained in an asymmetrical relation to each other. As long as professional upper- and middle-class women do not question their role in reproduction in a world structure that draws upon ideologies of nature versus culture to further this profit generation, the system will remain intact. Reproduction is subordinated to production for profit (Cotter, 2003: 20) within a capitalist economy that is based on the principles of private ownership and profit generation.

Racializing labor within the international division of labor in turn allows for the reproduction of global power in sexual, racial, and class terms. Neoliberal capitalism as a structure does not shy away from creating markets where none existed before, from boosting existing ones, or from finding new areas and bodies to colonize. There was indeed a time when racial and sexual capital wanted nothing to do with the "backward" Cypriot, Greek, and Turkish capital.[6] The crises resulting from aggressive transnationalization and expansion are forcing core capital to exploit and consume along with peripheral capital something previously unacceptable (Alexander, 1998: 293)[7] with the masculine and "white but not quite" capitalist class at the top, "black" females of working-class at the bottom, and women of other peripheral contexts as the co-implicators (the racialized sexed bourgeoisie) in the production of transnational capital.[8]

LABOR OBJECTIFICATION

Women who work as sex and domestic workers are objectified and commodified. Within Cyprus, Greece, and Turkey, women work as *artists* or *Natashas* in dance and nightclubs. In Cyprus in particular, women dance and offer their sexual services to not only Cypriot men, but tourists, business men, UN soldiers, and men working at the British bases in Cyprus. In Greece, sex workers work in hotels, cabarets, taverns, and bars and offer their services to Greeks, Albanians, and Arabs. In Turkey, they offer their services to mostly Turkish men and arrive from many countries of the former Soviet Union and Eastern Europe, including Poland, Rumania, Russia, the Ukraine, and the CIS (Gülçür and İlkkaracan, 2002; Morokvasic and de Tinguy, 1993) and they work in hotels and cabarets. Domestic workers in all three countries work in private homes and arrive from countries such as the Philippines, Sri Lanka, India, Myanmar, Bulgaria, Albania, and Moldavia. These women are subject to strict surveillance at their jobs, and some of them, depending on the conditions under which they enter the country, are not allowed to shop unsupervised. These restrictions are implemented because their bodies are seen as property and commodities (sexual in the case of sex workers) and thus any kind of opportunity to develop non-monetary relations undermines the employers' monopoly of their commercial value.

> No matter how upset we were, the customers persisted in wanting us to sit on their laps and drink with them. I couldn't speak to them because they were mostly Greeks and Arabs. We had to act sexy knowing quite well that if we didn't we were not going to make enough money to pay back what we owed. We had to share drinks because we were expected to sleep with them. (personal interview with Irena, 1995)

In Irena's interview, both Greek and Arabs buy access to sex workers' bodies, the object of desire for constituting "white but not quite" heterosexual masculinity in Cyprus, Greece, and Turkey. These men expect "unbridled sexual access to willingly objectified women" (O'Connell Davidson and Sanchez Taylor, 1999: 41). In addition to their locations as migrant workers, commodification of racialized sex also plays a major role in positioning these women in the global political economy and also how they will be treated. Because many of these women conform to the circulating global/Western images of sexy feminine women available to many in the peripheries through the global media, they are constituted as desirable objects in the peripheries by both men and women who will hire them in pursuit of the image and status of "whiteness" through their economic power. Despite the knowledge that her needs are marginalized in the relationship between her and the client, the sex worker decides that her labor is deeply bound in changing practices of consumption for herself, her family, her customer, and potentially for the larger context in which she finds herself. Since access to the clients' money requires her acting sexy, Irena proceeds to do so irrespective of her exploitation and her "othering," which in turn constitutes the power of her client and his masculinity through the consumption of her sexuality and body.

> My boss constantly tells me that I need to be careful when I go out on Sundays. I shouldn't become involved with any guy because I can become pregnant, which can create a lot of problems for me if I want to continue working with them. Sometimes, I get angry because I am a human and I need some love and affection myself. I now have a boyfriend from Greece and we are spending Sundays together till we decide to be with each other permanently. (Aung, a 25-year-old, Myanmaran domestic worker in Greece)

Aung provides examples of the ways she challenges or resists her boss's control. She is dating a Greek boyfriend who is considering a long-term relationship with her. The special combination of economic goals along with social desires (generation of cash and pleasure-seeking through a boyfriend) accords her the choice to enact a form of resistance against her employer who is in an antagonistic relation with her. Her female employer demands that she not have a boyfriend because such a relationship could reduce the surplus-value of labor she can extract from her because she can no longer control her personhood (Anderson, 2000). At the same time, sex and domestic workers are not the passive victims of globalization and their employers. They may be forced to participate in their own exploitation but they also challenge conventional boundaries of gender, race, and class by their presence in the households of the upper and middle-classes as well as their move in and out of these households. For example, Aung's response to the employer who wants to own her is that she has a life of her own above and beyond her identity as just the domestic worker of a Greek woman. These negotiations and assertion of agency are crucial for feminists and IPE theorists interested in a critique that exposes the politics of capitalism in order to build up a movement that produces an alternative to property relations. According to Aguilar (2002: 11–12),

> female employers' responsibilities in the household hinder their full participation in the way that men can and do.... it is also this very role that permits their formal incorporation into society.... Although qualitatively different, women's work is vital to the social order, perhaps the most important component of reproductive labor being the biological reproduction of the race. Anderson connects the latter with the historical development of nation-states where membership in the community was determined by race, a circumscription that is constantly being negotiated.... this racialized setting of women's positioning as citizens acquires significance, as it is here, too, that domestic workers play their major role: "the fact that they are migrants is important: in order to participate like men, women must have workers who will provide the same flexibility as wives, in particular working long hours and combining caring and domestic chores." Anderson observes further that the duty of "a woman with good...genes" is to ensure their biological reproduction in the next generation. But bearing children is not enough. The European woman is additionally entrusted with the inculcation of morals and values in her offspring, an obligation she can now fulfill minus the burden of their physical care. (citing Anderson, 2000: 190)

In a process similar to that which Anderson writes about above (and she includes Greek women here), the owning and middle female class of Cyprus, Greece, and Turkey sustain its power in the international division of labor by hiring female migrant working-class women of color to take care of their children and to take care of their households. As members of the owning-class or members with bourgeois privileges, they possess the power to exploit the working-class woman despite feminist traditional understandings that women share common interests in a capitalist-patriarchal system that naturalizes women's labor (Kollontai, 1977). Maria, the 48-year-old Cypriot employer, buys access to her domestic worker's life and organizing of that life while she "chooses" to work with her. The female employers expressed feeling responsible for their domestic workers. Partially, they are interested in their well-being, however, at the same time, they are also concerned about the complications a boyfriend in the life of their domestic worker can create. By getting pregnant, a maid may challenge the assumption that many employers have about their domestic workers: in order to be a domestic worker, one has to unsex herself.

> She may begin bringing her boyfriend over if she develops such a relationship and he may begin to linger around when I am not here. Who knows what can happen? My friends tell me stories, warning me that once their maid had a boyfriend she is not interested in working as hard as she used to. Also, one or two boyfriends came in and stole jewelry from their madames' houses. And what if she becomes pregnant? (Fatma, 46-year-old domestic worker's employer in Turkey)

These women are racially targeted on different levels: from racisms embedded in structures, and from imperialism refracted through international discourses on prostitution, domestic labor, and the invisible hand of globalization and its different markets. The *homo economicus*, the racial–ethnic ideal, is applied by the market to decide who will enter as a prostitute or as a female domestic worker in the global market. For example, images of the exotic are intertwined with ideologies of racial and ethnic difference: the Natashas and artists are defined as "other" and always in comparison to the racial and ethnic background of the client and his attached property, women of his own ethnic, racial, and class background and domestic workers. In all three countries, women who are considered legitimate workers for the sex trade are the "exotic" green- and blue-eyed, white-skinned women from Rumania, Russia, the Ukraine, and Moldavia.

It should be noted that other issues of difference such as "virginity" and age complicate this story. A Turkish woman shared the following story:

> He teaches at our university. We have two kids together, a son and a daughter. He and I were together for 20 years till he found this Rumanian, green-eyed, blond woman. He came home one day and he gushed to a friend of ours: "She is beautiful and she worships me, unlike Turkish women who want your money but will not give you all you want in bed." I was so angry at him for leaving me for this younger blond woman and also concerned that he might catch AIDS. What does she have more than me?

There is a racial separation of who works as a sex worker and as a domestic worker in Turkey as well. Similarly to Cyprus and Greece, women from the Eastern bloc and the former Soviet Union are working in the sex industry. However, many women from Georgia, Albania, Azerbajian, and Middle Eastern countries (and the Philippines) are working as domestic workers. In addition, many Turkish women from rural areas are working as domestic workers in Turkey.

The neoliberal corporate logic guides the political economy of sex in the market. It draws upon scripts of colonialism, which still inform the construction of the hierarchical stages of a female worker: a woman who is "white but not quite" with green or blue eyes becomes the object of ultimate masculine "desire" and sexual exploitation. This heightened exoticization of the sexuality of "white but not quite" women is a way of doing two things: valorizing peoples and cultures and "concurrently also constituting them as projections of western [and eastern] fantasies" (Rousseau and Porter, 1990: 7) who can be super-exploited because of their commodified "beauty" and "sexuality" at higher rates. Furthermore, these women's sexualized and racialized labor becomes a marker of danger and pollution. They are here to sell their "white but not quite" bodies but at the same time pose danger for the tourists who buy them, and also cause "pollution" of public morality, health, and the family if they are left unsupervised.

Altink (1995: 96) argues that some of the women from Colombia, when going through Cyprus, were not even provided condoms despite the public rhetoric of regular examinations of these women's health by the state. Such investment reduces surplus-value and increases costs that in turn increase production costs, something the state tries to avoid to allow for "efficiency" of production. This is what a Greek Cypriot working-class woman, a 35-year-old domestic laborer, had to say about these racial distinctions:

> Most of the domestic female workers are from Sri Lanka, the Philippines, and sometimes from Bulgaria. These women could not find a job back home and they all have kids that need food and clothes. They come here because somebody tells them in their country that there are jobs out here and they can earn money for their children. These women are not considered to be "sexy" and "dangerous" enough to steal the husbands of women who hire them because most of them have children and families. These women are expected to be good servants for the rich women in cities. I know this woman, called Lito, and she has a black maid.
> Author: What do you mean by "black"?

She is from Sri Lanka. Not only she cleans their house starting at the crack of dawn but she is also teaching their kids how to speak her language. The kids know her language better than Greek.
Author: How is Lito treating her domestic laborer?
Ah....she is treating Houanita quite a bit better than Eleni, who used to beat up her domestic worker. Hers is from the Philippines. (Maria, 1998)

Within the desire industries, reproductive labor is hierarchized commercially. Distinctions are made between the "black" female working-class worker who lacks sexuality in a Western sense and the "other" prostitute female worker who is "considered sexy and dangerous." Such racial distinctions between the "good" and the "sexy and dangerous" female servants end up reinforcing limits on national and ethnic membership in the "private" powers of the global market and the entry of labor in the gendered and racialized informal market of the desire industries as well as the rate of exploitation.

The men and women who can afford to buy the services of sex workers do so by commodifying their services in bars, hotels, and cruise ships. For them, the labor of these workers is a commodity to be bought and sold, especially the labor from "white but not quite" bodies. Women's participation in this commodified reproduction process is expressed consistently through comments like the following:

She is Rumanian.... He lies in bed fantasizing about her and I ask him all the time if he is thinking of her and he nods "yes" as if we are acquaintances and not husband and wife with two children. (interview with Kostantina, a 30-year-old Greek Cypriot, 1999)

These comments reveal the heterosexual/patriarchal myths and expectations by which women in these countries abide. Cypriot, Greek, and Turkish womanhood (and depending on class) is marked as either traditional, national, and maternal, or cosmopolitan. When the Cypriot, Greek, and Turkish men "go out" and exploit women's sexual labor, Cypriot, Greek, and Turkish women point to a few Rumanian sex workers as evidence that Rumanian women are all "loose" husband thieves. They are considered threats to the social/national/transcosmopolitan cultures as they are taking men away from their traditional or cosmopolitan roles. However, these comments make invisible the violent processes of recolonization and control of women's bodies by a production process that is guided by the logic of profit extraction, whether Rumanian, Greek, Turkish, or Cypriot. Moreover, this logic silences that the bodies and labor of sex and domestic workers are commodities as much as the bodies and labor of bourgeois "white but not quite" women. This logic further makes invisible the middle-class women's stakes in imperialist capitalism. This social relation of "private" powers begins with racism as much as it does with sexism and economic exploitation. The liberal capitalist-patriarchal relation that allows men to ignore their wives' needs is the same that enables them to be the rational and free consumer in the market who uses women as commodities. It is also this relation that makes possible women's complicity in the violence of the migrant female working-class.

Policed and controlled through particular rules and laws, these relations render sex and domestic workers vulnerable to their employers' and clients' practices once they are out of public spaces and in private homes, hotel rooms, bars, and cruise ships. A Bulgarian woman who worked on Louis Cruise ships said she started working at 5:00 a.m. in the morning, making beds, doing laundry, fending off her employers' advances, followed by two nightly shows (dancing and performances). Of course, depending on the night, some of the men (Greek, German, British, French, and Arabs) on the cruise ship were also provided "companionship." When I asked her what she thought about all this work, she replied, "It is okay because I will be able to save enough soon to be stable financially."

A construction worker and a man who owns a grocery store, frequent bookers of cruises on this line, said that two things made the trip worthwhile: gambling and the "blonds" from Rumania. The middle-class manager stated: "I met this woman on one of the cruises from Cyprus to Egypt. She was Rumanian. She talked to me at the casino, we went to her room and I gave her 30 pounds" [moves thumb in and out of his mouth]. This quotation reveals a set of social relations defined by commodification in which the woman is a means to the upper- and middle-class man's (and woman's) pleasure. Sex and domestic workers often discount the risks of violence and AIDS when faced with the potential payoff of financial stability. Working as sex and domestic workers is a more certain path to financial gain than other kinds of work back home.

One may wonder why women place themselves in a context of violence and uncertainty. The decisions of these women are determined by both local factors (e.g., change of socialist economies into market economies, and ethnic conflict) and by the location of Cyprus, Greece, and Turkey in the international economy of tourism. Their decision is also a consequence of transnational forces, such as foreign investment in tourism in these countries. Just as international investors see Cyprus and Turkey as a site of cheap labor, and offshore activity that brings "white but not quite" clients, international tourists know it as a place to buy "cheap" sex. Other factors influencing their decision are "ideoscapes" or the images about social relations that the international media produces and disseminates. As Appadurai suggests, these media images permit "more persons in more parts of the world to consider a wider set of 'possible' lives than they ever did before" (1991: 25). The state regulates the country's image and adjusts to international market demands through the concerted efforts of the office of tourism. These tourism offices have extensive networks that influence all sectors of the domestic tourism economy and play a major role in shaping how these sectors operate, everything from taxation to image. The government tourist bureau is basically responsible for sending messages about which illicit activities it will ignore (and possibly promote via carefully constructed images), and, therefore, is complicit in sustaining these industries and in supporting the interests of private powers.

One could make a similar argument about domestic workers in that when the host state turns a blind eye to this sector, the definition and rights of a domestic worker become subject to wide interpretation to make it possible for private powers to carry out its exploitation. The government looks the other way in order to respond to the competitiveness of the global market place, because middle- and upper-class women are either working (and therefore contributing to the economy) or at the very least providing a "subsidy" by hiring domestic workers so that the government does not have to provide any benefits to them and they might also contribute to the economy by spending their salaries.

THE LINK BETWEEN THE POLITICAL ECONOMY OF SEX AND DESIRE: EXPLOITATION AND RACIALIZED, SEXUALIZED (IN)SECURITIES AND VIOLENCE

In discussing the desire industries, employers and domestic and sex workers reveal an interesting subtext: that the link between the political economy of sex and desire is violence. The sex and domestic workers' search for opportunity and success, the impresarios' desire to fight formal economic marginalization and the feminization of poverty in the larger social context all push them to use particular strategies of survival and advancement. This is what Marina, a sex worker from Moldavia, had to say:

> I went to Greece two years ago. There was this guy who would come everyday at the bar where I was working. He wanted a relationship with me, and I finally decided "I do not have anything to lose." He

would take me out to the best restaurants and buy me the best cloth-ing. He would spend a lot of money on me every day till one day his wife discovered us at this hotel. She pulled my hair and started scream-ing, telling me that I was the cause of their problems and his not going home to his kids. I got angry and I said: "Take him...I am not keep-ing him from you." Unfortunately, she knew people in the immigra-tion office and they kicked me out of the country. Life there was easier for me than here in Turkey. I want to go back sometime and find him.

Irena is a 23-year-old Russian sex worker who works in Turkey. She left Russia after a friend told her that she could make a lot of money working in a cabaret. Her first stop was Israel, where she came across a handsome, Jewish man who "fell in love" with her.

I love him too...He is very handsome and he is only 27-years-old. He still sends me money and he calls me several times a week. He knows I am in Turkey now and he is hoping that that one day he and I are going to get married. I am hoping that time will come, although at times I am not sure. I am not ready to stop working and he wants me to stay home once we get married. I want to live my life. I am still very young.

Another woman, Elena, a 24-year-old Ukrainian sex worker, currently works in Turkey. Her story is one of a long-lived "success." A married, rich, 50-year-old famous lawyer in the country rents a fur-nished luxury apartment for her and supports her, making it possible for her to send money to her mother back home who was taking care of her four-year-old daughter. Elena was living the fantasy, sharing a household with a professional Turkish man who takes her out to high-class restaurants and buys her whatever her heart desires. While she has moved up socially and economically, at times she wonders if it is all a mirage. The man of her dreams may leave her, since he has not divorced his wife. Yet, she finishes her story by saying: "Maybe not...I am beautiful and young...why should he want to leave?" Other women are not so fortunate in their search for advancement.

Malavi is a 32-year-old Sri Lankan domestic worker who came to Cyprus three years ago. She lives with a family of four, and during her days off, she developed a relationship with a man from India with whom she rented an apartment in the capital. He was supporting her by giving her money to send to her family back home and also by pay-ing the rent. However, after two-and-a-half years of a great relation-ship, Raj felt that she was using him and his money. He told her: "You are always asking for money. You think I am rich." They fought con-stantly over this issue until one day Raj left her and now she carries the lease (seven months to go) and a "broken heart . . . I am still hoping he will come back. I felt secure and happy with him."

The four women tell different stories of varying degrees of "success." Two of the sex workers established romantic relationships with men who made it possible for them to move up socially and economically. Irena feels secure about her relationship with the man from Israel and wonders if she wants to give up "single" life for him. Elena feels lucky and attributes her success to her beauty and youth. Marina did not have the same opportunity to get rich quickly and continue her fantasy with a man she really liked. Malavi lost the security of a compatriot and she is still hoping for a reconnection with her boyfriend.

Simultaneously, the participation of the managers and employers of sex and domestic workers in the market is full of contradictions. The impresarios seek a job that brings fast money into their hands: a job that makes it possible for them to generate $700 per woman.

> Impresario: I decided to do this job because it has very good profits. A friend of mine told me. "Since you are on welfare, help me do this job and I will give you $200 for each woman we bring." I realized that the profits were very high and I said to myself, "why don't I do this on my own?" I have been doing this job for four years. Each woman gives me $700 clean profit. How do I find these women? There are women who worked with me in the past and I know have good characters and I advise them before leaving to go back to their countries: You do not have to come back and be "jumped by." Why don't you get a phone and find other women and send them to me in Cyprus?

Another impresario expressed similar feelings about choosing this line of work:

> I was born poor and I will die poor. I own a tavern. I have been doing this job now for six months and I first had three Rumanian women, afterwards, two Moldavians and one Rumanian, and I had some women who ended up getting married in Greece and are now citizens. Their job was to serve and keep our clients company. These women cannot find employment and they come to Greece to work. Greek men are now obsessed because impresarios find women who have good looks, are tall, and young.

However, impresarios' marginalization in the formal economy of the market does not stop them from exploiting and colonizing women located in the margins. On the contrary, these impresarios work toward creating networks of women in the former Soviet Union and

Eastern European countries who can find them "the cargo" to sell in Cyprus, Greece, and Turkey respectively.

Most impresarios indicated the drive to make money was a strong motivator for their decision to enter the desire industries. Not having much education or access to the formal economy, they seek out a place in the "informal" or shadow economy of desire. They see sex trafficking and prostitution as a "fact" of life for them. These men's masculinities and women's femininities are rationalized in the principle of commodity exchange. Exchange value—what is in fact unequal exchange of money for labor and sex—becomes an acceptable and taken-for-granted "equal exchange." Both impresarios and the female employers of domestic workers talked about the security that their employees feel under them. Here are excerpts of interviews with an impresario and a female employer of a domestic worker:

> As soon as the girl arrives in Cyprus, I am responsible for her. They feel a sense of security with us as impresarios, they trust us more than their boss because if they do not make as much money for them the bosses can scream at them and beat them. Their bosses, of course, are afraid that if these women complain to us, we, as impresarios have the power to write a complaint letter to the ministry of labor stating that this employer beats up women. Once I make this statement, as an impresario, that this employer abuses women when they do not desire to be sold, the ministry of labor takes their visas away and charges them fines. Author: Did you ever report any employers for violence against the women?

> Impresario: I was thinking to do it once, however, he came crying to me that he is poor and does not have money and I felt sorry for him. It seemed that he beat up the woman while he was angry. I did not report him because he would have lost all his visas if I did and then would have been fined $1,400 and his shop would be closed for life. I knew he is a bad man, but he is a family man with children so I did not report him because he and I could have gotten into a beating session. In Nicosia, I know around six of these men but I do not put women in their shops now. I used to before.

> Priti always talks to me about how other madames treat their maids. She always tells me how she feels secure being in our house because we treat her with respect, as one of our family. As long as she is respecting our family and follows my guidance why shouldn't we be nice to her? As long as she responds to my requests why shouldn't I support her? (Sevgul, a 45-year-old Turkish employer of a domestic worker)

Both impresarios and employers of sex and domestic workers seemed obsessed with the need to show how their employees feel secure with them. However, at the same time, their idea of security draws upon the neocolonial logic of their power and control over these women. In the desire industries, security takes the form of colonization and submission of women's bodies from lower-income peripheral economic states to the upper- and middle-class of other peripheries. Thinking about the desire industries and what the role of men (impresarios or pimps) is materially, women clearly as a group suffer inequalities of income and life chances. Men who sell women explain it away as "I am forced" to have women who sell sex, otherwise, "I cannot make any money." Women who hire domestic help explain it away "as changes in the market" and the demands put on them by social expectations regarding their life styles.

However, the issue of violence within the gendered, sexed, and racialized market is a far-reaching problem that raises all sorts of issues about the social organization of desire, the process of socialization, agencies of social control such as the immigration office, hereto— patriarchy, and the state, and the constitution of gender relationships with regard to power and labor in our societies. Some of the pimps want the women to be submissive to them, that is, produce as many profits as they deem desirable, and if they are not, they may beat them:

> The people who make/implement the laws in Greece know what jobs these women do here. I had three women who were supposed to be servers but it was not to my benefit. I ended up serving so that my women could go out with clients and sell sex. We usually do not protect these women. We are there to make money. If a woman is beaten by a client and the pimp is on the scene, then obviously he'll intervene because the client is damaging our worker. I always tell the women that work for me: you work for me and I work for you. However, there are many bosses who do not do that. They want the women to respect him and tell him where they are going and when. If the women do not want to do that, they beat them up or call them names or threaten them to send them back where they came from.

Once more, respect for the impresario and the employer of the domestic worker is about exercising power and control over the personhood of the women that work for them especially when they feel that their role in the society is marginalized.[9] "White women but not quite" and "black" working-class migrant women are there to serve him/her and the "white but not quite" impresario, female employers, and clients: the women are supposed to be gracious, smiling, praising, gentle in explicit comparison to the local women. This second kind of service (as opposed to the one he is doing) suggests a sense of feminine "authenticity" because it expresses voluntary human kindness ("you work for me and I work for you") and market relations. Despite the moralizing aspect of these discourses, patriarchy and racism are used as material practices of labor in which the labor of the female migrant working-class women is made available to capital for less than the labor of men and women of Cyprus, Greece, and Turkey.

The reproductive labor of sex and domestic workers is desired, exploited, used, and abused by the impresarios, and the middle- and upper-class citizens of the peripheral economic states. The desire industries in the peripheries depend on racism and sexism as material practices of labor. "Owning the means of production and exploiting labor power" becomes a sign of "white but not quite" masculinity and femininity, which, in turn, entails the power to dominate others. These privileged, gendered, and racialized positions of Cypriot, Greek, and Turkish men and women in the international division of labor is sustained through their continued exploitation of wage-labor in the desire industries. Its consumption under globalization brings to the fore that the link between sex and desire is exploitation and violence (physical and structural). Violence seems to be a permanent fixture of the social fabric, not merely a reaction to a crisis in which racial working-class migrant women are scapegoated for the structural insecurities peripheral economic states are facing. As capitalism restructures itself to generate more profits, peripheral economic states rush to generate for its owning-class profits by grabbing a few slices of the capitalist pie: the cheap labor of other peripheral economic states. It moves to devise strategies and methods to seek security and freedom of capital albeit at the expense and the exploitation of the working-class "white but not quite" and black women. The peripheral economic state rushes to seek cheap labor and make it available to capital despite its further political marginalization in the transnational economy.

CHAPTER 4

DESIRING POWER IN THE EUROPEAN UNION: PERIPHERAL ECONOMIC STATES' PARTICIPATION IN CAPITAL ACCUMULATION

Desire as a strategy of colonization is not new in world politics (Stoler, 2002, 1995; Young, 1995). Ann Laura Stoler (2002) exposes the linkage between colonization and desire by focusing on the complex household arrangements through which white colonizers officially mandated a system of superiority and disdain against local natives. Yet the former would not have survived without the latter's reproductive labor, especially from nannies, maids, houseboys, gardeners, prostitutes, pimps, soldiers, and other workers utilized or coerced by the colonial state. For this reason, Stoler argues that sex was a material foundation for the colonialist projects and not just a metaphor for colonial inequalities (Stoler, 2002: 14). Others, such as poststructural theorists like Robert Young (1995), argue that, desire for territorial expansion and self-reproduction led colonialism to become a machine that "forced disparate territories, histories, and people to be thrust together like foreign bodies in the night" (98).

Today, colonial desire has been transformed into a distinctly transnational political economy of desire (Robinson, 1998; Ebert, 2001; Hennessy, 2000). Within the imperative of the market, desire has become a strategy that hides the exploitation of people's labor by suggesting that if one desires labor one can exchange it for cash. Thus, the logic of the market of "equal exchange" becomes centralized and supported by a bourgeois democracy that draws upon difference to constitute desire for sale. However, the public intellectuals, including the state, silence these ideological moves. Applying this idea in the Chinese context, Rey Chow (1990) argues that "cultural specificity" has become the basis for a social division of desire. For example, the insistence on China's difference from the West has been generated from within China as much as from without. Among those perpetuating a "culturally specific" context are the sinologists who desire to vouchsafe Chinese culture from modernity. As China is becoming increasingly modernized, the Sinologist is overcome by the loss of his beloved object (Chow, 1995:4). The "Maoists" respond similarly in their desire to be located in the other. They valorize the other's deprivation and espouse a self-righteous politic of lack, subalternity, and victimization (Chow, 1995:13). Additionally, many of the Chinese intellectuals are "vanguards" (in Barthes's sense) who draw upon traditional knowledge to justify their methods and "authenticity" rather than ask "What does it mean to be Chinese?" (Chow, 1995:93). Further complicating matters are American universities that recruit "area specialists" and, in the process, "ghettoize" Chinese culture along geographic, rather than disciplinary, lines. These strategic moves of focusing on cultural specificity silence the class contradictions in its racialized and sexed appearances of politico-economic relations in the production of knowledge about desire and its sale for more profits.[1]

Rosemary Hennessy (2000) critiques many of the psychologizing/ psychoanalytic frames about desire. She argues that many poststructural theorists conceptualize desire as the force of social reproduction and relations. For them desire is a "psychic process whose materiality is rooted in the drives and conveyed through the symbolic order" (69). This understanding individualizes desire. Engaging Deleuze and Guattari's (1983) work, she states:

> [D]esire in the form of energy flows between organ-machines—or what they call "desiring production"—is the starting point of social life. No longer understood in terms of lack, desire or libido is the primary connective "labor" of desiring production. Indeed production is social production. Opposed to psychoanalytic theory and practice for the ways it tames or "territorializes" desire by anchoring it in the Oedipus complex, Deleuze and Guattari dis-organize subjectivity, unchain it from socially restrictive forces, and recode it around concepts of plurality, multiplicity, decenteredness. In their schema, desire becomes the basis of social production. Instead of being the product of history, desire is historically invariant matter. The material of desire is the primordial matter of energy flows or of things connected by energy flows—"menstrual flow, amniotic fluid spilling out of the sac; flowing hair; a flow of spittle, a flow of sperm, shit or urine." (Hennessy, 2000: 70 citing Deleuze and Guattari, 1983: 5)

Hennessy's critique of poststructuralists is crucial. These theorists focus on desire as being productive itself and an autonomous force that is not socially determined. For them, desire shapes the social. Deleuze and Guatarri (1983) argue that desire is a material entity and contest the classical view of desire that there is a dreamed object behind every real production (25–26). For them, desire produces and whatever it produces is real. This move divides the relation between need and desire, which, in turn, separates the relation of support between use value and exchange value. This separation is an ideological move. If desire is a materialist force in its own right, then one can conclude in capital-labor relations the source of profit is the managing skills of the owners and the managers of the means of production. Moreover, their strategy of separation makes it possible for them to further the relation between need and desire and move to argue that need is a product of desire. This move ends up supporting that desire is a "self-propelling social force."

> Desire is not bolstered by needs, but rather the contrary; needs are derived from desire: they are counterproducts with the real that desire produces. (Deleuze and Guattari, 1983: 27)

Deleuze and Guattari's theory justifies the strategic moves of a class that is able to routinely satiate its desires and does not have to struggle to meet many of its needs. The argument of Deleuze and Guattari that classical theorists' understanding of desire is idealist, a critique of Marxist theory, is an ideological move that erases the class racialized struggles. They recognize that

> capitalism liberates the flows of desire from the clutches of an oedipalizing culture, but it does so under social conditions that continually reterritorialize the desires it unleashes in order to accrue surplus value... Desiring production is revolutionary and capable of demolishing social form.... Despite their references to capitalism, here the separation of sexuality from historical and material production has become complete... the structures of exploitation in which capitalist production depends have completely disappeared. (Hennessy, 2000: 71)

In an epistemological move that parallels Hennessy's, Teresa Ebert (2001:19) argues that "desire is a practice, not simply a performance, and as such is historical and material" (1996: 48). She states that every woman's and man's very sexuality, "the ways in which her desires are constructed and the ways in which she is able to act on them, to be heterosexual, to be lesbian, to be a mother or not—is conditioned by her position in the historically specific gendered division of labor"

(Ebert, 1996: 48). Based on this logic, she further argues that sexual difference is the "basis for the social division of desire" which in turn becomes the basis for the social division of labor (Ebert, 2001: 19). Put differently, the neoliberal capitalist power project comprises a series of practices, discourses, as well as fantasies in satiating the desires for endless growth, appropriation of economic and natural resources, and self-reproduction.

This newer circulating theory about desire is part and parcel of the politics of the peripheral state and has turned into the ideological alibi of a structure that prioritizes the desires of the haves and marginalizes the needs of the have-nots as unreal and idealist. Using an understanding that "social production . . . is purely and simply desiring-production itself" (Deleuze and Guattari, 1983: 56), these peripheral states draw on this kind of desire and rely heavily on the desire industries as one way of cementing the allegiance of privatized national capital to transnational capital.

In this chapter, I investigate why the peripheral economic states of Cyprus, Greece, and Turkey use these newer ideologies of desire to justify their exploitative and consumptive patterns (similar to those of core economic states in the EU, represented by France, Germany, and the United Kingdom). Through the import of reproductive labor, sex and domestic work alike, the state is being transformed into a transnational *social* form, albeit in contestable ways. Many women and the local working-class through different organizing strategies challenge this transnational, neoliberal strategy of commodifying everything and everybody (ISAG, The Global Change Institute, Caritas Greece, Caritas Turkey). That is, the peripheral economic state's desire for "white" power within the transnational nonliberal project (such as access to labor and other markets) depends on employing the methods of hypermasculine, regional, capitalist elites within the EU (Rudolph, 2002 citing Krugman and Obstfeld, 1997; Krugman and Venables, 1995; Ricardo, 1955). Neoliberal globalization or restructuring of world economy occurs at the expense of certain sectors of itself such as the covert racial and sex trade in reproductive labor through licit and illicit activities, thereby criminalizing specific identities in the local and transnational working-class. In the next section I address how the peripheral economic state uses the desire of the owners of the means of production and their managers and redirects its resources to make possible its integration in a transnational world economic power, albeit by marginalizing and displacing the needs of the female migrant working-class, as well as the local working-class.

PERIPHERAL ECONOMIC STATES: FROM A WELFARE, DEVELOPMENTALIST STRATEGY TO NEOLIBERAL TRANS/NATIONAL PRIVATIZATION

The neoliberal international project has seemed bent on restructuring the world economy through privatization, competition, and state rescaling since the global economic crises of the early 1970s. Four major processes account for the peripheral economic state's privatization of hypermasculine neoliberal power, especially within the EU: (1) the serviceability of "white, but not quite" states (like Cyprus, Greece, and Turkey) to market openness and regulation (e.g., migration) that promotes global competition and economic integration; (2) the cooperation of different local "progressive" owning-classes within the Mediterranean toward implementing this serviceability, thereby "avoiding trade disputes and improving trust and mutual confidence across borders" (OECD, 2001: 8); and (3) the commodification and fetishization of the peripheral economic state's desire to "fit into" the capital accumulation machine by normalizing whiteness and masculinity in the neoliberal world order through the covert trade in reproductive labor; and (4) the prioritization of the desires of the upper- and middle-classes.

Serviceability of "White, but not Quite" States to Market Openness

Many argue that the world has been transformed into a system of trading states where power is increasingly based on Ricardian notions of comparative advantage, free trade, and free movement of capital (Robinson, 2002; 1998). Fewer states resort to military-territorial strategies to maximize their power; they turn instead to trade and commerce (Mueller, 1989; Kupchan, 1994). Proponents of the "Washington consensus" (Williamson, November 6, 2002) argue that the more economies move toward a Pareto-optimal frontier, the more "an [economic] rising tide" will lift "all [nation-state] boats," albeit unevenly (Rudolph, 2002; Krugman, 1995; Krugman and Venables, 1995; Krugman and Obstfeld, 1997). Yet, this globalization strategy of the trading state has sustained global inequalities even when it has made possible the free movement of capital, and trade (Rudolph, 2002: 2).

Since the 1970s and 1980s, a transnational state apparatus has emerged (Brenner, 1999; Robinson, 1998). It reflects the goals and objectives of the neoliberal world project: that is, "endless growth and self-reproduction" (Stoler, 1995). This restructuring has affected sites differently. For core countries like the United States, it has meant the end of the Fordist era where industrial workers undertake mass production and consumption within the boundaries of the nation-state. Information-based industries, such as banking and finance, have moved to the current mode of flexible production and consumption.[2]

For countries of the so-called socialist Second World, neoliberal globalization has permitted the rise of a transnationalized aspiring upper class to negotiate with the core global bourgeoisie and "artic-ulate a project for full (re)integration into world capitalism" (Robinson, 1998: 22). For Third World countries, or what I call here peripheral economic states, neoliberal restructuring has given impetus to a transnationalized local elite's displacement of various class devel-opmentalist projects (Robinson, 1998: 22). Amid these class contes-tations, another model of development is presented as a viable option for accessing the capitalist pie, the neoliberal project of unbridled cap-ital accumulation. Within this project one "no longer [focuses on] national economic growth, but a successful 'participation in the world market'" (Robinson, 1998: 26).[3]

This transnationalized strategy of participating in the world market intensifies the peripheral economic state's serviceability. National pro-duction now shifts to global production while the state now more than ever trumpets individualism, consumerism, and labor's global flexibility. EU member Greece is expected to muster all its services toward market openness despite its citizens' protests against such a project. As a "small, import-dependent economy" with "chronic trade deficits" being "balanced by strong invisible receipts, mainly tourism and shipping" (OECD, 2001: 9), Greece's owning elites are arguing for a privatization of the public resources which the nation-state manages: Greece needs to implement policies and programs that would enable "major reforms and the ensuing pro-competitive effects on the economy" (OECD, 2001: 9).[4]

While Greece is opening its markets to the world economy through harmonization and liberalization of its economy with the EU, the OECD still evaluates Greece as "lagging behind." This estab-lishes European countries such as Germany, France, and Great Britain as the states with open markets *properly* serving the needs of the neoliberal world order. Accordingly, they have the economic and political power and authority to structurally "force" Greece to "fit" into the family of the EU and serve it by contributing "to the highest sustainable economic growth and employment and a rising stan-dard. . . . while maintaining financial stability, and thus . . . contribut[ing] to the development of the world economy" (OECD, 2001: 2). The state of Greece moves despite many struggles between capital and the working-class to further privatize the social resources by responding to the desires of the emerging transnational owning-class. To ensure its complete integration in the global capitalist economy, Greece follows closely six principles: (1) transparency and openness of decision making; (2) nondiscrimination; (3) avoidance of unnecessary trade restrictiveness; (4) use of internationally harmonized measures; (5) recognition of equivalence of other countries' regulatory measures; and (6) application of competition principles (OECD, 2001: 11).

Turkey, currently not a member of the EU, and with the Republic of Cyprus, just gaining accession in May 2004, have actively reconstituted their legalistic practices to gain entry. Their Pre-Accession Economic Reports reveal a desire to serve transnational capital and more specifically the owning-class by adhering to the principles of liberal bourgeois democracy. The reports outline the major principles that these peripheral states must follow to "whiten" themselves by becoming viable forces in the continuation of the capitalist world system: a movement away from national to EU-oriented production to "complete [the] liberalization of markets," and increase private consumption including goods and services.

> Achievement of a satisfactory rate of growth, under conditions of internal and external macroeconomic stability, full employment and social cohesion.... The liberalization of the economy and the promotion of its restructuring and modernization as well as its further diversification, in line with the comparative advantages of the island and the harmonization process with the EU....The labour market policies are directed towards promoting macroeconomic stability and fostering competitiveness. (Pre-Accession Economic Programme of the Republic of Cyprus, 2001: 3 and 13)

This report is an ideological call to facilitate the fulfillment of the desires of "white but not quite" capital of the peripheries. The peripheral economic state needs to further liberalize, that is, open its borders for capital to move freely and do whatever it so decides. Moreover, it has to design labor market policies that "promote macroeconomic stability" and "foster competitiveness," codes for maintaining the highest rate of profit possible through lowering the wages of labor irrespective of its point of origin. Similarly, we read in Turkey's Pre-Accession Economic Report:

> In response to unsustainable trends in public finance and substantially high real interest rates during 1999, a comprehensive macroeconomic programme covering the 2000–2002 period was launched at the end

of 1999. The IMF, through a three-year Stand-by Arrangement, supported this programme.... based on the following four pillars: tight fiscal policy, which aims at a considerable improvement in the primary surplus of the total public sector... forward looking incomes policy, rule based credible monetary policy in combating inflation, structural reforms in areas of agricultural support system, social security, privatization, fiscal transparency and regulation and supervision of the financial sector. (Republic of Turkey, Pre-Accession Economic Programme, 2001: 3)

This report is replete with codes about the desires of capital and the expectation by the transnational state apparatus (i.e., Western European capital) and international institutions like the IMF for the peripheral economic state to work together to create conditions that capital requires: freedom to move anywhere and without any constraints. Corporate liberalism (van der Pijl, 1984: 10) with its contingent global trading regime saw liberalization as more than tariff reduction. They came to push for "harmonization" processes that entail bringing national "formal" domestic rules governing production relations and business under the control of this transnational regime. More specifically, the EU demands that all three countries encompass "harmonization" of their domestic rules and regulations with those of Western European countries by removing tariff barriers.

Additionally, liberal corporate globalization supports the enhancement of the "private" powers of capital by making it possible for financial capital to prevent macro-policies aimed at increasing employment or wage levels (Rupert, 2000: 46). The European regime in Brussels increases the incentives of all three governments, and more specifically of Turkey, through high-aid packages to seek national macroeconomic strategies such as "tight fiscal policy," "forward-looking incomes policy," "rule-based credible monetary policy in combating inflation," and "regulation and supervision of the financial sector." These strategies appeal to global financial markets, which in turn, will bring more capital to the pro-EU actors, that is, the middle and owning-classes of Turkey. All three governments closely follow strategies that make them attractive sites for financial institutions and transnational corporations. These sites are turned simultaneously into the cheap labor sites by the standards of higher-income economies as well as the sites that possess skilled and semi-skilled manageable and disciplined labor (Agnew and Corbridge, 1995: 169). At the same time, these sites become attractive for migrant labor since they are reasonably "well managed" and show signs of economic growth. More and more, all three governments find themselves integrated into and affected by transnational social relations, and, more and more, all three states are privatizing these relations and subjecting them to the power of capital instead of norms and rules of substantive democratic governance.

"Progressive" Local Capital and Its "Welcoming Mat"[5]

As more transnational factions of local owning-classes subscribe to the neoliberal world order and its contingent ideologies in world politics, they are consolidating new, transnational economic activities that further subject the working-class, both local and migrant, to the discipline of the market. For example, the Greek and Turkish owning-classes (historically construed as "ethnic rivals") are cooperating with one another to serve the world market, an unprecedented development in Greco-Turkish relations. Consider how the owning-classes mobilized expressions of citizen solidarity and the new political term "seismic diplomacy" (after the two countries were shaken by devastating earthquakes) to achieve market openness within the EU/global economy:

> Through their actions, our citizens sent a powerful message to their respective governments: they urged us to deepen the process of reconciliation and dialogue that had already begun on a diplomatic level. They taught us that mutual interests can and must outweigh tired animosities. . . .Greece firmly believes that Europe has much to gain from accepting a European Turkey. In January, I, (George Papandreou) made the first official visit to Turkey by a Greek foreign minister in 38 years, to sign the first of nine agreements with my Turkish counterpart, Ismael Cem. . . .He reciprocated only weeks later, becoming the first Turkish foreign minister to have officially visited Greece in 40 years. Greece and Turkey have now embarked on a process of cooperation in various fields of common interest, such as trade, tourism, security, illegal immigration, energy, and the environment. (http:www.greece.gr/POLITICS/EuropeanUnion/GapGreekTurkishOpEd.stm)

Cooperating around "seismic diplomacy" and economic development, Greece and Turkey ally themselves toward supporting capital. This, in turn, makes it possible for their local pro-EU owning-class to reap benefits. However, cooperation is not enough. All three states need to contract domestic markets and cheapen labor through casualization, migration, and social austerity programs to render themselves competitive worldwide, and within the EU. In addition, they must open their public sectors, protected industries, and natural resources to be "commercially exploited" (cited in Robinson, 1998: 26; Yilmaz, 2003; Malaos, 2000; OECD, 2001) if they desire more benefits.

Linking development and serviceability to the world market, and the disciplining of the neoliberal market are all strategies guided by linear logic. It is a development that further opens the national borders and economies to the whims of corporate globalization. As long as the three states proceed without any "derogations that [may] delay...major reforms" (OECD, 2001: 9), then the world economy seals an unholy bond between "white but not quite" and "white" capital, resulting in the imperial desire to accumulate profits through the expropriation of surplus-value, irrespective of the violence that may be committed to achieve these goals. Peripheral economic states speed up their integration through their participation in sustaining the new historical structures that embody an enhancement of the social powers of capital. One such strategy is the commodification and fetishization of the peripheral economic state's desire to access these capital powers, but at a cost: dismissing the needs of both the local and migrant working-class as unrealistic and irrelevant. Following Deleuze and Guattari (1983)—"desire does not lack anything; it does not lack its object.... Desire and its object are one and the same thing" (26)—the peripheral economic state and its owning-class lack nothing because they are free to desire power within the EU and the surplus-value of the migrant female worker and make it their own anytime they so decide. In the process, they can use strategies that subject the majority of their populations as well as other peripheral economic states to the powers of capital.

COMMODIFICATION AND FETISHIZATION OF THE PERIPHERAL ECONOMIC STATE'S DESIRE TO "FIT" INTO THE NEOLIBERAL WORLD ORDER

"Fitting" into the neoliberal world economy requires more than just the strategies of harmonization of domestic rules and regulations. It also requires intensified exploitation, commodification, and fetishization, irrespective of the ideologies of desire that make invisible the increasing integration into transnational relations and the further subsuming of social relations under the "private" powers of capital. Reproductive labor, in turn, is used by the owning-class to facilitate the serviceability of the peripheral economic state to the discipline of the market. However, peripheral economic states exacerbate their economic precariousness precisely by importing labor to meet the "competitive" demands of neoliberal restructuring.

Feminization of the Peripheral Economic State:
Constituting the Desire Industries

More than trade, migration has become a major venue for capital accumulation (Hatton and Williamson, 1998; Rogowski, 1998). For this reason, peripheral states solicit migrant labor, both high and low skilled. In using the exploitative and violent strategies of masculine neoliberal development, the peripheral economic state also feminizes aspects of its economy. It designs policies that structurally support the owning-class. Many of the peripheral economic state's policies and practices may seem to mimic the rich-income countries. Following Homi Bhabha (1994) who first articulated the notion of mimicry as a survival tactic for the colonized, Ling argues that the colonized try on

> like a new accessory, the colonizer's reflected image in the body/site of the "native." A moment of political destabilization rather than fawning flattery, mimicry subverts the hegemonic convention that the colonizer is always separate from and superior to the colonized. Mimicry's artifice shocks the colonizer into accepting a possible parity with the colonized. (2002: 116)

Ling updates Bhabha's insight by differentiating mimicry into two analytical types: formal and substantive. Formal mimicry refers to superficial, direct borrowing; substantive mimicry indicates a deeper integration of old and new. Ling's model, albeit more complex than Bhabha's remains static. Mimicry may "shock ... the colonizer into accepting a possible parity with the colonizer," however; we never come to know whom the colonizer comes to accept as equal and an agent on his/her own terms. Thus, the political implications of this model in its class, gender, and racial configurations are never made explicit. Mimicry in both its formal and substantive forms becomes a class strategy in the hands of the local owning elites. Even when the colonized shocks the colonizer, he is not necessarily awakening him to the needs of the marginalized classes and peoples but rather he, himself, is awakened to his freedom (desire) for "private" power, that is, capital ownership and control. That is, the owning-classes may use formal and substantive mimicry as strategies to simultaneously achieve their integration into transnational social relations and mystification practices that make invisible their powers which end up supporting the owning-classes, and the managers of the owning-classes at the expense of the local and migrant working-class.

In the Mediterranean, the peripheral economic state integrates liberal masculinist capitalism (economic man) with local patriarchal traditions (family and the patriarch-state) to mystify the exploitation of particular genders, races, and classes. It argues that women's labor is for utilitarian, economic production ("nimble fingers") and self-sacrificing, generational reproduction ("good wife," "hardworking maid"), that "white but not quite" women are the "Russian sex queens," and "black" women are hardworking, generating lucrative remittances for the nation-state (maids, nannies, nurses, and "entertainers" overseas). In turn, the state draws upon the dialectical relationship of substantive and formal mimicry to produce creative ideologies (Ling, 2002: 116)[6] in order to further subordinate itself to the power of capital while attempting to reproduce its power within the EU economy. For example, all three states draw upon patriarchal understandings of male privilege to exploit Russian sex queens for the generation of profits in the desire industries.

According to Ling, core capitalist states tolerate, even encourage, formal mimicry of capitalist development. They become punitive, however, when the peripheral economic state begins to embark on substantive mimicry, thereby challenging core states not only economically but conceptually. This leads to contestations for power. Nonetheless, this elite competition and conflict "reveal an underlying hypermasculinity at work" (Ling, 2002: 117).

> The players in and site of hypermasculine competition since colonialism may have changed, but its script of colonial power relations and under-developed hearts remains the same. Hypermasculine capitalism reconstructs *social* subjects, spaces, and activities into *economic* agents that valorize a masculinized, global competitiveness associated with men, entrepreneurs, the upwardly-mobile, cities, and industrialization. Relatedly, it assigns a hyperfeminized stagnancy to local women, peasants, the poor, and agrarian production. Hypermasculine capitalism, in short, is *reactionary* in nature.

Ling's critique is important in that it brings to the surface another appearance of capital: that of the peripheral economic state. However, the birth of this capitalism, though, is not *necessarily* reactionary. On the contrary, this hypermasculine capitalism, as Ling coins it, fights with core owning-classes over the significance of their own power, desires, and social reproduction. The contestations between hypermasculine and core capitalism are not really whether needs of people are as important but how to fulfill the desire of the owning-classes, irrespective of the exploitation and violence (such as the assignment of stagnancy to women of the Third World). The dialectics of formal and substantive mimicry may end up pushing aspects of the peripheral economic state into their own feminization, sexualization, and racialization. Exploiting reproductive labor and commodifying it in the desire industries, the peripheral economic state finds itself in a precarious economic position. However, this is not a problem for transnational capital, whose major interest is subjecting all to its power, and securing its reproduction, irrespective of the violence upon women, migrants, the working-class in general, and even historical national elites:

> Within the global city alone, a tiered structure of public economy professionals with their clerical, janitorial,...other so-called support staff as well as women who can offer them sexual services "install...a private economy of migrant labor, legal or otherwise, which provides much-sought support but non-taxable services." (Saskia Sassen quoted in Ling, 2000: 145)

Cyprus, Greece, and Turkey have put themselves up "for sale," if you will, to satiate the new emerging local owning-class' desire for transnational material power both within the EU and the capitalist world economy. But this "opening up" of migration of skilled and unskilled workers remains anchored in less well-off states. Herein lies the fundamental contradiction of this policy: the peripheral economic state feminizes, that is, opens up itself to structural adjustment, including privatization, cutbacks in healthcare and benefits and social services, itself, in order to masculinize itself, that is, to increase its power like other EU core states in the world economy. Note this OECD report (2001: 8) on Greece's "selling" of its public/domestic sectors to the private powers:

> The momentum of and commitment to reform and the general policy stance towards international market openness have been largely shaped by the membership of Greece in the European Union....In particular, concerns are widely shared about the effects of a restrictive domestic environment, of important state control over the economy and of extensive recourse to command and control regulations, on the competitiveness of domestic enterprises and the attractiveness of the country to foreign investors....

The European Union managers of capital challenge the nationalization (e.g., code for social access to resources) of the economy and the controls that could potentially exercise on the transnational freedom of regional capital. These same managers argue that Greece's ability to take an open stance toward the freedom of movement of capital within its borders results from its membership in the EU. What these discourses silence is that once national/social capital becomes privatized citizens lose their power as well as their ability to hold the state accountable. "Private" powers are neither accountable to the working-class nor are they interested in being democratically accountable. More concretely, an opening up to the EU's harmonization process transfers the citizens' power into the hands of an emerging transnational elite (policymakers, investors, and others) headquartered in Brussels whose primary interest is the reduction of tariffs on capital. The former Greek EU president and experts on migration had the following to say about migrant labor and its importance to the development of the European Market:

> Europe with its ageing population and greying workforce must begin to focus on the benefits of managed migration to maintain economic growth and competitiveness.... by allowing the debate to become monopolized by illegal migration by placing all of our collective energy in devising ways to keep immigrants out we have failed our publics....demographic experts from the United Nations and the European Commission warned that pension ages will rise and Europe's share of the world economy will shrink unless migration is embraced as one of the tools for combating the alarming decline in fertility. (http:www.greece.gr/POLITICS/International/migration .stm)

The peripheral economic state finds itself questioning the masculine strategy of the EU to target the illegal migrant. As long as substantial amounts of energy are focused on finding and managing the illegal "other" within EU borders, the public will lose. As a broker for multinational capital and facilitator of cheap labor, the peripheral economic state too is not worrying about all people and more specifically the working-class, both local and migrant. The Greek EU president is more concerned that many Europeans may not support migration if the focus remains on the "illegal" migrant who is identified as the cause of many problems such as crime and diseases. Thus, it is important for the managers of capital to redirect the discourse on how Europe can be helped by migration. Of course, what this text is silencing is how Europe facilitates the extraction of labour from Third World countries or other peripheral economic states.

Greece began to import cheap reproductive labor in the 1970s. Part of a larger migration phenomenon in Southern and Southeastern Europe, many people migrated from countries very close to the borders of Greece such as Albania, Bulgaria, Poland, Rumania, Russia, the Ukraine, Moldavia, and Georgia. Many others arrived from the Philippines, India, Ethiopia, Pakistan, and India (Kethi, Human Resources Information, 2002; Ministry of National Economy, 1999, 1998).

Despite stringent migration controls introduced in the early 1990s and attempts to put into place the Schengen provisions, a large number of undocumented migrants persist in Greece (Kethi, 2002; Lazaridis, 2001; Anderson, 2000; Fakiolas and Maratou-Alipranti,

2000; Lianos, 2001; Kandaraki, 2000; Roubani et al., 2000; Valencia, 1995). Recently arrived migrants with work permits number about 25,000–30,000 and make up 0.6–0.7 percent of the total labor force (European Employment Observatory). Because illegal migration is said to be "statistically invisible" (Lazaridis, 2001: 75; Cothran, 2001), the number of undocumented migrants in Greece is difficult to estimate. According to data, the total number of immigrants is said to have increased from approximately 400,000 in 1993 (Commission of the European Communities, 1993: 16) to 600,000 in 1999 (Lazaridis, 2001: 75 citing Fakiolas, 1999; "from around 4.1 percent to 6 percent of the population"), to as many as one million in 2002 (General Secretary of Public Order Ministry, 2001; Chair of Labor Ministry Committee on Migration, 2001; Kethi, 2002: 1; Spartacus, 2000; Katsoridas, 1994; Tsanglaganou, 2000). Almost all female migrants are absorbed into the service sector.

> In particular in domestic service, tourist-related activities and in various forms of sex-related entertainment, all of which have experienced a rapid growth in recent years. (Lazaridis, 2001: 75)

According to Kethi (2002), out of the 50.2 percent of the female migrants in Greece, 80 percent are working in three sectors: 55 percent are working in private households (domestics), 14 percent in the hotel–restaurant industry, and 10 percent in other industries. This research focuses mostly on the 372,000 migrants who applied to become legal residents of Greece in 1998.

In 1995 the (OECD) claimed that about one in twelve employed persons in Greece are from another country and are earning half of the going rate of compensation. In 2001, the U.S. Department of State reported that 40,000 women, mostly between the ages of 12 and 25, are trafficked to the country each year for prostitution (U.S. Department of State, Country Reports on Human Rights Practices, 2002; Trafficking in Persons Report, 2003, 2004).

Turkey and Cyprus are following in Greece's footsteps. Their pro-Europe owning-class envisions itself as part and parcel of Europe. Germany uses racially based obfuscation to reign in Turkey's imperial desire to enter the European family of capital and power. However, the Turkish pro-Europe owning-class, or Turkish elite, defy this mystification. For example, in 1997 German Chancellor Helmut Kohl stated: "Turkish membership in the EU is not possible," and that the EU was "a civilization project" within which "Turkey has no place" (Kuniholm, 2001: 7). Yet, Germany and the United States remain Turkey's favorite trading partners (Allen, 2000: 2).

Until very recently, Turkey was considered a "sending" country with three million of its people having migrated to Western Europe (Içduygu, Sirkeci, and Muradoglu, 2001; Gülçür and İlkkaracan, 2002: 2). However, today, it is both a "receiving" and a "transit" state (Narli, 2002). Its "migrant population has diversified to include individuals from the former Soviet Union and Eastern Europe" (Gülçür and İlkkaracan, 2002 citing Karaduman-Taş, 2001: 413, personal communication, State Institute of Statistics, Turkey; Narli, 2002).

While Turkey has become a major transit and receiving country (Narli, July 9, 2002; IMO, 1995), it has no immigration law to inform its public, police, or the media. Turkey has a regulation on asylum seekers entitled "Regulation on the Procedures and the Principles Related to Mass Influx and the Foreigners Arriving in Turkey or Requesting Residence Permits with the Intention of Seeking Asylum from a Third Country" (Regulation on Asylum Seekers, November 30, 1994). Many migrants arrive in Turkey from different countries of the Middle East because of political persecution there, or from Asia and Africa, primarily motivated by economic opportunity.

While some of these migrants use Turkey as a transit site (IMO, 1995), they must "work to survive" while there (Narli, 2002: 1). Studies (IMO, 2003, 1995) found that migrants arrived in Turkey from Iran, Iraq, Bosnia, the continent of Africa, and the continent of Asia (Philippines, Sri Lanka, Pakistan, Afghanistan). For Asians and Africans, the major reasons for traveling to Turkey were economic (60 percent for the former and 50 percent for the latter), for Iranians, social/cultural/religious (69 percent), and for Iraqis, war informed their departure to Turkey (56 percent). Most of these migrants entered Turkey without a passport or a refugee document. Iraqi citizens with "ethnic" identities (such as Kurds, Chaldean/Assyrian, or Turks) extensively used networks of recruiters or traffickers to enter the country (IMO, 1995: 20). Around 50 percent of the migrants entering Turkey had to pay bribes in their country of origin or at the border of the neighboring country. The average cost of migration differs depending on the country of origin. The maximum cost was paid by Iranians ($10,500) and the lowest cost was $5 by Iraqis (IMO, 1995: 27).

Cyprus is also participating in the transnational project of migration to lower its costs of labor. Despite 29 years of division into Greek and Turkish states, the Republic of Cyprus moved to unify with the EU justifying its move by arguing that its integration could possibly lead to the Cyprus problem's solution: "the integration of Cyprus is not linked with the political solution of the Cypriot problem.... Locating the Cypriot problem in the political circles of the European Union opens possibilities for resolving it. It partially identifies the content of the solution and becomes a lever and invitation to moving towards European Integration with resulting advantages for both communities" (Kranidiotis, 1996: 90). These neoliberal principles (separating politics from economics; advantages) guided the opening of the borders within Cyprus in April 2003 and led to debates among the Cypriot elite about how to proceed together with the European integration irrespective of the socioeconomic gaps existing between the two communities. The Cyprus Republic

> intends to continue with the process of gradual liberalization of the remaining restrictions on capital movements in accordance with the commitments made vis as vis the EU, so that by accession Cyprus will fully comply with the acquis requirements.... the labour market in Cyprus can be considered to be relatively flexible and well functioning. (Pre-Accession Economic Programme of the Republic of Cyprus, 2002: 80–81)

An assessment by the managers and policy makers of the European Union and Republic of Cyprus affirms that the state is moving toward implementing "fully and completely" neoliberal policies and that it follows capital's rules: extraction of maximum surplus-value. Nevertheless, it still needs to orchestrate better strategies to extract more surplus-value from the local as well as the migrant working-class. Yet, according to the EU, the Republic of Cyprus still has room for improvement in the area of labor.

These neoliberal strategies of globalization (e.g., development) are anchored in migration of mostly unskilled labor[7] from comparatively less well-to-do countries such as the Philippines, India, and Myanmar, and economies in transition such as socialist European states and the former Soviet Union. One official from the Republic of Cyprus explained this labor migration in the following way:

> There is a huge demand for maids and artists in Cyprus. It is cheap labor...people have money and they want to hire others to do their work or give them pleasure...the society has changed...social mores have changed and women and men relate differently to each other.... Moreover, the demand for these workers is on the rise, there just aren't enough Cypriots who want to come in and clean somebody's house for only 150 pounds...regarding the artists, there is demand for

Russians and Eastern Europeans...and we benefit as a whole when we hire foreign workers; again, it is cheap labor. (Interview with a Cypriot Migration Officer, 2001)

This officer articulates the social and economic reasons (mostly pull factors) that are used to justify the Cypriot import of sex and domestic workers, an idea that Anderson expresses in her book when she describes the benefits that receiving states have from importing women to do the "dirty work" of the nation-state. The receiving-state benefits in a variety of ways because the labor power of the domestic and sex workers has been produced without any "outlay from...[the importing] state and, theoretically at least, [sex and domestic workers] are to return to their countries of origin one day, thereby saving the receiving-state any expenses associated with their old age....Again, theoretically, they do not bring their children with them, saving the host state associated health and education costs....In practice, immigrants are less likely to draw on social provisions than citizens, and yet they do pay taxes" (Anderson, 2000: 109). The import of female migrant labor ensures low reproduction costs because the receiving state does not have to pay costs "incurred in labor migrant subsistence prior to migration" (Chin, 1998: 109).

The Neoliberal State Exploiting and Colonizing Migrant Reproductive Labor

Paradoxically, the peripheral economic state itself has been overtly hostile to female migrants. From a strictly economic standpoint, "a worker is a worker" irrespective of their racial background and color of their skin. If we followed the neoliberal economic logic, one would expect preferences to be based only on a country's economic needs and the skills a migrant possesses to fill such needs (Rudolph, 2000: 4). However, this is not the case in Cyprus, Greece, and Turkey.[8] Unskilled labor immigrant policies display racial and gender preferences in the allocation of immigrant visas or temporary work permits. More specifically, the rich generating income "peripheral economic state" *facilitates the sale of* reproductive labor in its racialized and sexed configurations, enabling the exploitation of migrant women's labor and the colonization of their bodies through violence.

Most female migrants who work in the desire industries face a number of problems such as sexual exploitation and violence in addition to the ones usually faced by people who have to move. Many of these women in all three countries do not feel that they can go to the authorities to seek protection because they are afraid they might lose their work permit; some of them may have no work permit at all. For example, a study on violence against foreign women in Greece in 1998 revealed that 415 women (with the majority under age 15) faced violence within 5 months of arrival:

> The offenders involved in sex trade were 114 men and 16 women, 103 of who were Greek, the remaining (27) cases being foreigners. The social status of the offenders varie[d] widely, with doctors and lawyers involved, businessmen and policemen.... regarding arrests of foreign women prostituting themselves in Greece. Over the last three years, the newspaper "EXOUSIA" reports 6,100 arrests in 1996, 10,500 in 1997, and 12,800 in 1998. (Roubani, et al., 2000: 4–5)

> Madame always looks at me like I am a machine. She orders me around, she wakes me up at 1:00 a.m. if the kid is crying even after I finished my job because she thinks I am here to work for her 24 hours a day, despite my contract requiring me to work much less than that. She always says that I "have to be available" and respond to the needs of the family that provides me with my bread. (Tricia, 25-year-old Filipina working in Greece)

Migrant women are bearing the burden of violence, exploitation, and the "flexibility" of deregulation of peripheral economic states' easy-hiring, easy-exploiting labor markets because many migrant women and their female employers must find a way not to neglect their family/communal/national obligations. This heterosexual expectation is justified because of the ideological mystification that women, migrant and local, should be the ones responsible for reproductive work instead of men (e.g., their husbands) or the state.[9]

In Turkey, the peripheral heterosexual/heterosexist economic state, "in its need to secure its social and geographic boundaries vis-à-vis . . . the Others," produces certain "desirable" sexualities and intimacies in "relation to other configurations of desire that may fall outside whiteness" (Kaur Puar, 2001: 173). It regulates reproductive labor through acts of omission that result in violence for women migrants. Anastasia, a 21-year-old sex worker from Moldavia, lifted up the back of her blouse to reveal five burns on her back. She explained:

> My pimp got angry because I did not want to go with two of his clients. He got really mad at me, cuffed my hands, and tied them together to my feet. Afterwards, he pushed his cigarette on different parts of my body and then he locked me into the hotel. The next day he returned for some more tricks. In the beginning I wanted to go to the police after I spent a week at the hospital, but I did not have the

heart to do that. I was also scared and finally after a lot of thought I decided to return to him. He is one of the few people in my life that treated me as good.

Similarly, in Cyprus, we see a reassertion of an heterosexual state that is due in part to immigrant working-class bodies that threaten or destabilize the boundaries and borders of the nation. Many of the women, both sex and domestic workers, are sexually exploited and live with the constant fear of violence and regulation of their labor and lives. The hidden, privatized, and, at times, illegal nature of the work aggravates their situation. Many of the sex and domestic workers are violated by their madams, managers, pimps, law enforcement officers, or customers, who may beat them up or verbally abuse them with racist statements such as "you stupid filipina," or "you little flat face." The murder and death of prostitutes and even domestic workers is not uncommon in these countries (IMO, 2003), and yet, the licit/illicit border on which the desire industries are located isolates these women, preventing them from seeking what meager resources and help that is available (Kostopoulos, Trimis, Psarra and Psarra, July 21, 2001). In all three countries, sex workers talked about how difficult it is to report rape. The police consider its occurrence "impossible" especially when women choose this job, and, thus, sex workers like Anastasia rarely choose to report their abusive and violent johns, pimps, or police officers.

HIGHER INCOME MEN AND WOMEN EXPLOITING MIGRANT REPRODUCTIVE LABOR AND OTHER FEMINIZED SUBJECTS

Hypermasculinizing (that is, making sure that it secures bourgeois heterosexual private powers) the peripheral economic state participates in hyperfeminizing, (that is, exploiting and sanctioning violence to extract surplus-value and their ensuring gaining flexible access to their personhood) all others, including migrant women and their labor, local women, and other racialized groups. This hyperfeminization of migrant women and their labor is apparent in several discussions with men in these three states as well as some of the agencies who try to "sell" these women. Consider what some agencies said about the women they bring to Greece for sale:

> Wedding with trial.... When the right woman is identified, the agency stops the search and the dates. "The last day before you leave," is explained in the instructions, "you arrange the details for a visa and the

day of the trip of the lady. This duration of the visa means that the lady can come for a while in your place, to live together in order to see how you are doing under the same roof." (*Eleftherotypia*, November 11, 2000: 2)

Moreover, women from ex-socialist countries and the former Soviet Union are described as follows by several of these market agencies:

Our women-members are serious, they look good, are honest, gentle, respectful and interested in serious relations.... Bulgarian women do not make exaggerated demands and claims from a man that perhaps women from Greece may make and that is because they have lived in poverty and they have learned to be satisfied with little.... (*Eleftherotypia*, November 11, 2000: 3)

These women are hyperfeminized in relation to the middle- and upper-class Greek women who are hypermasculinized by becoming "less attentive to their men" and losing their femininity. They are supposedly not the dedicated and very hardworking slaves that patriarchs look for in these countries. For local women, hypermasculine competition entails more than just working as professional women in the market. It entails flexibility in the labor market and at home. It pushes women to hire domestic workers to clean and take care of the domestic "dirty" work. These "localized" strategies, in turn, make it possible to contain the structural contradictions that emerge among men and women. For men, it requires migrant women who can satiate their desires and provide them with pleasure and sex especially after a day's hard work in the market. This process, in turn, lulls them into oblivion rather than moving them to challenge structural contradictions that privilege them by costing them their alienation.

A prominent psychiatrist in Cyprus was asked the following questions: How do you view the phenomenon of the cabaret in contemporary Cypriot society? How do you understand the issue of foreign "artists"? Here is his response:

On this issue I have very strong opinions. I believe that Cypriot women are the most negative women in the world. In the development of our society, women have become very demanding. They have lost every sign of gentleness. They get so attached to their kids and expect their husband to be the one who buys everything for the house. The masculine sex in Cyprus is not treated as a man. The woman works for many hours with the child and when the man comes home she does not even give him food. And do not forget that the Cypriot women are very thin and as soon as they get married they become like boats. When

the man goes to the cabaret and the Bulgarian, the Rumanian (her ethnicity does not matter) responds to him like he is a man, things are
different. These women see the man like a man. They are thinking that
this man has to fuck. No Cypriot woman thinks that she has to give
him oral sex.... These things are necessary. What do you think the
"artists" do to them? She will tell him "My love," she will touch his
face, will give him oral sex, and will make him feel like a man. (Zenios,
2002: 67)

This psychiatrist suggests that Cypriot women are not responding to
their "naturalized" feminine role of "making a man feel like a man,"
whereas the "artists" know how to treat the masculine gender. Again,
the dream of the patriarch in these states is to have a woman from
Rumania or Bulgaria who can serve his desires. Despite the psychiatrist's comment that ethnicity does not matter, clearly ethnicity and
race *do* matter. Men choose women from countries of the former
Soviet Union and Central Europe, societies in deep economic crises,
ostensibly because they are "beautiful, dedicated to their families,
they are excellent housewives, and behave gently toward their husbands and they know how to support, they are not spoiled and do not
give a damn about material interests" (*Eleftherotypia*, November 11,
2000: 4). In sum, these women are the patriarch's dream: beautiful,
traditional, and satisfied with little. This approach is both heterosexist and racist toward all women, those who work in the desire industries, and those who do not. It renders invisible the real problems
women in the desire industries face, such as trafficking, and renders
invisible that Cypriot women are demonized in the process in order
to justify the hetero-patriarchal desires to exploit and consume
women's bodies and labor as a form of "freedom" and as a method
of inclusion in the global economy (Demleitner, 2001).

CONCLUDING THOUGHTS

The Cypriot, Greek, and Turkish governments, along with different
agencies, for example, are urging their women and men to buy
migrant women's reproductive labor as a way of responding to their
consumptive desires, which supports the development of (re)produc-
tion relations' into a neoliberal social formation. Buying women's
cheap labor decreases the costs for economic development and
secures these men and women bourgeois privilege and frees them to
spend more time toward professionalization (support and management of capital relations) and in entertainment. Cypriot, Greek, and
Turkish official rhetoric has recast this development as an opportunity

for them to become viable economic members in the family of the EU. In sum, this inclusion makes them "white." Today, the move to join the EU or cast oneself as a viable economic and power broker requires more than just individualistic consumption. It requires deploying tactics in negotiations with NGOs and other human rights organizations which challenge these neoliberal practices and ideologies.

Almost all the women that work as sex workers in Cyprus, Greece, and Turkey are "white but not quite" and come from countries in deep economic crises where new entrepreneurs are:

> Plunged into a hellish free-for-all of "grabification"—a brutal struggle to steal everything they could get their hands on. They plundered [these nations'] wealth of natural resources, sold state-owned gold, diamonds, oil, gas, Siberian forests, even plutonium, and unloaded them on to the West to amass their private fortunes. And, as we have seen in the money-laundering scandals of late, they also privatized billions of dollars of western aid. (Holmstrom and Smith, 2000: 7)

This "transfer of property into private hands" has led many "propertyless proletariat [to be] dispossessed of the means of production and subsistence and, consequently with nothing to sell but their capacity to labor" (Holmstrom and Smith, 2000: 2). The processes of privatization and dispossession in the countries from which these women come destroyed "social property rights" and pushed women to seek opportunities in other states. In many of their countries, these women did not own the means of production, however, they did "own" their jobs. After many struggles they "had long-established rights to housing, state-provided medical care, childcare, and numerous subsidies from the state ... Divested, 'freed' from control, possession, or ownership of the means of production, the majority of people in the[se countries] are forced to come to the market with, in Marx's words, 'nothing to sell but their skins'" (Holmstrom and Smith, 2000: 6).

Following the logic of feminists and political economists who want to "de-colonize global restructuring" (Chang and Ling, 2000: 33) and also put forward an alternative understanding of community, this chapter focused on the racialized and gendered nature of the peripheral economic state. In particular, I examined the effect of these relations on the subaltern working-class woman whose reproductive labor becomes the major element of exploitation in the "regime[s] of labor intimacy" (Chang and Ling, 2000: 33).[10] This focus makes it possible to recognize other "social processes, practices, meaning-structures, and institutions" and "how [they] assign and reflect historically constructed notions of 'masculinity' and 'femininity' that are also class-based, racially specific, and culturally defined" (Chang and Ling, 2000: 34).

A resultant patriarchal power structure values white men and masculinity and devalues women and femininity even while depending so crucially on female reproductive labor throughout the economy. This racialized gendering may apply to whole groups of people, certain sectors, and particular members and institutions of the world economy regardless of their biological sex. For example, a woman may have use value in the schema of gendered society but little exchange value, since gender can never be fully exchanged within the patriarchal structure that constitutes her subjectivity and social agency as production- less. This racialized gendering also applies to the peripheral economic state, which desires to constitute its power by restructuring itself through integration into a neoliberal institution of the world economy that can mediate capital accumulation through the "structur[ing], facilitat[ion]…and sustain[ance]…[of] a globalized service economy" (Chang and Ling, 2000: 35). Within this restructuring, women and men of lower-income countries are sexually and racially exploited.

In importing and exporting reproductive labor, the peripheral economic state is complicit in the development, facilitation, and structuring of the desire industries—in the name of neoliberal development and progress or restructuring. While the state's complicity in this service economy is not a recent development of globalization (Chang 2004; Chang and Ling, 2000; Glenn, 2002), the state's role is being changed in the process of responding to transnational restructurings because of an intensification of these industries and their economies (Ebert, 2001). Thus, it needs to be creative in drawing upon ideologies and circulating discourses to justify its transformation.[11] Herein lies the dilemma. While peripheral economic states view the desire industries and migrant reproductive labor as economically central, these same industries exacerbate a sense of *national insecurity*.

Let us now examine how the state works toward mystifying its own insecurity and the majority of its people's lack of safety, including those of the migrant working-class, who produce surplus-value for it by focusing on the working-class migrant as a threat and the creator of insecurity.

CHAPTER 5

NATIONAL DESIRES FOR SECURITY

> In the colonial countries, the spirit of indulgence is dominant at the core of the bourgeoisie; and this is because the national bourgeoisie identifies itself with the Western bourgeoisie, from whom it has learnt its lessons. . . . the national bourgeoisie will be greatly helped on its way toward decadence by the Western bourgeoisie, who come to it as tourists avid for the exotic, for big game hunting, and for casinos. The national bourgeoisie organizes centers of rest and relaxation and pleasure resorts to meet the wishes of the Western bourgeoisie. Such activity is given the name of tourism, and for the occasion will be built up as a national industry. (Fanon, 1963: 153)

> Security firms do the biggest business in the cities where the gap between rich and poor is greatest. . . . It now seems that these gated compounds protecting the haves from the have-nots are microcosms of what is fast becoming a global security—not a global village intent on lowering walls and barrier, as we were promised, but a network of fortresses connected by highly militarized trade corridors.
> (Klein, 2002: xxiii)

Fanon speaks of how the national bourgeoisie is complicit in setting up centers for Western capital following the territorial decolonizations in the Third World. He brings to our attention the strategies that capital employed, drawing upon racism to dominate and exploit the labor and lands of the Third World. Today, Naomi Klein talks of how corporate globalization, a continuing manifestation of neoimperialism (such as development and modernization), has not brought the riches it promised people and how the gaps between the rich and the poor are becoming vast, so much so that the owners of private property are building security/military corridors to protect their riches from those who produce it for them. Constructing walls and barriers separating labor from capital, the agents of corporate globalization are armed and ready to build new fortresses to protect the property of the haves from the have-nots. Simultaneously, the peripheral economies' upper class, the bourgeoisie, are expanding industries to acquire their own pieces of the profit pie.

The owning-class of both the core and peripheral economies not only constitute desire as a commodity, a strategy of colonization and imperialism (Aguilar, 2002; Ebert, 2001), but also conceal these exploitative and violent relations by reifying a desire for *sovereignty*. In other words, the basis of the nation-state logic resides in classic liberal visions of a nation-state as integral to itself within its borders-sovereign. It's the same logic that also creates the liberal individual image of the migrant who makes "choices" and brings "his" or "her" culture wherever "he" or "she" migrates.[1] This restructuring of capitalist social relations is a crisis-ridden process (including the crisis of the agency of the national state itself) that engenders new forms of power and domination. Fomenting a desire for things from abroad, for persons and ("others") for reproductive labor, globalization simultaneously induces a corresponding rise in the desire for "security" (Bigo, 2002; Içduygu and Keyman, 2000; Campbell, 1992; Müftüler–Bac, 2001). This link between globalization and the desire for "security" can be seen clearly through the migration of reproductive labor, which is increasingly interpreted and presented as a security problem.[2]

In this chapter I examine the peripheral economic state's complicity with imperialism. By imperialism, I refer to the monopoly of corporations and their compulsion to export capital anywhere for higher profits (Lenin, 1939). This definition of imperialism is very different from the prevailing meaning of imperialism today, which still focuses on the territoriality of the state and the silencing of the cultures and the voices of others. Lenin's definition focuses on imperialism as a global system of exploitation and a military–economic–political practice (Aguilar, 2002; Ebert, 1995). Through the exploitation, exclusion, and violence (i.e., physical, emotional, psychological, and material) of the migrant female working-class, the state works along with corporate capital to sustain the structures that make possible its own economic precariousness in the European economy. More specifically, its active participation in the desire industries (by both licit and illicit practices) leaves it flexibly vulnerable to the whims of the neoliberal financial institutions and multinational corporations. Concealing structural insecurities by operating through a set of assumptions similar to those of core economic states, the peripheral economic state manages and controls potential crises that can challenge the organization of capitalist relations. These states work toward managing and technocratically governing social relations of capital and labor in the process of competing for markets that each is willing to colonize. Simultaneously, they make invisible the sources of social and human insecurity rooted in the hegemonic structures of inequality and injustice. This chapter examines how in the process of integrating themselves into a neoliberal state transnational formation, Cyprus, Greece, and Turkey sustain an ideological stance that presents migrants as a security threat disturbing and destabilizing the national order (Içduygu and Keyman, 2000: 4; General Directorate of Security, Turkey, 2001). This framing occurs even as the changing dynamics in the world reshape migration and migratory regimes into transnational processes "necessary" for capital accumulation.

The peripheral economic state's desire for "security" is anchored in the following practices: (1) traversing an imperial geography in a search for certain markets/theaters of consumption, such as the facilitation of the influx/migration of foreign workers to satiate the desires of capital by maximizing its economic power (Alexander, 1998: 284), (2) eroticizing the desire economies while blaming immigrants and citizenry who participate in these industries (e.g., illicit trafficking) as the contributors of societal anxieties and insecurities, (3) drawing ideological mystifications from the same neocolonial frameworks to indicate that it is not "asleep at the wheel," but monitoring the borders, and counting, documenting, and disciplining migrant labor, and (4) making invisible the structural domination by powerful actors of the world economy, be they states (strong European states), class (the owning-class), or international institutions such as the IMF.

TRAVERSING AN IMPERIAL GEOGRAPHY: CONCEALING CAPITAL ACCUMULATION AND EXPLOITATION

The purchase and sale of reproductive labor did not begin with Cyprus, Greece, and Turkey. It is a dynamic, transnational process. The structural, forced migration of women for reproductive labor began with the slave labor that took place from the sixteenth to nineteenth centuries (Anderson, 2000: 129; Glenn, 1992). The labor of black and indigenous peoples was exploited, that is, forcefully appropriated by what came to be known as the owning-class (e.g., slavery) or through market transactions involving the purchase of other people's labor time by the owners of the means of production. Despite the fact that slavery is illegal under bourgeois democracy (Marx, 1990) so that the fraudulent notion of free exchanges of wage for labor power is made invisible, today the sale and purchase of reproductive labor is done legally but forcefully as part of licit and illicit exchanges. Many women migrate legally to seek labor and opportunities, and yet millions are forced into trafficking every day from poor-income generating states into higher-income sites for affluent consumers.

Though the organization of the desire industries and the trafficking trade is not the same as the slave system in the antebellum South, it still draws upon understandings and practices of slavery, recolonization, exploitation, and racism in its everyday constitution and reproduction. Exploitation and violence along class, physical, sexual, emotional, and spiritual lines is part and parcel of the relationship among employer, the wife of the employer, and the employee (Anderson, 2000: 131; Jacobs, 1988; Davis, 1984). As Anderson (2000: 128) argues, "the distinction, if one wishes to make it, can be extremely complicated, but perhaps the key point to make is that slavery and wage labour ('wage slavery') are not diametrically opposed" when looking at the ways the trafficking of women and children is organized. On the contrary, the seemingly free relation between the employer (capital) and labor (the female migrant laborer) is guided by compulsion. The legal blocks against slavery have not ended it.

> Wage labor is a hidden form of slavery (through the exploitation of "surplus labor"), and prostitution and other forms of sexual slavery are an integral part of bourgeois democracy and the free market. (Ebert, 2001: 14)

Both sex and domestic work are forms of slave wage-labor irrespective if it is "legal" or "illegal." Legalistic notions that sex trafficking and other kinds of trafficking are illegal in the EU and in the peripheries of Cyprus, Greece, and Turkey serve to mystify that sexual slavery is an integral part of neoliberal capitalism and bourgeois democracy (Conference on Trafficking in Human Beings, International Women Lawyers Federation, Instanbul, 2001; Europe Against Trafficking, OSCE Report, October 2001; Erginsoy, 2000). The peripheral economic state facilitates and manages potential crises of imperialist capitalism and plays a crucial role in sustaining structural/ social insecurities. It conceals them by drawing upon the epistemic imperial political ideological frameworks that end up making the working-class, and, more specifically, female migrant workers, the scapegoat. Despite EU laws and policies legitimizing the import of this waged labor and protecting against the "illicit" aspects of this population trade, the recruitment, transportation, harboring, receipt of women depends extensively on trafficking and smuggling (İçduygu, 2003; Lazos, 2002). Trafficking and smuggling of women happens through

> the threat or use of force or other forms of coercion, or abduction, of fraud, of deception, of the abuse of power or of a position of vulnerability or of the giving or receiving of payments or benefits to achieve the consent of a person having control over another person, for the purpose of exploitation. Exploitation shall include, at a minimum, the exploitation of the prostitution of others or other forms of sexual exploitation, forced labour or services, slavery or practices similar to slavery, servitude or the removal of organs. (Convention against Transnational Organized Crime and its Protocols. (Doc.A/55/383/ www.odccp.org/palermo/convmain.html)

While not all domestic and sex workers face the same "slave conditions" and are not recruited through trafficking and smuggling,[3] many are recruited through trafficking even when they legally traverse countries' borders. Trafficking and smuggling are a transnational market that involves well-organized networks and includes countries of origin, of transit, and of destination, worldwide. This $7–12 billion annual market is driven by a desire for cheap waged labor by capital through the facilitation of the flows by the state. In the desire industries, ideologies about economic mobility, visas to Europe, and the existence of men interested in "rescuing" working-class women from a lifetime of foreclosed opportunities and poverty conceal that the sale of their surplus labor generates profits for traffickers, police officers, and state officials (Di Nicola, 1999: 3).

Through migration, modes of governance, and regime performance as well as the neoliberal market (desire industries and trafficking), the states collude with each other to perpetuate socioeconomic inequalities by sustaining in place property relations and social insecurities for the majority of their people, as well as for the domestic and sex workers who are vulnerable to exploitation and violence. Despite the state's continued focus on itself as the referent object of security, it conceptualizes the female migrant as a transnational agent, a threat to interstate relations. In one of Turkey's top circulating papers, *Istanbul Sabah*, the Ankara edition, we see how the media regime makes invisible the structural violence and anxieties generated from capital relations by stating that Russian prostitutes are posing a threat to Turkey's national security.

> A majority of individuals, who have financial gains from the ... Natasha Activities show these women as married on paper and make them Turkish citizens. If no measures are taken, the number of people who have acquired Turkish citizenship in this way will increase to hundreds of thousands. This situation will become an important security issue for Turkey.... It will also be an important threat factor in terms of the effect it will have on our human resources.... Most of these women are university graduates and they provide the intelligence units of their countries with intelligence on various issues. It has been established that the intelligence units interrogate some of these women for days after they return to their countries. The state officials, who have been involved in the Natasha activities and who are in important positions, may leak extremely important information regarding the general security of the state, to these women. It has been established that some of these officials have illegal relationships with these women. It is known that the important strategic natural sources and the human structure [of Turkey] are being examined with this method. (http://www.cdi.org/russia/johnson/6064-11.cfm)

In this newspaper text, we read how the women are creating a problem because they use relationships with Turkish men to acquire citizenship and they will in the end overflow the country.[4] Additionally, these women are a danger because they "have ways" of drawing out crucial information from officials about national security that may compromise the sovereignty of the state.[5] On focusing on the individual female migrant as a threat to the national security of the peripheral economic state, this text serves to silence the class struggles ensuing, the state's collusion with the multibillion dollar industries of desire, trafficking, and smuggling to ensure their continuing, profitable operation while also infantilizing the men as being used by the women. It likewise hides how numerous individuals from these countries, as well as outside their boundaries, are faced daily with abject conditions. Even when reports refer to the role officials play in the "Natasha activities," they still characterize women as violators of state security and "exploiters" of the Turkish economy. The focus on the Russian woman and its relation to the Turkish official makes invisible the structural racialized and gendered relation of labor and capital as well as the state and the other terrors that migrants face daily.

As in the James Bond movie "From Russia with Love" (1963), the Russian woman is constructed as the devious expropriator of national security information from Turkish officials. Most of these kinds of portrayals and information the newspapers circulate come from the state. For example, what we read earlier was from a "Natasha Activity Report" (NAF), which has been drawn up by the National Intelligence Organization (MIT), the General Staff, and the Interior Ministry. These constructions of the Russian woman silence the structural exploitative relationship of the working-class, by the owning-class the expropriation of its labor under terror.

Such reports by the state render invisible the different kinds of structural insecurities that female working-class migrants and children face. The working-class of female migrants is exposed to exploitation of their labor and bodies daily. Many of the men and women who manage the desire industries come from working-class backgrounds and find themselves "choosing" the best option out of the few available to them to generate fast cash and integration into the middle-class. Despite increased cash flow, these men and women who employ the same methods that the agents of formal economy use to expropriate the surplus-value of the working-class labor and with the use of force remain the "underclass" who engages in illegal activities. International/regional institutions act as intermediaries between capital and labor to manage crises. They constantly use harsher methods of surveillance and control within these illicit industries to control antagonisms and conflicts that may emerge. An elaborate national security set of ideologies is set in place to justify capital's "permanent state of war" against the working-class and other anti-corporate globalization movements. These systematic strategies of terror contain popular discontent and disarticulate mass organizing (Petras, 1987: 103; Pigem, 2003). In the 2003 International Migration Report on Irregular Migration in Turkey, a man involved in smuggling that İçduygu interviewed states:

> In this region, smuggling is part of the economy. If it weren't for animal husbandry and smuggling, the people in this region would not have survived for centuries. Smuggling is a way of life here and it is not something negative. Being a doctor or an engineer is no different from being a smuggler. Years ago, we used to bring sugar from, and take animals to, Iran. Tobacco smugglers and porters have even inspired the poems of Ahmet Arif, for instance in the poems "33 Kursun" or "General Muglali Vakasi." Smuggling is the basis of the region's economy. Everything you can imagine travels over the border. You just ask for it. This has now become a necessity. There is no cultivation and animal husbandry is dead. The government gives no money to the municipalities. Unemployment is high. I studied but I am still unemployed. The business of my father and grandfather is more profitable....In a

system like this, it makes no difference if we are carrying spare car parts, diesel fuel, or people. The fundamental rule of capitalism operates here; it is a matter of supply and demand. On the thousand years old Silk Road, whatever item is needed is smuggled. At that time, the borders we have now did not exist. Travelling that route was not considered smuggling. There were only different taxes at different stops. But now on paper they say this is Iraq, this is Iran, this is Turkey, and it is illegal to cross without notification. My relatives on the other side of the border are larger in number than the ones on this side of the border. I live in Turkey but more than half of Khvoy is my kin. This kind of a relationship is an advantage for all sorts of smuggling including the smuggling of people. It works like an insurance.[8] (Içduygu, 2003: 79 citing Alevi, 37-year-old Kurdish male and a local smuggler in Turkey)

Alevi's narrative, brings to the fore the many contracts that capitalism generates in order to sustain its expropriation of surplus-value from the working-class. His narrative makes apparent the arbitrariness of borders in the ways capital works to organize its regime by drawing upon the mirage of licit and illicit economies as well as the artificial boundaries between nation-states. As Alevi states, in both licit and illicit economies the fundamental rule of capitalism operates. The artificial boundaries between these economies do not stop capital from exploiting the racialized working-class female labor in the desire industries. It also makes apparent the many contradictions facing the organization of migration as well as understandings of security within a transnational context. As long as migration is understood through the categories of the state, its sovereignty and the national, then any movement and crossing of borders is considered dangerous to the "homogeneity of the people." Alevi brings to our attention the multilayered complexity of the world structure and the ways the body politic or the state narrows this history because of the myth of sovereignty embedded within it. These modern concepts of state, sovereignty, security, and borders are strategic methods in the hands of "private" powers in their search for more profits and expropriation of surplus-value. As Bigo argues, these discourses:

always structure our thought as if there existed a "body"—an "envelope," or "container"—differentiating one polity from another. The state justifies itself as the only political order possible as soon as it is accepted that sovereignty, law and order, and single body are the prerequisite for peace and homogeneity. It justifies the "national" identity that the state has achieved through a territorialization of its order, by a cutting up of borders. (Bigo, 2002: 67)

Bigo does not though explain the reasons the state participates in cutting up of borders and how such a cutting ends up securing the privileges of some at the expense of many. A lack of structural security in both sending and receiving peripheral economic states (such as prevailing sources of livelihood and protection of the resilience of life-supporting conditions of people) pushes many men and women into crossing borders to seek opportunities and employment. For example, smuggling is currently considered an illegal activity within a capitalist structure despite the fact that these activities could not exist without the legal contracts the state generates and justifies through the rule of supply and demand, and other fraudulent formal rules of exchange. The traffickers and the migrants come to be seen as major violators of the integrity of what is "inside" the state as well as a danger and threat to the homogeneity of the state, society, and the polity. Alevi's explanation of his participation in the trafficking industry, his understanding of the regional history as well as his experience with the formal economy within Turkey complicates our understanding of interstate "national" security. Unable to find employment in Turkey, he draws upon his own resources—relatives on the other side of the border—and actively participates in the smuggling of people and things to make a living. Another 50-year-old, Kurdish male, interviewed by Içduygu for the International Migration Organization Report, a smuggler since he was 11, had the following to say about trafficking and smuggling:

> There was this guy Ahmet from Masshad, one of the biggest smugglers. He is now in jail for having killed his wife. He was good at establishing connections with police officers. He was like a police officer himself. Migrants would come to him, he would arrange their accommodation, and then Ahmet would tell the police he was sheltering illegal migrants. He would then take these people to Istanbul. There are people now who work outside Van and Istanbul. Most are Kurdish like myself. Seydioglu is one of the biggest smugglers to Istanbul. He has a shop across from the mosque. The salaries of Iranian police officers are very low. The salary of a high-ranking soldier is equivalent to the salary of a low-ranking [police] officer in Turkey. For this reason they encourage smuggling so that they themselves earn money. In Turkey we also have police stations that take bribery but usually there is no need. (Içduygu, 2003: 83)

This narrative by a Kurdish male involved in the trafficking of humans, reveals that the illicit exchanges of the economies of desire depend extensively on the instruments of the state such as police officers perceived to be licit. Thus, the state's focus on the migrants and the unease they create within its national boundaries seems to make invisible how the global/local nexus in a transnational world is increasingly becoming more the context for the production of social inequalities and insecurities: "globalization makes security a multidimensional form of relationship whose scope ranges from state to identity" (Içduygu and Keyman, 2000: 4). This understanding and conceptualization of security presupposes the state as the container of politics (Bigo, 2002: 65) and it is anchored in the narratives of political elites who are concerned about their power and ability to control territorial boundaries. This central presupposition that peripheral economic states can control the flow of migrants to their borders is becoming more important at a time when political elites know that they cannot control money and credit (Strange, 1994) and even flows of people. These elites are finding daily that their attempts to seal the borders conflict with the transnational movement of capital as well as with the transborder social practices and activities of millions of people who are forced to migrate from one country to another for a better life even when these activities are labeled illegal and illicit due to their involving violations of formal rules generated in a capitalist transnational structure and implemented by the state. The many artificial boundaries such as licit and illicit economies, rich-income and lower-income nation-states that so far have separated the racialized and sexed female workers are being transformed. More and more people are now able to see that capitalist ideologies have prevented them from recognizing possible alliances and producing solidarity relations toward constructing alternative classless, raceless, and sexless communities (Ebert, 2001).

Clearly many of these police officers, the male clients, the impresarios, and other representatives of these countries are exerting their power upon women in order to generate their status within their communities. However, many of them are "small potatoes" within contemporary class society and end up becoming intermediaries among the working-class, capital, and managers of the crises of capitalism. In addition, they participate in a cycle of reproducing the same capitalist relations: exploitation, violence, and even their insecurities in the world economy.

Globalization as a process engenders new forms of transnational marketization for cheap wage-labor and trafficking of humans to serve others and new cooperative/domination relations among different states. Yet the state and its political agents continue to present both the controlled (licit) and uncontrolled movement of people as a security threat. For example, a report that was prepared by the National

Intelligence Organization, the General Staff, and the Interior Ministry in Turkey warned that the "Natasha Trade" threatens the security of the state: "our first consideration is the security of the country. As Turkish citizens, we live in an uncomfortable area. We have to consider the internal security of our country when implementing domestic laws and regulations. All of our regulations respond to the logic of stabilizing the security of our country" (Frelick, 1997: 47). However, this securitization of migration is a pedagogical tool and a mode of governmentability[6] that both new emerging transnational institutions and states use to affirm their role as providers of protection and security and to mystify anxieties about their structural economic precariousness in the world economy as well as conceal the violence exerted on migrants from private powers. As Bigo (2002: 70) argues:

> This "will to mastery" on the part of the politicians has only one effect, but an important one. They change the status and stay (at the national—or, in the contemporary European context, Schengen—borders), declaring legal or illegal the arrival and they stay in the country, but they know that a person who wants to enter will succeed anyway. Thus, in an illegal situation, the immigrant becomes, for the politician...the personal enemy. Politicians see themselves as insulted by the incapacity to enforce the integrity of the national body they represent. The "migrant" is seen as both a public enemy breaking the law and a private enemy mocking the will of the politician.

The activation of narratives focusing on the migrant as public and private enemy of the state and its agents links migration and security, and this linkage blurs the ways categories such as sovereignty and security are associated with a "particular way of governing—that of the so-called Westphalian state and its modern...variations" (Bigo, 2002: 68) as well as property relations. Moreover, this approach obscures many unresolved structural questions (such as exploitation, unemployment, poverty, and urbanism) that converge in a space that lacks political solutions. Defining the female migrant as a "third-country" national as opposed to a European makes possible particular practices and the continuation of social relations of exploitation and inequality:

> I make 100 pounds for my boss for each client. If on a particular night, I sleep with 20 clients, it is 2,000 pounds for him. How much do I get out of this? 400 pounds per month. Then, I have to pay back my travel expenses to Cyprus of 1,500 pounds, 1,500 pounds to the agent who found my impressario here...and then what is left for me after so much

work?.... At least, in Russia, before Perestroika, we had food, housing, and access to the health system. This newer life for us is good in the sense that we can make cash faster but it is disastrous because we are constantly exploited without any recourse. (Anna, Russian sex worker in Cyprus)

This is not a job. It is closing your eyes, surviving, and if you finish your "ambassadorship to Turkey" with some money in your pocket, you are in good shape... you know cabaret is only for sex and prostitution and, of course, I can't ever say anything negative about the Russian, the Moldavian or any other impresarios even when they steal your money and do not do anything for you... and you know the reasons behind this silence. (Elena, Russian sex worker in Turkey)

He is renting this 10-story apartment and he has imprisoned us in here like we are slaves. At times, when I feel desperate and scared for my life I want to run and tell the police. But for what purpose? So that I can be exported back to Belarus? (Joanna, Belarusian sex worker in Turkey)

My madame treats me very well. She allows me to eat with them at the same table and she also buys me some extra clothing. However, the money we make as foreigners is very minimal: $300 per month and the hours are long and difficult. I am glad though I am not beaten or sexually abused like some friends of mine from Sri Lanka. (Patmini, domestic worker from Sri Lanka in Greece)

In Anna's, Elena's, Joanna's and Patmini's stories we see that sex and domestic workers are faced with different kinds of issues: Anna speaks of the freedom that she is experiencing with the new capitalist system, however, she is also aware of the exploitation. Elena talks of knowing how the impresarios use women but she cannot talk of this exploitation because she "knows what can happen to her," a metaphor for being found dead. In the story of Joanna, another picture about the free market unfolds: its slavery underpinnings. She is very clear about the state and its agents as the controllers of the interest of the desire industries that she keeps silent as well. Her fear of being deported to Belarus is stronger than her fear of slavery and threats to her life. Patmini raises the issue of her meager salary but at the same time she is also thankful for not being in a worse situation that her friends find themselves in. All these narratives speak of the same structure that generates the exploitation of "white but not quite women" and "black" women as well as the culture of terror. All these actions are possible, all in the name of protecting European citizens and their security. These strategies by the impresarios, the state, the women themselves sustain a wage labor ("wage slavery"), which, in turn, ends up supporting the further feminization of aspects of the economy of the peripheral economic state (State Department, 2002; Gülçür and İlkkaracan, 2002). The police, local business, employers, and impresarios participate in sustaining social arrangements that render security to a select few nationally and transnationally: those who access profits and fast money from exploiting the labor and the bodies of female migrant women, and the working-class and those who in turn benefit from keeping in place the neoliberal world order even with its illicit activities. As stated earlier, the peripheral economic state's responses are justified in the name of sustaining its sovereignty, a code for securing capital's freedom of movement and practices. It adheres to state laws and policies to govern social relations within borders, thereby providing "security" to its citizens.

> When the police show up in the cabaret where I am working and want to ask me questions about my relations with specific clients I am very careful. If they think I am not cooperating, I get afraid, and I offer them services or money.... One night I was walking with a friend of mine in the streets. We did not want to work that night, and they stopped us and they took us to the police station in Ayios Dhometios. There they asked us many questions and also wrote a report stating that we slept with two clients for 250 pounds each and thus, they have to fine us. We refused to sign the report because we did not understand what it was saying. Then, they started threatening us, calling us names, telling us that if we want to go back where we came from, the land of gypsies, then we could continue doing what we are doing now. At one moment I asked them: What do you want from us? If it is money just let us know and we can give you money. One of them smiled and said: "No beauty, you know what we want from you. After all, aren't you here for that?" After a few hours, they called our boss who came and picked us up at the station. (Vera, sex worker from Bulgaria in Cyprus)
>
> Ten of us are renting this apartment. We come here every Sunday for relaxation and support. This apartment as you can see is of substandard quality and yet we pay 250 pounds per month with no central heating and with many broken tiles all over the place. Also, the locks do not work in any of the rooms. (Chandra, domestic worker in Cyprus from India)
>
> One day the police raided our hotel. They wanted to take my passport away and took me into custody. While at the police station three policemen kept calling me names and another one kept singing this popular song Natasha Disco.... Girls have come from Russia, the coast is full of them, it is OK for the single men, But what happens to the married ones?.... he kept repeating this last line. They decided to write a report claiming that I slept with a client charging him 800,000 Liras. I started screaming: What kind of police are you? What kind of protection are

you providing us who came here to work? Finally, they took me to a "Can-Can" [Turkish Slang for the hospital for sexually transmitted diseases] and when they discovered that I did not have any sexually transmitted diseases, they let me go. (Marianna, sex worker in Istanbul Turkey)

The narratives of these three women unfold other aspects of the desire industries: the economic and political ways women are being surveilled by the state and the manners the market further manages their meager wages they earn under slave and violent conditions. In the case of Vera we see how the police, official agents of the state, are taking over "the role of 'pimps,' by taking a percentage of the women's profits" (Gülçür and İlkkaracan, 2002: 7) and in the case of Chandra, the businessmen who own property are able to exhort as much rent as they can for substandard housing. Indirectly, the peripheral economic state is placed "in the role of the pimp." It mediates the relation between the working-class of female migrants and for this it gains access to "extra salaries" for the police, and also it gains through the investments women make (Gülçür and İlkkaracan, 2002: 7) in the housing, hotel, and other industries.

Even while they sustain the focus on the migrant female worker as a force that constitutes political disorder instead of the "desirable order" within the national boundaries of the peripheral economic state, agents of the market and political security (the state) end up centralizing the desire industries as economically and politically vital when in fact the desire industries are one factor responsible for exacerbating the economic precariousness of the peripheral economic state within the EU (Department of State, July 2001). Its focus on boosting its allegiance to transnational capital, and making capital relations appear as "integral to the 'natural' order of things" (Alexander, 1998: 281), is based on a few assumptions: European political identities are "universally desirable" and the criteria employed by them are the most effective. Thus, anyone or anything that evades and rebels against the "truth" embedded within those assumptions becomes labeled right away as the enemy of this identity and its rules.

Migration and the active participation of the peripheral economic state in it is a calculated feature of globalization. Economic interventions such as SAPs and free trade policies facilitate migration and more specifically forced migration of women and children from lower income to higher income generating states. The state and its agents whose interest in securing openness for capital to move and exploit cheap labor make the female migrant the "object of eroticization" or just an "object" ("she is my Filippineza"; "What do you think I am? Your Filippineza?"; "Russians are the queens of sex"; "foreign female migrants do the jobs that no Greek, Turkish, or Cypriot woman wants to do") while all the time attributing a threat to difference.

SECURITY AND CLASS RELATIONS: THE RACIALIZATION OF THE FEMALE MIGRANT FORCE AND SECURITIZATION OF "FREEDOM"

Girls have come from Russia
They are all over the coast
The river in our valley
Flows in excitement
Oh, Natasha
The border at Sarp has been opened
Trade has begun
Family fights have started
Those fed up with their wives
Now sleep with Natasha

Come, let's have a meal
And go to a hotel together
I am in trouble because of the infidel's daughter
(Excerpts from song by Erkan Ocakli)

These popular discourses (songs, stories about migrants, and media reporting) play with fears of insecurity exacerbated by corporate globalization by designating sex and domestic workers as potentially dangerous to the security of their citizens. The opening of the borders (e.g., Sarp in Turkey), the popular Turkish *Natasha* song informs us, makes possible the trading of a female migrant labor force that excites the passions of the men so much so that they leave the Turkish women "without love." When these discourses focus on the working-class female migrant labor that makes a choice to traverse its borders to seek opportunity, work, and love affairs, they make invisible the larger social, political, and economic context within which their movement becomes generated.[7] Moreover, this method of governing—which focuses on the female migrants—aims to master the "havoc" with minimal management and change in asymmetrical social powers distributed according to class, gender, and race.

Blond hair, plucked eyebrows, gauche broad brush, ink stains and a hole in the stockings....Adults, under age, women and men, gays and lesbians, transsexuals all report "present" daily to not only the free trade of flesh, and its long-term duration but also with the hope for...a lenient acceptance of this industry. (Kouyioumtzi, *Eleftherotypia*, April 3, 2001)

In Greece, *Eleftherotypia*, a very well-established newspaper, describes the "free trade of flesh" by painting a picture for us of the colors, bodily inscriptions, and the different kinds of people it takes for it to concretize itself as a legitimate industry. This quote indicates a highly contested racialized geography traversed by migrant sex and domestic workers in choosing to seek employment and opportunity within countries that do not accept these industries fully. Despite the freedom to "move" flesh back and forth, this industry is tightly controlled since it has to do with the most intimate aspects of social relations: flesh, sexuality, and gender relations both in the public and the private sectors.

Limassol and Paphos are turning into "ghettos of legal and illegal workers" where "prostitution and drug usage and crime flourish." (*O Phileleftheros*, October 4, 1996)

Instead of every house and a Castle, Every House and an Asian Woman. (*O Phileleftheros*, February 14, 1997)

Two reports in *Phileleftheros*, a Greek newspaper in Cyprus, discuss the migration of sex and domestic workers in Cyprus. In the first piece we read how different cities in Cyprus are turning into ghettos, sites of drug and criminal activity. In the second piece, the author mocks Cypriots' strategy of gaining prestige by hiring Asian maids. However, this social satire does not expose or engage the reasons behind such desires. What made possible the decision to hire Asians within Cyprus in 1997? It paraphrases a well-known comment made by Lyssarides, the veteran leader of the socialist party EDEK in Cyprus, who was advocating that "every house be a castle" in the face of Turkish expansionism or territorial imperialism. However, these newspapers *do not* ask: how does the expansion of the desire industries intensified by the last stage of imperialism become challenged?

All the aforementioned discourses from songs and popular newspapers speak of understanding freedom as the desire to constitute one's identity through the commodification and consumption of the female migrant worker. This consumer also appropriates the migrant's "side" product such as sexual intimacies, pleasures, status, and power within one's "castle" or home while explaining it as an individual choice (e.g., the infidel's daughter creates trouble for me; the painted face of the Eastern and Balkan woman is irresistible; I can do anything I want in my castle). These discourses make invisible the social relation of inequality and the position that the different subjects in that relationship occupy in the division of labor.

> Legalized slavery and pimping! The Migration law (Article 34) conceptualizes the women in the sex industry as artists. (Avgi, 2000: http://193.218.80.70/cgi-bin/hwebpressrem.exe)

Avgi, a more critical newspaper in Greece, raises the issue of how the law is legalizing slavery of women through pimping rather than popularizing the idea that sex and domestic workers make individual choices to migrate to these countries.

> Migrant workers [are] useful in making Cypriot products more competitive ... and low wages paid to migrant workers will yield high wages for Cypriot workers (in the long term). The increase in profits and productivity, it is suggested, will lead to ... a reduction in unemployment and crime, and eventually to increased wages for Cypriot workers (Trimikliniotis, 1999: 156 citing Anastasiades, *O Phileleftheros*, December 4–5, 1996). One woman from Sri-Lanka was working from 7:00 a.m. till 10:00 p.m. every day, except Sundays, serving four related families with very low wages. (Trimikliniotis, 2001: 30 citing the newspaper *Phileleftheros*, February 14, 1997)

The process of reproductive labor is transformed to maximize the generation of profits in all three states. Laws and regulations about the eight-hour workday are suspended in the case of selling domestic labor, and race, class, and gender become the determining factors for the employers. In seeking to maximize output of the female workers, many Cypriot, Greek, and Turkish employers lengthen the workday, and rent their domestic workers to relatives for further use and with minimal compensation. Women of color from poorer-income generating states become the objects of exploitation. Racism and class social power work together in keeping in place a system of private ownership by appropriating the surplus of the working-class women of color of Sri Lanka, Philippines, India, Myanmar, and of the "white but not quite" women of Russia, Rumania, Albania, and so on.

When locals face the migrant women, deeply entrenched racist behaviors and assumptions come to the surface. They complicate dichotomous relations between the secure and the nonsecure on different levels: structural, institutional, and personal. Yet, in policy and political and popular discourses, the domestic and sex worker becomes framed as the referent object of insecurity—societal insecurity (Waever et al., 1993; Weiner and Russell, 2001) as if security in a transborder context can be so narrowly punctuated. Transborder collaboration among the different bureaucracies structures relationships and practices about people's movements and especially "Third World" nationals between administrations and executive powers of each country. These transborder relations strengthen security services to the detriment of health, environment, employment and poverty, violence against women both local and migrants (Greek Helsinki Monitor, 2002) by transforming these services into auxiliary services and always justifying these decisions by attributing to the migrant responsibility for crime, delinquency, and deviance (Greek Helsinki Monitor, 2002; Parliamentary Commission Report in Cyprus, 1997). The discourses circulated by the state, the media, and the market itself attribute responsibility to the individual migrant. These discourses end up supporting the investment of more resources in security services (Bakker and Gill, 2003).

> You read in our newspapers about the "self-proclamation as a community" by the Filipino workers. It is because of Filipino, Russian, and other migrant women that we have all these slums in our major cities such as Nicosia and Limassol. These are becoming a fairly permanent condition. Many of these migrants live in these areas, which are proving to become more fertile ground for community organizing. Perhaps one day they will wake up and want to overtake the state. So it is crucial for us to invest resources in technologies that can enable us to protect ourselves from any kind of destabilization. (Migration officer in Cyprus, 2002)

> Turkey has to "increase the number of bilateral security co-operation agreements especially with the countries of origin (44 countries). (Ministry of Interior, Coordinated Action against Trafficking in Human Beings in South-East Europe: Towards a Regional Action Plan, 2000)

The migration officer in Cyprus raised the issue that the state is concerned about migrant movements in its attempt to sustain this image of sovereignty. It is afraid that one day female migrant workers are going to politically organize against it and dismantle the media image used to justify capital's exploitation of their labor. Thus, the state has put into place laws that prevent labor migrants from politically organizing, and it further invests resources to build up its security to crush any possible uprisings. Similarly, in Turkey the state wants to build official security connections with the peripheral states of origin to subvert potential movements against them. The coordinated actions against trafficking in human beings are really creating codes for protecting the private property and the class that owns it from potential uprisings of the working-class in both the receiving peripheral economic state and in the peripheral economic state of origin. While creating more laws to protect trafficking in human beings is vital in a world economy that exploits bodies for profits, these actions are short-term "reformist" strategies that do not address the structural conditions that generate such trafficking in the first hand. This constant focus on the migrant as a danger to the state's order hides the structural, institutional, and social insecurities experienced by local and migrant women, the working-class, and other marginalized groups. Forced migration and the sale of women's labor daily under slave conditions to increase "private" powers ownership and generation of profits is made invisible. The state addresses fears, rather than the transnational movements of people resulting from major restructurings the world over and the insecurities that are being generated transnationally and instantiated locally. Globalization links migration and security as a multidimensional relationship whose scope ranges from transnational neoliberal structures, to state, to households to identity.

The glocal relations that make possible the linkages between migration and security act as the context. The peripheral economic state draws upon these racist, classist, and gendered epistemic frameworks to mask its role in facilitating these industries and its contribution toward its own feminization/economic precariousness and crisis of agency (Içduygu and Keyman, 2000) within the regional world power of the EU. Focusing on societal insecurities, the political rhetoric of peripheral economic states converges with the ideologies of leaders from core states of the neoliberal world order to recolonize and sanction further violence against the working-class. This rhetoric divides the working-class contaminating the local working-class with visions of "freedom," "law," and "order" and attributing the existence of crime, threat, danger, and deviance to the migrant working-class.

Glossing Over Transnational Inequalities/Insecurities

European countries, are dominated by discussions of the threat that the new and feminized migration of poor-income generating countries represents to national security and identity (IMO, 2003). In all

Table 5.1 Registered housemaids and artists in Southern Cyprus, 1995–2001

	Category of female migrant workers	
Year of arrival	"Artists" (sex workers)	Housemaids
1995	991	1,995
1996	2,743	2,815
1997	2,945	2,522
1998	2,730	2,809
1999	2,794	3,221
2000	2,472	4,392
2001	1,602	3,494

Source: Official statistics provided confidentially by a migration officer.

three countries, laissez-faire recruitment of foreign female labor led to a gradual transformation of the migration inflows. In effect, migration flows present a challenge to states wishing, on the one hand, to keep intact a traditional control of territory, and on the other, to exploit a cheap and flexible supply of labor. So, the state "fences-off" the migrants and the desire industries when faced with critiques about the destabilization of Greek and Turkish identity, but complies with middle- and upper-class demands for sex and domestic workers. (See table 5.1.)

Several women who had worked previously in Cyprus, Israel, Turkey, and Greece communicated to me the constant anxiety and lack of safety associated with the expectation that they could be transferred at any time to other locations as "the market necessitates" (see also Lazaridis, 2001 and Psimmenos, 2000). Most employers saw them as "cargo" that could be moved around and in accordance to the desires of the clients.

> He walks in and wants to offer me a couple of drinks. The two drinks turned into 12 and we ended up finally in a hotel. He wanted me to be his mommy....the next day, he wanted me to embrace him while he was holding a pacifier in his mouth...this went on for days...I became tired with his stupid demands but I also wanted the money. What could I do? My boss was always a few miles away...(Interview with a 21-year-old Ukrainian sex worker in Greece)

The sexual distortions that men impose on sex workers may be dismissed as "stupid" by them; however, these cannot be resisted in an "equal" relationship of exchange: money for services. Many of the women feel frustrated about these distortions and yet are afraid to challenge them either because they think they will lose the client or their impresario will beat them if they do not follow the client's requests. The personal and social lack of safety migrant women experience in the desire industries (sexual and class exploitation, violence, murder) daily are made invisible by the industry of surveillance and control:

> She left Russia with the promise of a job in Greece...It turned out to be prostitution. Then she was stashed in a stifling apartment bordello in the port of Salonica. She and the other women there were rarely allowed to leave. Clients visited at all hours. The anguish for Ira Penkina ended last month, in the apartment's narrow bathroom. She tied black pantyhose around a pipe above the toilet. The other was knotted around her throat. There was no suicide note....What the inquiries have uncovered has staggered the nation: claims of sexual slavery, accusations of corruption—including alleged police protection for the groups. The revelations suggest Greece has become a European Union foothold for prostitution rings with links throughout the former Soviet bloc. (http://friends-partners.org/[partners/stop-traffic/ 1998/0376.html)

Ira's story is not the first or the last. It is a common one. The slave conditions sex workers face in all three countries as well as the state's complicit role in sustaining in place these unequal relations is well established. The deaths of women in the industry that eroticizes sex, race, and violence are not unexpected. Yet, the peripheral economic state's discourse on surveillance and control of sex workers' lives and bodies, which conceptualizes them as contributing to its domestic "crises" (*Simerini*, October 10, 1996; *Fileleftheros*, March 4, 1997; *Alithia*, March 4, 1997), glosses over these violences as just individual aberrations in an industry that individual women choose to be part of. Despite recognizing that such industries could not exist if it was not for the networks of pimps, impresarios, states, and bureaucracies of control and surveillance and against the backdrop of the existence of class society, the state continues to make invisible the economic relations that make possible these supposedly "equal" exchanges. Faced with daily violences, working-class migrant women negotiate these multilayered relations and understandings about racialized class by figuring out ways to secure for themselves the conditions that will enable them to live a life that pushes them to be more than fenced cargo:

> This guy, a very famous lawyer, went crazy for me. He always told me
> how he liked Belarussian women. He was not as interested in the Russian
> women because they were too arrogant and too demanding. He loved
> being around me all the time, so much so that my employer was very
> happy. He would take me to the most expensive hotels, buy me the most
> expensive jewelry and clothes and then one day I said to him: Why don't
> you rent me a place so that I can be there for you whenever you want,
> and he did! (Interview with a 28-year-old Belarus sex worker)

In this story, a sex worker decided to employ her knowledge about
the pecking order that exists in the ranks of sex work in the desire
industries. She successfully exploited the asymmetries within the
working-class of female migrants to make some personal headway.
She was able to get her own place and to escape for a few hours the
brutality of the trade. Asymmetrical racialized relationships *among* sex
workers are a factor affecting action within the desire industries
among the different agents: the state, the agents of the networks
of trafficking, women, employers, and sex workers themselves.
Sex workers know the score in their own business, and use it in nego-
tiating their security, that is, access to fast cash albeit short-lived at
times, within the desire industries.

> Russians are the best women in sex, the Greeks say. Then the Ukrainians,
> and then the Rumanians. The client will not go with a Filippina. He
> wants a white woman like us. (26-year-old Russian sex worker)
>
> Russians are beautiful, tall, with green eyes. Men prefer them over the
> black women. Who will choose to go with an African or a Latina the
> moment that they can have crystal water in their mouths? (50-year-old
> Greek employer)

At the top of the scale we find the Russians, the Ukrainians, the
Belarussians. At the bottom of the scale we find the Latin Americans,
the Albanians, and the Africans. During interviews with sex workers
in Greece, it became apparent that this racialization has been
internalized as common knowledge and used in the negotiations over
money among the sex and domestic workers themselves.

> My cost is sometimes $400 and sometimes $500 depending on the
> client. My boss knows the clients and he sends me to them when they
> enter the shop. (24-year-old Russian sex worker)

I know that some men prefer the Russians for sex because they will do anything for money. Unfortunately, we do not make as much money as they do. Men who are serious do want us [Bulgarians] though because we have a heart and we are not going to do it just for fun. (Vera, 35-year-old Bulgarian ex-sex worker)

The above ex-sex-worker focuses on how Bulgarian women "have a heart" and are morally superior to Russian "loose" women. The racialization and sexualization practices of the neoliberal capitalist project regulate racialized poor women by presuming them to be sexually available and aggressive and also active in the sphere of work. Many racialized poor women work toward "climb[ing] out of bad girl space into respectability" (Razack 1998: 346) and in the process making invisible the sex-worker. In this case we see a similar logic at work. Despite being a prostitute, Vera draws upon this discourse of morality and respectability. The existence of such racialized asymmetries within the desire industries (re) positions the women in conflict and competition with each other. This strategy displaces accountability from the "private powers" and sustains in place the unequal social relations of production on the racialized and gendered working-class itself. Within the distribution of sexual services for pleasure the logic of colonialism and competition is prevalent. These ideologies not only divide the sex workers among themselves, they also lead them to divisions among themselves, in addition to determining who will sell the most sex for the most money. However, these gains are short-lived. In the short term, they receive money but they do not become self-determined. As long as the structures remain the same, women cannot become truly free and equal. (See table 5.2.)

This asymmetrical racialization is based on the colonial logic of "us and them" and is used extensively by networks of traffickers in women, the employers, and the clients. Antidemocratic and disabling as these practices may be, these class-based powers are contestable in principle and contested in fact. These social relations of exploitation are reproduced by alienated or estranged labor. The working-class participates in its own domination by involving itself in the practices of production and reproduction that are organized by property relations and guided by the logic of privatized expropriation of surplus-value of labor.

The classed, raced, and gendered powers of the state and the employers of the reproductive labor are reciprocal, constituting a "dialectic of power" subject to ongoing contestation and restructuring. It is not incomprehensible that the sex and domestic workers

Table 5.2 Asymmetrical racializations within the desire industries: Greece*

Worker	Categorized worker in the desire industries	Employment sites	Clients	Normative discourses about the workers
Sex	A	Clubs Striptease Joints Massage Parlours	Upper class	Beautiful Tall Educated Thin Sexually sophisticated Mostly Russian
Sex	B	Hotels and houses Local newspapers Mobile telephone "red lines"	Mostly middle class	Beautiful Tall Thin Young Mostly Russian, Ukrainian, Belarussian
Sex	C	Streets	Mostly lower middle-class and working-class men	Cheap "animals" Ugly, uneducated Mostly Greek and Albanian sex workers
Domestic	D	In private households	Mostly middle and upper middle classes	Organized Clean Civilized Mostly Filipinas
Domestic	E	In private households	Mostly lower middle class	Albanians

Sources: Lazaridis (2000: 87) and my interviews with sex and domestic workers.

themselves use this logic to decide how to make sense of a world that wants to "consume" them in every way. And as Kollontai reminded us, the political economy of sex is not a politics of morality. It is a politics of profits, violence, and exploitation. Thus, it is not surprising to see these same politics applied "strategically" by the workers themselves.

The sale of women's labour, closely and inseparably connected with the sale of the female body, steadily increases, leading to a situation where the respected wife of a worker, and not just the abandoned and "dishonoured" girl, joins the ranks of the prostitutes: a mother for the sake of her children, or a young girl like Sonya Marmeladova for the sake of her family. This is the horror and hopelessness that results from the exploitation of labour by capital. When a woman's wages are insufficient to keep her alive, the sale of favours seems a possible subsidiary occupation. The hypocritical morality of bourgeois society encourages prostitution by the structure of its exploitative economy, while at the same time mercilessly heaping contempt upon any girl or woman who is forced to take this path. . . . All forms of prostitution flourish like a poisonous flower in the swamps of the bourgeois way of life. . . . Prostitution, under capitalism, provides men with the opportunity of having sexual relationships without having to take upon themselves the responsibility of caring for the women until the grave. (Kollontai, 1977: 263–264)

Kollontai focused on prostitution to substantiate how modern productive relations make possible the exploitation and subordination of the working-class. What she states about prostitution applies also to domestic labor. The domestic worker finds herself forced to take care of the bourgeois family by cooking, cleaning, and taking care of children and elderly for the sake of her children and/or family. At times, she supplements her income by "selling sexual favors."

As in Cyprus, Greece is committed to open migration within the EU, however, Greece's location in the Southern European context makes it susceptible to several insecurities: threats from the south (Algeria, Turkey, Egypt, and the Palestinian territories), the proliferation of weapons such as the spread of weapons of mass destruction (Snyder, 1996; Kemp, 1991), the emergence of regional conflicts (Cyprus; the Gulf war conflicts; conflicts in Algeria; and Libya), and the worsening of economic and social conditions in Southern Mediterranean states (Niblock, 1996; Joffe, 1996). These conditions lead to "an increased migration from the southern to the northern shore of the Mediterranean . . . frequently referred to as a 'threat,' 'population bomb' or 'time bomb'" (Tsardanidis and Guerra, 2000 citing Lister, 1997: 101).

Immigrants in many Southern European countries (e.g., Italy, Greece, and Spain) may be perceived as competitors in the local labor market, as a burden on social and welfare services, or as the ones responsible for the lowering of wages and as impeding the restructuring of the economy into a capital-intensive one. In addition, many "immigrants are [also] attracted by the existence of a large underground economy" (Tsardanidis and Guerra, 2000: 330). Within EU countries, uncontrolled migration is increasingly perceived as a

> threat to public order...public opinion, the media, some political parties and police officials often associate irregular migrants with various criminal activities, such as drug trafficking, thefts, armed aggression or even terrorism against both the receiving country and the country of origin. While this feeling of insecurity may be based on real facts, the overall impact of immigration on the crime rate and the internal security of receiving countries tends to be overestimated. (Tsardanidis and Guerra, 2000: 331)

Problems of public security and order are at the core of political debates about migration within these three countries. For example, the influx of Albanians in Greece has created many social problems and tensions. Liberal social scientists attribute the "allegedly high and rising crime among Albanian immigrants" to their lack of knowledge and familiarity with capitalist models of consumption (Tsardanides and Guerra, 2000: 331). Yet, the recorded criminality rates of Albanians in Greece are not higher than would be expected given their living conditions within the Greek society (Psimmenos, 2000, 1995). I focus here on the official state documents on public order within Greece. In Article 50 of *Public Security* we read:

> Whoever exits or attempts to exit the Greek territory or enters or attempts to enter it without the legal formalities, is punished with imprisonment of three months or with money of at least 500,000 drahmas...(paragraph, 1). If the alien enters the Greek territory or exits without the legal formalities, the judge of criminal court, after the approval of the court of appeals...can move to send the alien to his/her country of entry or origin. (paragraph, 2)

In Article 53 paragraph 4 we read:

> Whoever is employing an alien without the permit of stay is punished with imprisonment of at least three months....in case of a relapse the employer is punished with imprisonment of at least six months.

Both of these articles bring to the fore contestations regarding public security by the state. The aforementioned text demonstrates that the state "perceives" migration as an issue with which to be dealt. Although it is not a clear and direct securitizing discourse about migration, the approach toward the migrants is influenced by public opinion on migrants and insecurities. Described as "criminals" and "deadly threats," migrants (*Kathimerini*, April 28, 1999) are viewed, nervously, as "the domino of the Balkans. The chain reaction that started with the prevailing of the Albanians in Kosovo will spread the fear of dissolution from country to country" (*Ethnos*, October 31, 1999). The passing of the new immigration law in the Greek Parliament cements this as a crucial issue that will organize social relations in Greece. When the general principles of the migration law were outlined on July 28, 1999, the government Interior Minister Vasso Papandreou said, "this policy will involve improved guarding of the country's borders to prevent the entry of even more illegal immigrants" (Papandreou, 1999). Moreover, she added "that measures taken recently to increase border security [are] already paying off and would be continued at an even greater pace....the need for entry into the country to be controlled...this would be achieved through bilateral agreements between Balkan countries; employment agencies expected to be set up in Balkan capitals and within the framework of the Stability Pact for the region—something being discussed at present by the European Union...This was the only way to secure a labour market which was competitive rather than a 'black' labour market" (Papandreou cited in *Athens News Agency*, July 29, 1999). This project to intensify the external security at the frontiers emerges out of the belief that Greece, along with other Southern Mediterranean states, are to become the gatekeepers of the EU and Europe's Southern frontier (Perni, 2001).

The Greek government's migration policy and articles by the police to create public order have come under considerable criticism from feminist organizations, other migrant NGOs, and the Left (*Avgi*, 2002, 2001, 2000). Due to such critiques, some of the articles were changed. Nevertheless, the debates around the immigration law and the contestations about its formulation indicate how difficult an issue migration and security has become for the Greek government (*Athens News Agency*, 1999).

Perceptions of immigration and Greek governmental policies in recent years have been influenced by a variety of factors: a strong Left, feminists, and migration nongovernmental organizations (*Athens Agency News*, 1999; *Avgi*, 2000, 1999), public opinion, and concrete violent incidents by two Greeks who embarked on a "crusade" to rid Greece of as many non-Greeks as possible by killing them (*Nea*, October 25, 1999; *Ethnos*, October 24, 1999; *Ethnos*, October 23,

1999). The politicization of migration as a security issue by opposi-tional political forces pushes the state to "deal" with migration. However, as it pushes for further liberalization of its migration poli-cies and as it puts "sovereignty of the state and border control at the heart of regulatory efforts" (Sassen, 1996), it contributes to its own further peripheralization and the "fencing-off" of migrants and their human rights without substantively changing the asymmetrical social relations of production.

As in Greece, the focus on security unfolds at the national level in Turkey. National security was framed through the November 1994 law entitled *Regulation on the Procedures and the Principles Related to Mass Influx and the Foreigners Arriving in Turkey or Requesting Residence Permits with the Intention of Seeking Asylum from a Third Country*. It has

> led to the a priori codification of asylum seekers as security threats. . . . The state-centric logic that defines the 1994 regulation has deepened rather than resolved the migration crisis. . . . The increased globalization of societal affairs (although it renders prob-lematic and untenable the equation of society with nation-state) forces us to take the linkages among the global, the national, and the local much more seriously than we did before. . . . the problem of modernity has been expanded to—in a sense subsumed by—the problem of globality. Many of the particular themes of modernity—fragmentation of life worlds, structural differentiation cognitive and moral relativity, widening of experiential scope, and ephemerality—have been exacerbated in the process of globalization. (Robertson, 1992: 55)

This "a priori codification of asylum seekers as security threats" effects the lives of sex and domestic workers. In light of Turkey's desire for a position in a regional power bloc to secure the movement of capital (even when its integration into the EU is consistently blocked by different Western European core states' elites) (*Vima*, October 3, 2002), this codification of migration as a national security issue becomes a tool in protecting the interests of its upper and middle-classes. Major criteria that Turkey must fulfill in order to be integrated in the EU include those "of competition, fishing, trans-port, of culture, . . . the free movement of capital. . . . it has fulfilled partially the criteria of the economy, . . . criteria regarding employ-ment, energy . . . justice, internal affairs, and the national program of development" (*Vima*, October 3, 2002; Ergüvenç, 2000). Turkey also has to transform its methods of governance by finding diplomatic ways to address border conflicts, and dealing with the problem of corruption and the issue of human rights.

In addressing global flows of people within the EU, European leaders and countries have treated Turkey as a "buffer zone" in their efforts to create Fortress Europe. Turkey's response to this global mobility of people has been to control and limit their migration within Turkey. In its attempts to address international migration, Turkey, like Cyprus and Greece, has placed a premium on security of capital relations. This strategy is

> an effort by Turkish authorities to replace the previous practice, which they now consider too liberal and threatening to Turkish security, with one they believe will enhance their control over asylum in Turkey. However, the security concern and its practical applications have failed to limit the growing movement of asylum seekers, refugees, and transit and undocumented immigrants. (İçduygu and Keyman, 2000: 7)

However, this narrow "a priori national security" approach to governance is problematic because it does not take into consideration the material realities of globalized migration and the new emerging role of the state in the restructuring of the world economy. Its very narrow focus on the control of borders and the fencing-off of politics into mere questions of security as protection of sovereignty, identity, and citizenship limit the possibilities of understanding the feminization of migration and masculinization of security as two sides of the same coin: global restructuring generates various types of migration, and, thus, security is not simply a "reference to the national and territorial constitution of societal affairs" (İçduygu and Keyman, 2000: 7) but also to the freedom of movement of capital. Globalization has brought to the fore that with the "decline of territorial constraints" the state's role has not dissipated. On the contrary, what is at stake is the "qualitative change of governance" (İçduygu and Keyman, 2000: 7). Migration, and more specifically, feminized migration, are not simple internal affairs that states can easily resolve. Turkey's desire for security may be understandable in a changing world that is increasingly oriented toward restructuring, yet the violence that the state commits upon the female migrant workers by focusing on them as a threat misses the complex configuration of the politics of migration, security, and globalization.

> [I]f globalization means the process of increasing interconnectedness between societies and is beset by contradictions, clashes, and crisis; if global restructuring generates or amplifies various types of migrations;

and if it is no longer possible to think of security with reference only to the national and territorial constitution of societal affairs, then we can conclude that a crucial need exists to reconstruct the way we deal with migration flows. And such reconstruction should be based on new thinking that views migration as a postnational social form in a globalizing world, that sees migration flows as multilayered processes, and that forces the nation-state to come to terms with the complexities involved. (Içduygu and Keyman, 2000: 7)

Thus, the desire for "national security" by nation-states that view "migrants as a priori national security threat" limits the creativity necessary to effect real change in how the global world is governed, and more, specifically, the reconstruction of regional governance toward the safety of the majority of the population.

The peripheral economic state's desire to become white by including itself in the "new" global economy pushes it to collude with the world hegemonic leadership such as multinational corporations, and core European capital, and it plays along with the game of securitizing itself by focusing many of its citizens' resources on control and surveillance. In addition, the state collapses its own structural insecurity and makes invisible the conflicts of interest (that is access to more surplus-value) among different state and class actors within the EU and the world economy.[9] This racialized, classed, and gendered division of labor for which the neoliberal world economy is pushing poses social and institutional challenges for the peripheral economic state. Yet, the peripheral economic state's collusion with the core hegemonic powers to collapse its economic precariousness in the world economy as a threat and the orchestrated unease with which female migrants are viewed make invisible the real challenges about safety the hegemonic economy poses for, communities, women, and children in the peripheries, and secondary processes of globalization such as states.

BY WAY OF CONCLUSION

As Klein argues, the world is changing, turning into a global security formation. The borders of sovereign states are turning into "a network of fortresses connected by highly militarized trade corridors" (Klein, 2002: xxiii) despite the promises of globalization that walls and barriers among different states will be lowered. This global security formation depends as much on the core state of the world economy as the peripheral economic state. While the end of the Cold War in 1989 served to decrease external threats among trading states, the peripheral economic state feels the pressures from citizens and national political elites to sustain its power in a fast pace changing world economy. Sovereignty, law and order, and the unified body of the polity are seen as prerequisites for peace, homogeneity, and wealth. The state attempts to address these concerns by focusing on migration. However, its responses end up justifying the "national" identity it has achieved through a territorialization. It focuses on migrant workers as one of the key problems. In attributing the fears and unease experienced within its borders to the working-class female migrant, the peripheral economic state makes invisible the transnational changes that further feminize and racialize its economy (the peripheral economic state constitutes its wealth through the desire industries and through trafficking economies). Even when political elites know the limits of their " 'fable' as much as the Greek knew that their gods were part of the fairy tale" (Bigo, 2002: 69), they still open or restrict the entry into the country. This political response further generates some profits for the global security economy while creating insecurities and a lack of safety for the majority of its citizens and the working-class of migrants who do not have access to the profits of the desire and security industries.

Looking at the responses of the peripheral economic states of Cyprus, Greece, and Turkey in the context of the globalization, migration, and security and the complex configuration of those politics in these sites, we see that migration of reproductive labor cannot be contained as an internal "national" affair for these states. Therefore, the solution to this problem does not rest in mere securitization of the "national" state. Migration of reproductive labor has an impact on the migrant-sending and migrant-receiving state, the migrants and their families, the citizens of these peripheral economic states, and the transnational community. Since the restructuring of the world economy generates the movements of reproductive labor the world over, it is no longer possible to think of these movements as occurring across one or two borders, and it is no longer possible to understand security by referring only to the national and territorial constitution of world and social politics. The reductionist approach of considering the working-class of female migrants as an a priori national security threat glosses over both the insecurity within a global capitalist economy and the lack of safety that is created on different levels (structurally, institutionally, and personally) in the process of restructuring the neoliberal world economy and its contingent institutions. In sum, the state's desire to respond to the desire and interests of its owning and ruling class pushes it to resolve migration by linking national security to privilege and by deflecting attention from an underlying political economy of exploitation and violence. Therefore, it is now crucial to interrogate whose desires and whose needs are privileged and whose desires and needs are marginalized under the neoliberal regime of capitalism. Chapter 6 puts forward a new materialist global political economy of sex, a model that challenges the idea that a neoliberal legal framework of freedom of choice, which redresses inequalities of women in the world economy, will transform the conditions of exploitation and violence against the working-class, both male and female. This model is a conscious effort toward the encouragement of the development of solidarity and an intervention to fighting against all that hinders the development of safe social relations of public (re) production and safety.

CHAPTER 6

A GLOBAL POLITICAL ECONOMY OF SEX: FEMINIST POSSIBILITIES FOR TRANSBORDER DEMOCRACY AND SAFETY

> There will be no feminist revolution without an end to racism and white supremacy. When all women and men engaged in feminist struggle understand the interlocking nature of systems of domination, of white supremacist capitalist patriarchy, the feminist movement will regain its revolutionary progressive momentum.
>
> (hooks, 1995: 107)
>
> Women and their fate occupied me all my life and concern for their lot brought me to socialism.
>
> (Kollontai, 1977: 30)

In the previous chapters, I delineated the connections between capital and the culpable state in the exploitation of the wage labor of sex and domestic workers. In this final chapter, I ask: How might we break this systemic hold? What role can feminism play in challenging the structures of a global ruling class that tightly adheres to a hegemonic doctrine and uses all means possible to obfuscate its politics?

Most of us seem to be bystanders to the spectacle of security and "globalization with a human face," a mirage promulgated by capital, multinational corporations, the states, IR, and even feminist theorists. Instruments of justice themselves presuppose the export and import, abuse, and near-enslavement of numerous migrant women (Trepanier, 2003; Rajalakshmi, 2003; Lepp, 2003). The peripheral economic state seems to follow closely the doctrine of capital and designs policies to sustain low inflation, fiscal retrenchment, and flexible labor markets, to facilitate the free flows of goods and capital to promote the interests of investors, employers, as well as the interests of the owning-class through the exploitation of working-class peoples. Ideologies about "globalization with a human face" and flexible labor (Psimmenos, 2000) obscure the politics of neoliberalism including its weakening grip even among those who have been its proponents (Rupert, 2000). It is within this context that ideological contestations and struggles as well as feminist critiques are crucial in the creation of solidarity among different active transnational grassroots movements such as women's groups, NGOs, labor unions, indigenous groups and environmental groups. They enact a critique of transnational capitalism, its property relations, as well as its antidemocratic politics and governance that further loosen the grip of neoliberalism on people's lives.

Accordingly, intellectuals cannot understand themselves as mere professionals or neutral bystanders. Only through working as a movement to produce collectively a vision with an alternative ontology and progressive social change by incessant critique and expanding the horizons of limiting social self-understandings (Gramsci, 1971: 164–165, 375–377) could we transform the conditions that subordinate all of us, women and men of color, indigenous and transgender peoples and working-class peoples to the logic and coordinates of capital. In this book I offer not only an analytic framework to help us analyze the conditions that sex and domestic workers face daily in the peripheries. I am also offering knowledge and practice that challenge the dominant, feminist ivory tower as individuated from and independent of the struggles of migrant workers. This critique not only explains the situation of women in the peripheries, dealing with problematic racial relations, but it also shows what could be instead of simply what is. Women in the peripheries exemplify what academics talk of: desire as an expression of freedom. Indeed, they reap the brunt of that desire on their bodies daily and experience its ineluctability on their personhoods (Anderson, 2000). Their daily struggles along with the work of several NGOs that address the exploitation and violence they face (Kadin Kapisi in Turkey; the Association for the Solidarity with Asylum Seekers and Migrants; Istanbul Inter-Parish Migrants Progamme; Caritas; Catholic Migration Commission; Social Center in Cyprus) constitute a "movement in progress" to change the racialized and gendered division of labor.

Working together, they find the self-determination to change their conditions. Sex and domestic workers are beginning to make connections previously unimaginable, resisting in many different ways the neoliberal structures and institutions that exploit their lives. This "movement in progress" challenges private property relations, the relentless accumulation of capital, and the brutality of its agents, employers, and investors. These struggles may have contradictory moments, but women, men, and trangender peoples draw upon understandings of sex and desire that challenge the neoliberal separation of economics from the production of ideas, sex, class, and race (Altman, 2000; Aguilar, 2002; Ebert, 2001) as well as other de-reifying social relations of capitalism (e.g., national working-class vs. migrant working-class). They circumscribe territorial discourses and practices of nationalism and citizenship that open up possibilities for collectively building the emancipatory subjectivities we need for truly sustainable safe communities. How does this work?

POSTCOLONIAL MATERIALIST CRITIQUE AND ITS DEMOCRATIZING PROJECTS

Exploitative and violent capitalist relations are transformative. Progressive projects require that we witness, remember, and explore new possibilities to work with one another toward a different world where freedom from necessity and violence (e.g., where people do not depend on exploitation for their survival) becomes a reality. Democratic projects must simultaneously engage conventional sources of power as well as its nodes of disjunction and production, including location (household, office, factory, cabaret), different social relations (labor, social movements, nongovernmental relations), and the process of power (organization of social relations, social reproduction of identities).

Desires and needs are not private matters. They are rather historically produced gendered and raced relations: "historical practices that develop in response to the development of the forces of production as they come in conflict with the relations of production" (Cotter, 2002: 24). It is important for feminists to recognize the significance of the private ownership of the means of production as well as the command over the labor power of women of color and the working-class worldwide. Such understandings help us recognize whether the current system and its structures allow for the freedom of all people from exploitation or whether they need to be transformed to do so. Freedom to experience pleasure at the expense of others' labor and bodies cannot be changed unless we question the privileged status of private property, the powers of the class that owns it, the apparently private social relations of desire, the allegedly universal and apolitical economy within which these relations take place, and the liberal understandings of individuals as isolated and autonomous.

Many feminists and critical theorists of IPE articulate a non-hegemonic intellectual and political project (cf. Baker and Gill, 2003; Cotter, 2003; Mohanty, 2003; Klein, 2002; Anderson, 2004; Rupert, 2002; Ebert, 2001; Ling, 2000; Hennessy, 2000; Wong, 2001; Muppidi, 2002; Singh, 2001). They connect the neoliberal project of global capitalism to social relations created by the market and the state, as well as to the racial, sexual, and class divisions of labor, indicating that coercion and consent politics are part and parcel of the (re)production of neoliberal power. They show that neoliberalism's agents, a multinational coalition of financiers, businessmen, and trade unions, and globalizing elites such as intellectuals and political leaders sustain free-market policies worldwide in the name of democracy and freedom (Tumino, 2003: 1), while attacking an emerging movement of social justice (Zapatistas, 1998; World March of Women; Lesbian Avengers; Anti-Capitalist Convergence; Labor Notes; United Students Against Sweatshops; Ruckus Society; Direct Action Network; Indy Media, The Immigrant Support Action Group in Cyprus; KEDE, Greece; Hands Across the Divide, Global Change Institute). According to some theorists "inter-state" and "intra-class" tensions exist within the ranks of globalizing capitalism, which relies heavily on nation-states to mediate and facilitate the reproduction of neoliberal capitalism and the conflict between capital and labor (Bakker and Gill, 2003; Rupert, 2000). Contradictions between national and globalizing aspects of capitalism are intensified in a process where global capitalist institutions are "transforming and incorporating—rather than simply displacing—nation-state based institutions, and being constructed on a terrain of intra-class, as well as inter-class conflict" (Rupert, 2002: 12 citing Robinson and Harris, 2000: 23).

THE DIALECTICS OF SEX, DESIRE, AND MATERIAL PRODUCTION

Property relations institutionalize exploitation and violence in the neoliberal world economy. As long as private ownership drives social relations through the expropriation of the surplus-value of working-class men, women, and sexual "others," then desire, sex, and love cannot be transformed.

> I love the fact that 90% of our prostitutes are from the Balkans and Eastern Europe. We get to taste all kinds of women "on the cheap."

We do not even have to leave our city to find the most beautiful women
in the world. (Greek male, 45 years old)

This Greek man samples women in a market that racializes sex for
profit. The market-state calculates that it is not cost-effective to
transform asymmetrical relations of power that exacerbate economic
insecurities. On the contrary, it uses racism and sexism to continue justifying the expropriation of surplus-value and its generating profits for
some at the expense of the majority. As Andrea Smith states, when talking about women of color in the United States "women of color
become particularly dangerous to the world order as they have the ability to reproduce the next generation of communities of color.
Consequently, it is not surprising that control over the abilities of
women of color becomes seen as a national security issue" (Smith, 2002:
123). "Women of color" include those who are "white but not quite."
They are constructed as the objects of desire for the upper class. Yet,
their moves, their labor power, and their reproduction are controlled
and managed by capital. Racialized and sexual divisions of labor are jus-
tified/mystified with racialized and sexualized ideologies. This racism

> does not merely arise in moments of crisis, in sporadic cleansings. It is
> internal to the biopolitical state, woven into the web of the social body,
> threaded through its fabric . . . Thus, communities of color become pol-
> lution from which the state must constantly purify itself. (Stoler, 1995)

These strategies draw upon an ontology of fear and insecurity
regarding the privileges accrued from the labor and surplus-value of
non whites and the benefits that emerge from a "de facto unequal representation and social reproduction" (Gill, 2003: 203). This pleas-
ure/desire of whiteness takes hold in the peripheries as well. The
upper and middle-classes feel anxious especially when they know that
they can access the transnational state apparatus, that is, the best
schools, medical care and also possess freedom from drudgery while
exploiting slave labor to attend their households, their sexual and other
distorted desires, their reputations and property (Gill, 2003: 203).
Violence against the migrant female worker through sex, domestic
work, surveillance, or control (all aspects of imperial social relations of
terror) enables bourgeois subjects to allay their fears about the true
nature of their relations with the colonized others. Yet, this fetish of
decorating "white but not quite" and black bodies with disdain to sat-
isfy a self-created desire to be "white" (or possess the freedom to con-
quer, exploit, and consume the "other's" labor and body) is a pleasure

for the bourgeois subject who is able to silence social conflicts and contradictions such as his/her incomplete access to "whiteness."

> White is a form of rape which perpetually redescribes itself as seduction. Whites and fellow-travelers enjoy their victims in the same way when they humiliate them through the act of racial labeling as when they all humiliate them through the discourse of racial categorization. There is no "race", there is race which humiliates and race which is humiliated. There is pleasure in humiliating the other through race just as there is pleasure in denying that is what one has done. This denial is accomplished by engaging in a discourse which naturalizes the social... This last pleasure, the pleasure of re-characterizing rape as seduction, or race as natural, is accomplished through ideology. (Farley, 1997: 476)

These racializations and sexualizations are not deviant behaviors on the part of some pimps or some white people. They are part and parcel of a whole system of racialized capitalist-patriarchal dominance over women, the working-class lesbians, gays, and trangender peoples, indigenous and other nonwhite peoples. Within these structures and institutions practices of direct physical violence and indirect methods (such as seduction) are used to keep the female migrant working-class, women, gays, lesbians, trangender people, indigenous and nonwhite people in their place. This seduction enables the "private" powers to accrue benefits and privileges through the expropriation of surplus-value. And it is not accidental. It is the method that many nonwhites use to "whiten" themselves, that is, to become the global social bourgeoisie. This pleasure/desire of whitening takes hold in the peripheries as well. The peripheral economic state uses these same methods (colonization and exploitation) to create and sustain its economic growth. It commodifies all social life ("sexy Russian queens" "my Filipineza"), privatizes public welfare ("hiring of maids"), colonizes male and female bodies ("men for sex," "bitches," "maids," and "birth machines" for the nation-state), draws legalistic lines, between the "private" unregulated violence from regulated state and market violence, and displaces grassroot visions of democratic life (cross-cutting interests, coalitions, and alliances).

Female migrant workers respond in different ways to these violences and violations. They (1) undermine and expose the arbitrariness of national boundaries while reinforcing nationalist identities, (2) choose to subvert commodified compulsory heterosexuality, and (3) work collectively in their immediate environment and the larger global economy to challenge the structures and their colonizing/exploitative logics. Let's now see how.

NATIONALISM AND IDENTITY: REIFICATION OF PLACE AND THE DIASPORIC COMMUNITY

Neoliberalism in its globalized form "democratizes" by decentralizing the movement of reproductive labor and creates a diaspora of national households worldwide. Many sex and domestic workers have connections to cross-national and cross-continental households—their household in their "home" countries, their household in their immediate environment, the household of their sisters and brothers in other countries.

Svetlana, for example, is from Russia. Her sister, Vera, works as a barmaid in Italy. Her youngest sister does sex work in Germany. Similarly, a domestic worker from Sri Lanka, Malavi, has a sister who works in Saudi Arabia, a husband working in Kuwait, and their daughter working in Greece. These cross-continental households sustain each other through letters, phone calls, and exchanges of food, cash and other commodities. If faced with difficulties and crises, these cross-continental households struggle collectively as transnational laborers while contained within the borders of national identity. "We are the new 'economic heroes' for the Philippines and yet the slaves of so many different countries" (Maria, 45-year-old domestic worker from the Philippines in Cyprus).

Despite the diaspora of these households, or because of it, many workers draw from a nationalist discourse of identity to explain their export abroad: "We are very proud as a community of Sri Lankans to contribute millions of dollars to our national treasury" (Malavi, 50-year-old domestic worker in Cyprus). Subsuming one's surplus labor within a nationalist identity does not recognize the structural inequalities that prevent income-poor states from providing employment for their workers. Instead, women are portrayed as active participants in the economic development of their countries. Paradoxically, this discourse empowers sex and domestic workers. As national "economic heroes," they send their remittances home to cover the billions in interest on loans accumulated from the WB and the IMF (Rosca, 1995). Accordingly, they feel they have the right to critique their state:

> Many times our country is interested in guaranteeing the smooth flow of foreign currency...it does not care about what happens to our children or us. What we need is a different community, we are already starting to do that—we get together on Sundays and spend time with each other and share about our global family. (Twethi, 40-year-old domestic worker from Myanmar in Greece)

Twethi and her counterparts understand that their states see them as cash cows. Yet many sex and domestic workers are still not able to challenge their low wages and the regime of private property that pushed them into the tentacles of diasporic labor movements:

> If it weren't for Greece, my family would be dead. If it wasn't for Mrs. Eleni and Mr. Andreas, I'd still be working on a farm for almost no money. Going back home is scary for me because I don't even know if I can get a job. (Rosalita, 38-year-old domestic worker from the Philippines in Greece)

Like Rosalita, many sex and domestic workers still nationalize the state and hierarchize them in terms of being good (if they provide a job for them) and being bad (if they do not provide employment). These logics of nationalism are coping mechanisms and draw from nationalist discourses to resist a democratic expression of "misery and hopelessness" (Zapatistas, 1998: 11). All are equal but some (those who own the means of production) are more equal than others (those who have nothing to sell but their labor). Yet many other workers resist "neoliberalism's historic crime in the concentration of privileges, wealth, and impunities" (Zapatistas, 1998: 11). They do so by focusing on their immediate sexual relations with one another.

HETEROSEXUALITY AS A COMPULSORY COMMODITY

Sex and domestic workers have also internalized various moral discourses. Many of the sex and domestic workers argue that they do not work as prostitutes. They are better than those women who sell their bodies for "sexual favors."

> We know that there are several Filipinas here who supplement their income with prostitution. On their free Sundays, they go out with men and get paid instead of going to Church and worshipping God. (Rosa, 50-year-old domestic worker from the Philippines in Greece)

Rosa criticizes those women who sell "sexual favors" and for their flexibility which enables them to earn more than a subsistence income. These divisions of women (e.g., moral and immoral subjects) serve the regime of private property. The entangling logics and mystifications of capital undermine women's collective and self-determination. Other women challenge this internalized compulsory heterosexuality and moralization. In order to challenge this regime, they break ties with their communities or become "tomboys" (Chang and Ling, 2000: 40). This is how two women migrants in Greece expressed their resistance to compulsory heterosexuality:

> Petra and I have lived together for the last three years. We left the cabaret life. Now, I work in a tavern just serving drinks and Petra works as a construction worker. We got so tired of having to sell our bodies all day long. Now, we are with each other and we don't need men in our lives. We are so much better with each other than with men, and better in expressing our love. (Marina, 35-year-old former sex worker in Greece)

Some women see this strategy as a freedom to relate to others without social prohibitions, to self-identify and orient themselves according to personal choices:

> Five of us rented this one bedroom apartment and meet each other on Sundays. Delia and I are now the best girlfriends. Everybody knows it and they let us use the bedroom when we want to be close with each other. She and I are the tomboys of our household here. We support a lot of other Filipina women to challenge their fear of being with each other—there is nothing wrong with being a lesbian. Is it better to constantly being asked by your boss to give him sex even though you do not care about him? You actually feel disgusted thinking that he wants you ... I am just paid after all to be his helper and not to serve him sex. (Gloria, 34-year-old domestic worker from the Philippines in Greece)

> I decided since I left the Philippines that I was always a lesbian. I always loved women and wanted to be with them. I could not do it though in a country that is Catholic and expects everyone to be with a man. Coming to Greece made me realize that I can now live my life and be free to love whomever I want. My family is not here—rather, my family that accepts me the way I am is here. I always tell my girlfriend who is from Sri Lanka that I love her and I will always love her no matter the color of her skin. (Tricia, 28-year-old domestic worker from the Philippines in Greece)

Recognizing these sexual, racial, and political connections is very important in bringing women together. Still, these subversions are not enough to challenge the compulsory heterosexuality and exploitative violences that domestic and sex workers experience "here and there." Domestic workers are still afraid to bring their lovers to the "home" they work in, which is both their public space of work but also their private personal space. Greece is not any better as a space than the Philippines for domestic and sex workers to express their love and sexuality for each other. Both of these spaces make decisions racially and sexually. They categorize women within an international division of labor that profits from the exploitation of women and their insecurities. Race and class "synthesize the new cartography of labour economics" (Salazar Parrenas, 2001) where sex and domestic workers occupy the lowest rung in the hierarchy of desire industries.

Forging Transborder Alliances for Social Democracy and Safety

Sex and domestic workers in Greece, Turkey, and Cyprus are forging alliances with working-class women and others to challenge both the state and the structures of slave wage labor and improve the quality of their lives (Agathangelou, 2002). They do so by: (1) exposing how the peripheral economic state's nationalist and transnational discourses of naturalization, commodification, and the myths of opportunity and "white but not quite" slavery are strategies of colonization that silence social personal freedoms at different places simultaneously; (2) understanding how these individuals and groups of people are exploited, oppressed, and the ways of organizing their lives is informed by "private" powers and their interests rather than their own. The agents of the neoliberal project use methods that "keep them in place"; (3) recognizing that they as agents who participate in making possible the profits of private powers can envision their futures because they carry not only the scars of oppression and exploitation, but also the memories of survival and self/collective empowerment; and (4) (re)interpreting the strategies utilized by capitalist and patriarchal structures, practices (nation-state, citizen, freedom, sexuality, serviceability, flexibility, and democracy) toward envisioning possibilities for global social justice and putting in place the material conditions (a feminist democracy) that could emancipate all people from exploitation and from violations of their safety.

These different transformative processes are ridden with internal and external contradictions and tensions. Women themselves are constantly faced with choosing what strategies to employ in changing their lives (Rupert, 2002: 15; Danaher and Burbach, 2000; Yuen, Katsiaficas, and Rose, 2001). Nonetheless,

> [a] non-essentialist position does not imply a nonbelonging to a group, nor does it imply loss of agency or of coalitions and solidarities. For some feminists of color, identity politics remains central . . . which can enable a politics through positions that are coalitions, intransigent, in process, and contradictory. (Grewal, 1994: 234)

Many of my interviewees talked about the different structures, practices, and discourses that constitute migration and migrants as a problem.

I left my country to come to Greece because of the debt that my country is facing. Many people like me are travelling abroad to seek employment. What else can we do? Unless our country becomes as rich as Greece, many more people are going to try to escape poverty and seek a better life. (Maria, Filipina domestic worker in Greece)

There were no jobs in Moldavia. I came here. Was it better for us to die? The system was closed for so many years and access to capitalism was limited. The system opened up with Perestroika and many people found themselves without money and everybody left. First, the women left because they did not have any jobs or money. If I wanted to keep men company and I did not have money I could not do it. If you do not have a job, you cannot have a good life. I want my child to go to school but I cannot send him. I did not want to stay in Moldavia any longer. (Vera, sex worker from Moldavia working in Turkey)

Much money goes to the policemen and the immigration office to protect their citizens from us. Wives call in and demand that they kick us out of their country, as if we cannot find other ways to get back in. One of my Greek boyfriends was married with three children. He used to spend a lot of time with me telling me all the problems he had with his wife. One day, two of the policemen who many times took us out for sex came to the cabaret and informed me that I had two days to leave the country; otherwise, they had no option but to kick me out because of a complaint. I questioned them for hours, but they said: "It is not our fault. We have a serious complaint from a citizen." They kicked me out and for what purpose? A few months later, my boyfriend came and found me in Bulgaria. Then we found an impresario who got me a new passport and visa. I was able to come back to the country with a new name and new identity [laughing nervously]. (Viktoria, 24-year-old-sex worker from Bulgaria in Greece)

As Kollontai surmises: "the world is divided into two camps" (51). Blaming sex workers for their men's promiscuity reflects the privileged class position of Greek and Turkish women in a capitalist-patriarchal structure, making invisible the larger order of economics and politics that contextualizes these relations. Greek and Turkish women are implicated and are complicit in these relations. Instead of choosing to ally with the women against the violence that is generated toward them by men, the Greek or Turkish woman chooses to protect her class interests even at a cost to her gender. Moreover, when the Greek woman transfers and collapses the conflict that she may have with her husband onto the sex worker, she colludes in sustaining an imperialist system that desires and consumes women's sexuality as a major means of generating profits and makes possible its efficient social reproduction. Similarly, the Greek husband chooses to be antagonistic to the sex worker despite her own racialized peripheralization to core capital.

Viktoria recognizes these contradictions within the system and seeks ways to subvert its politics. She is able to resist only with the financial support of her upper middle-class client. Together, they subvert the rules of law, which are rather arbitrarily set to protect the rights of some at the expense of others. Citizens of income-rich states rarely are asked to examine their attitudes toward poor countries and the women who are marketed as exotic, sexy, and/or flexible workers. Income-rich citizens are lulled into thinking that their desires are more important than any income-poor country's citizens' needs and desires. They do not even ask whether their lives could be possible without the labor of the women that serve them daily. Nor do they ask whether their consumption practices and patterns have larger implications on the poverty and forced labor they employ. In this way, income-rich citizens reproduce their identities and selfhood at the expense of "white but not quite" women.

> Instead, the liberal idea that we are autonomous individuals who contract with each other is used to annul the idea that prostitution is non-reciprocal sex and thus a violation of the personhood of the prostitute. The contract cancels the violence, although we readily recognize the violence of other financial transactions (such as Third World youth who sell their corneas to First World buyers). The space of prostitution, which Malek Alloula describes as "the very space of orgy: the one that the soldier and the colonizer obsessively dream of establishing on the territory of the colony," is the space of license to do so as one pleases, regardless of its impact on the personhood of others. (Razack, 2000: 107)

While transborder alliances do disrupt these structural relations, they can be equally problematic. As we saw earlier, a local man worked with an impresario to subvert the politics of the formal, legal economy by successfully bringing an expelled migrant sex worker, Viktoria, back to Greece. Even when the peripheral nation-state mediates with transnational capital to constitute the desire economies as a strategy to employ some disenfranchised people, it is still commodifying women's labor and their bodies. Local and transnationalized practices and ideologies of desire, servility, and serviceability, depend on a set of commercial productions that are consumed for sexual pleasure.

Public critiques from different NGOs (ISGA; KEDE; Global Change Institute; CAHT) highlight these economic and political contradictions. They challenge conventional constructions of race, the peripheral economic state, civil and human rights, security and insecurity, freedom, and democracy. Working-class peoples and, more specifically, working-class female women speak up and juxtapose their stories next to those told by agents of the state and the women and men who hire sex and domestic workers. These stories bring to the fore an alternative vision of how to organize our lives, our communities, and larger world orders.

For example, Sophia, a Cypriot 55-year-old working-class woman who used to be a domestic laborer, disclosed that her son had just hired a Filipina domestic worker:

> Did my son forget when I used to work as a domestic worker? I hope not. Otherwise, he could participate in the same torture I experienced when I was working to feed him and help him grow and go study abroad.... Why do the rich need their houses cleaned? Why don't they do it? I lost my job because they had to pay a little more to me than they pay the Sri Lankans and the Bulgarians who are my friends and are exploited. They work for nothing!

The crucial point here is that the emerging middle and upper class, some of which are children of working-class women, collude with transnational power structures by exploiting these women and treating them as slaves. Sophia's friendships/alliances with Sri Lankans and Bulgarians stem from these same structures of exploitation.

A friend of Sophia, Galena, who worked as a domestic worker for five years in Cyprus, is now married to a Greek Cypriot man and lives next door. These two women talked about their own exploitation and oppression and their need to work as domestic workers.

> I used to get up very early and catch the bus to go to work. I would leave my 5-year-old son behind with my sister and I would worry the whole day about his well-being. I would worry about being safe in the village. I would take care of Maria, Antonis, and many others and my sister would take care of my son. These were scary times for me. (Sophia, a 55-year old Cypriot)

> I was scared when I was in Bulgaria. My husband left me with two kids and I did not have any savings to take care of their basic needs: food and clothing. I left Bulgaria for a better life and I left them with my parents till I was able to bring them to Cyprus. I came here for a better life, but my boss was torturing me, so I decided to leave that family. I came here to find a job to make a better life, and I planned to be here for a short time. Now, I got married here and found a new country. (Galena, a 50-year old domestic worker from Bulgaria and now a Cypriot citizen)

The mobility of sex and domestic workers engenders the potential for developing new alliances toward collective deliberation and solidarity. When Galena says that domestic workers migrate with dreams of success but they remain unrealized, she makes the first step toward the creation of a critical consciousness regarding the capitalist myth of opportunity.

Their lived practices challenge the racialization, commodification, and nationalization of women's lives and bodies. Categories such as Cypriot and Bulgarian woman/worker, nation, race, and class are purposive categorizations that make possible the extraction of surplus-value. In this particular case, Galena's marriage to a Cypriot makes it possible for her to acquire citizenship. At the same time, she remains clear-eyed about capitalist structures, exploitative practices against the working-class, and the insecurities these sustain against female working-class women. She proceeds to talk about what is required for change:

> Sharing our fears, insecurities, and exploitation that we suffered is very useful because we are reminded that the state, here and there, are not for us. They export and import us at will. They use citizenship to subvert our freedom. They know that all of our energy is spent on trying to be safe within the context they have defined for us. However, what is important for us to remember is that we cannot fight individually while remembering the fears and insecurities we face alone. Many times, this way is what keeps us in place. But just sharing between us is not enough, either. We need a movement to support our work. That's the reason I am now a member of the communist party. I am a Greek Cypriot and I have citizenship and I can use it to help others like myself.

Migrant women are also organizing. On Sundays, their one free day, many domestic workers in Cyprus and Greece congregate in central parks of the major cities, socializing and networking with other domestic workers from Europe and the Middle East. Rosalyn, a Filipina domestic worker in Greece and a member of Caritas, a major NGO for migrant rights, told me the following:

> We come together and share stories and strategies to help women who are new in Greece and do not know how to rid themselves of their contracts when they work under very bad conditions. The state does not support them. On the contrary, the state always ends up supporting the employer. Domestic workers in the Middle East and Europe are working with us to mobilize the resources and legal knowledge that can be utilized against the local employers and also change the slave system we are forced to be part of. What we need now is an alternative vision like the one the Zapatistas espouse. We need a Greek Forum, like the World Social Forum (WSF).

Rosalyn and Galena raise crucial questions about women's agency and globalization and its remedies for "equality." "The fact that globalization provides jobs for the jobless in no way means that it changes the social relations of production" (Ebert, 2001: 398-399). We need to exercise our freedom to critique and challenge the exploitation and violence of neoliberal globalization and its agents of desire. We must enable a more social democratic participation in securing human dignity and quality of life for the majority of this world (Agathangelou and Ling, 2004).

Sex and domestic workers challenge, albeit embryonically, the material conditions of private, capitalist ownership that underpins their exploitation and violence. These struggles may be contradictory but they push us to extend IPE and feminist scholarship and politics such that capitalism's priority of profits, private property, and efficiency over human life becomes blatantly obvious. These women's struggles highlight the need for a transborder political economy that begins *with the dialectics of sex, desire, and the material relations of production* (Cotter, 2001; Ebert, 2001).

MATERIAL RELATIONS OF PRODUCTION

As I stated in chapter five, with transnationalized neoliberal insecurity (Escobar, 2001) the few feast off the many in the current symbiosis of national security. This creates the drive to find more markets and commodify more of human life. Peripheral and core economic states fuse capitalist ideologies with nationalist ones to produce exclusionary practices of consumption as freedom. Peripheral economic states appeal to a Self/subjectivity that needs consumption of cheap labor to be considered autonomous and free in order to boost their economy. We need, in short, an emancipatory approach to globalization.

This is happening already. Note, for example, the rise in popular protests at WB/IMF/WTO meetings as well as surging participation in the WSF, held in protest against the World Economic Forum (WEF).[1] Female migrant workers are also crossing borders to expose the underlying labor relations in the international division of labor by organizing against their exploitation. Women's labor unions have expanded, as well, with cross-national feminist networks precisely due to their common exploitation and oppression under neoliberal globalization (Chang, 2004; Moghadam, 2001, 1999; Raymond, 2003; Coalition Against Trafficking, Houston, Texas, 2004; Global Alliance Against Traffick in Women, 2003). Labor unions and other groups usually not identified with a feminist agenda now have reason to ally with women's organizations. Such linkages subvert hypermasculine violence and desire by engaging previously demarcated camps of hostility. They provide one venue for unraveling racialized, heterosexual, and gendered violences along with the privileges that have been accruing to a minority, whether in core or peripheral economic states.

THE NEED FOR AN ALTERNATIVE ONTOLOGY: MARXIST-FEMINIST HISTORICAL MATERIALIST METHOD

How we study a subject not only defines it but also affects our suggestions for social transformation. Steve Smith (2004) identifies ten major assumptions of mainstream IR that perpetuate, even if unintentionally, the dichotomized world of Self versus Other.[2]

Steps toward creating a world or a new historic bloc that is safe for the majority of the world, and addresses the majority's needs require a transformation of understandings. This, in turn, requires a historical materialist method of analysis. The desires and needs of people, their gender, sexuality, identities and differences, and their agency are not outside of and independent from the conditions that produce them (Marx, 1976: 42). They are historical material relations created through labor. "Materialism is not a matter of inference. It is a praxis: the praxis of labor through which humans act "upon external nature" and change it, and in this way simultaneously change themselves" (Ebert, 1996: 34 citing Marx, 1977: 284).

A feminist historical materialist critique explains the rise of the desire economies, the insecurities, and the lack of safety that are generated within them. It explains the process through which the employer of the female migrant sex and domestic worker extracts their labor in order to benefit their own class interest. It also explains the ideological mystifications that a supremacist white and masculine historic bloc constructs to socially produce itself. It is here that we, as intellectuals, cannot abdicate responsibility. A Marxist-feminist historical materialist critique begins with the social understandings of the female working-class migrant and engages the contradictions. Revolutionary struggles that expose these contradictions of the current imperialist, neoliberal practices do not automatically follow material changes in production relations. They have to be produced by us, as social agents of the different communities. Due to the methods, pedagogies, and ideological mystifications of the agents of "private" powers, many peoples' self-understandings are constrained (Rupert, 2000: 11 citing Gramsci, 1971: 164–165, 326, 375–377,

420). Gramsci's major point in his project is that engaging popular common sense and making explicit the contradictions latent within it may make possible the build-up of an "emancipatory political culture and a social movement to enact it" (Rupert, 2000: 11)—an alternative historic bloc where "private" powers do not dominate the majority of the world. Gramsci's philosophy of praxis requires "a criticism of 'common sense', basing itself initially on common sense in order to demonstrate that 'everyone' is a philosopher and that it is not a question of introducing from scratch a scientific form of thought into everyone's individual life, but of renovating and making "critical" an already existing activity. It must then be a criticism of the philosophy of the intellectuals out of which the history of philosophy developed and which, in so far as it is a phenomenon of individuals... can be considered as marking the 'high points' of the progress made by common sense" (Gramsci, 1971: 330–331). Simultaneously, the organic intellectuals' responsibility is to critique even the most critical theories produced in our academic communities and exposing their sociopolitical consequences as well as their ontologies.

We need, in short, a *global* political economy of sex analytic to understand and change our world. It begins with our everyday practices and subjectivities, recognized as "dynamic, contradictory and unresolved dimensions of experience" rather than reified or fixed (Bannerji, 1996: 80). Following Himani Bannerji, who follows radical feminists in the tradition of Marx and Gramsci, I posit that we—all of us—need to begin with ourselves and our lives as the launching point for our explanatory and analytical inquiries, especially if we are committed to a revolutionary and transformative politics. Our social analysis of theory and practice must involve ourselves, as political agents who work collectively in a movement to produce knowledge towards a transformative politics. We also need to de-reify capitalist social relations in their racial, class, sexualized, and gendered configurations, to make visible the practices, processes, and norms of globalization—otherwise known as the latest forms of imperialist capitalist-patriarchy—that so crucially shape our lives. For example, we can critique theories that separate sexuality and desire from class because they obstruct a project of emancipation. Theories that focus on "local" struggles also make impossible our understanding that a collective movement of anticorporate globalization struggles is required to put in place the material conditions to emancipate all people from exploitation, violence, insecurity, and their lack of safety. These assumptions, I suggest, uphold a class privilege in IPE and feminist pedagogies. They deny, marginalize, or exile alternative voices and identities that challenge established boundaries of community, self, security, and safety.

A Marxist-feminist historical materialist method allows us to analyze globally the political economy of sex through (1) Critique: Identifying Complicity in Exploitation and Oppression, (2) Self-Reflection: Deconstructing IR and feminist Communities' Knowledges toward Production of Collective Transborder Solidarities, and (3) Emancipation: Transforming the Relationship Between Research and Praxis and Crossing Borders Toward Collective Deliberation, Change, and creation of safe communities.

(1) Critique: Identifying Complicity in Exploitation and Oppression

As I stated in chapter three, John and Io each stated that they were helping "their" women given the poverty and lack of employment in their home countries. Interestingly, both employers acknowledged feelings of conflict in hiring women from other peripheral economic states to do their "labor" and, in turn, generate profits (in the case of John money and in the case of Io a securing of her bourgeois subjectivity as a professional woman) for them. Nonetheless, they easily racialized and sexualized their workers by comparing their value (e.g., the Sri-Lanka domestic worker was a thief whereas the Filipina is a trustworthy worker and closer to Greek ways of lifestyle).

Critical feminist materialist research points out that the perception of non-alternatives arises from erasing contradictions, which are part and parcel of social relations and reflect the differential power locations of the employer and employee. Both John and Io recognized the problematic issue of hiring cheap labor yet neither believed that they were participating in unequal power relations. As the conversation unfolded, they began telling their own stories of exploitation and oppression in the new global economy. John talked of his working-class background, his disability, and how the state pushed him to the margins of the formal employment sector to land, finally, in the shadows of the desire industries. Io recounted her relationship with her husband regarding household work and how every time she raised the issue of him sharing the household work, he would get angry and become violent. She also began talking about violence at work. She shared how there were several cases of sexual harassment but none of the top supervisors wanted to deal with them.

In this "dialectical dialogue," we moved beyond a "moralization" stance to an understanding of how the desire industries are organized and founded on exactly the same principles as the formal economy: property relations and expropriation of the worker's value. The only difference is that the ideological mirage between the formal and informal economies silences the complicity that employers have in sustaining structures and institutions that give them "freedom" to acquire as racial bourgeoisie the position of manager and profit-maker in their roles as employers of sex and domestic workers. Capitalist-patriarchy thus seizes upon this complicity and the pleasure it offers as another epistemological tool to ensure the exploitation of and violence against female workers of color.

A connecting moment for all of us came when I brought up the issue of my potential participation in the exploitation of the labor of sex and domestic workers. Using the conversations of employees without exposing the class politics that inform both relationships could turn into another exploitative relation. Important as it is to expose the exploitation between employer and employee, it is equally so to acknowledge similar processes of exploitation and violence through the agency of ideas, our class position as mental workers and its various social privileges. In so doing, we challenge the methods and pedagogies of a capitalist regime that requires certain divisions and binaries for its *ontological* survival (e.g., production vs. reproduction, formal vs. informal economies, mental vs. physical labor, licit vs. illicit economies, racial, class, and gender differences). However, these moments remain individuated unless they contribute toward creating an emancipatory political culture and a mass-based social movement.

(2) Self-Relation: Deconstructing IPE and Feminist Communities, "CommonSense" Understanding Toward Production of Collective Transborder Solidarities

Understanding the social relations of knowledge production exposes the connection between the "clean" offices of the state or academy and the "dirty" brothels or bathrooms of the desire industries. Feminists interested in transforming capitalist-patriarchy can work simultaneously to affirm the agency of sex and domestic workers as well as make explicit how IPE knowledge producers, politicians, and pundits alike work together in creating such environments of self-estrangement, estrangement from our labor, individuation of knowledge, divisions of communities, complicity, and exploitation. The neoliberal corporate logic that underpins the desire industries is the same that guides our activities as knowledge producers. As stated in the previous section, the more I came to work closely in the communities of desire industries, the more I began reflexively to go back and forth between the production of knowledge in the IPE community and methods we utilize to produce it. Content such as the sovereignty of the nation-state, the story of supply and demand, the invisible hand, and processes such as the estrangement of labor, divisions of communities, colonialist moves, racialization and genderization of labor, competition, violations and transgressions became apparent to me. Moreover, our complicity as a community to not challenge the capitalist-patriarchal ontology of individualism, separation of politics and economics, the national and transnational borders, and the hegemony of the market became more real and brought to the fore the ways, we, as agents of our diverse communities, embody these relations. The desire industries highlight the need to eschew re-colonizing the 'other,' an endeavor requiring a praxis that makes possible transborder collective struggles and solidarities. It is vital that we achieve awareness and make explicit how the desire industries and the ways we produce knowledges in our communities (e.g., the academy; the state) are informed by the same capitalist logic whose whole purpose is generation of more profits. These relations of production draw upon scripts of colonialism such as a woman who is "white but not quite" with green or blue eyes as the desired object; similarly, IPE and feminist theorists mystify these production relations by focusing on legalistic codes to challenge the nation-state's collusion with trafficking or the subjugation of Third World women, as if the nation-state is the sole participant in the regime of profit and the creator of this regime. Drawing upon these scripts of competition and estrangement from labor, IPE and feminist theorists can end up colluding with the mystification practices of capital-labor relations (e.g., expecting Tricia, the sex worker to provide us, as feminists who want to outlaw trafficking, insights about the patriarch Third World and its pimps), supporting a regime of profit and a gendered racialized world order that sustains in place the asymmetries and inequalities world wide. By bringing these two moments together, as knowledge producers or sex or domestic workers, we can make apparent the contradictions of the regime of private powers. We could, as critical IPE feminists, contribute toward a transborder/dialogue between the communities of desire industries and other communities. This crossing at times is difficult, and reveals another aspect of our social relations: the internalization of mystifications and the need to transform them. We can consider the following question: How did we, along with the other members of these different communities, internalize these epistemological tools of capitalist-patriarchy, so much so that we even experience pleasure out of this "distorted" production of personhood through making ourselves the "white but not quite" feminist bourgeois subjects?

(3) Emancipation: Transforming the Relationship between Theory and Praxis and Crossing Borders Toward Collective Deliberation, Change, and Creation of Safe Communities

It is not by shooting bullets in the battlefields that tyranny is overthrown, but also by hurling ideas of redemption, words of freedom and terrible anathemas against the hangmen that people bring down dictators and empires...(Emiliano Zapata, Mexican revolutionary, 1914)

Sex and domestic workers, a few employers in Cyprus, Greece, and Turkey, and knowledge producers, including myself, join in different collectives (Immigrant Support Action Group, CHAT, Greek Helsinki Monitor; Global Change Institute; Reintegration Centre for Migrant Workers, Greece) and work together to build solidarity by challenging trafficking and migrants' exploitation. Through critiques of the conditions in our communities and the desire industries, we come to recognize the importance of deliberation on the possibilities for connections, sharing, and action. In the Global Change Institute, and through CHAT, we held meetings and prioritized an agenda for change. In the process, we made explicit our differential power relations based on the position that each occupied in the international division of labor. The stakes in the struggle to solidarity are different for all of us; however, our entry point into this struggle is informed by a sexual raced division of labor and a vision for an alternative world. Our "different" locations in the transnational division of labor became an opportunity to share and discuss the violences as well as the privileges that it accords to each one of us. Discussions about the impact of globalization and capitalist-patriarchal values on sexuality, desire, and domestic work and its effect on households became part and parcel of our deliberations. Moreover, discussions about how to challenge nationalist boundaries were prevalent in our praxis of labor. We came to see that nationalisms are obstacles to an alternative vision that enables solidarity. The barbarism of migration regimes causes thousands of violations and deaths all in the name of democratic legalism. These practices require more than challenging border camps and detention centers. The dismantling of fences demands solid support networks.

Discussions and grassroots organizing helped us understand each other and the privileges/powerlessness that different women experienced because of public property theft such as privatization and fortune making. A major part of our deliberations featured problematizing the international division of labor that claims that it accords rights, privileges, and meets people's desires because of its equal exchange logic (e.g., women of color and white but not quite women are to respond to and serve the desires of "white but not quite" Cypriots, Greeks, and Turkish women and men because they get paid for their services). Artificially produced and institutionally supported divisions, such as Greek/other, researcher/activist, worker/activist, rich-income state/lower-income states were thereby deconstructed. These relationships do not occur on equal terms. For this reason, the process of research/activism can become part and parcel of work that challenges the larger exploitation regime or end up supporting the neoliberal world order and its practices. If the organizing, the analysis, and the collective work (social movements) remain just localized projects that do not attempt to make apparent the contradictions of the capitalist regime on a global level, then the possibilities for change become narrowly punctuated. Ontological/epistemological alternatives become marginalized and invisible and knowledge production itself ends up colluding with the racialized and gendered class politics of capitalism in our different communities (including the communities of teaching and learning). The same would apply to feminisms that do not engage the conditions under which propertied men and women are able to exploit the work of women of color from lower-income countries. If the "common-sense" stories of all of us, women, men, transgender, and indigenous people and their contradictions in the desire industries and outside them do not become part of a feminist praxis through a global political economy of sex analytic then possibilities for solidarity become reduced and remain within the nation-state boundaries or at best take shades of a neoliberal democratic discourse of human rights violations (Zatz, 1997; Reanda, 1991; Miles, 2003).

Our grassroots work made us increasingly aware of the exploitation that takes place within both the licit and illicit economies as well as the violences committed on different racialized/classed/gendered bodies. Thus, finding alternatives, including a different language, became central to our deliberations and struggles, both socially and personally.

Sex workers wanted to meet counterparts who worked at different sites (e.g., cabaret, hotels) and share their experiences with them. Sex workers also wanted to meet with domestic workers despite the hierarchical valuation of prices. Female workers started to organize and support each other especially when they faced sexual and other kind of violences. Lists of support organizations as well as personal contact information were made and distributed among us. Although these gatherings did not change the desire industries, their values and policies, female workers began breaking out of their isolated experiences and saw themselves/ourselves as agents in their/our work environments.

Hearing alternative stories in this nascent movement from various marginalized people opens up previously unimagined spaces for organizing. In the telling of stories, "revolutionaries" redefine the rules and roles of those who claim to speak for them, in ways previously considered "rationally" unimaginable. Understanding the social relations of sexuality, desire, security, and safety is significant for critical IPE. These dialectical relations will "determine...whether the social arrangements will be able to eradicate oppression for all, or whether they will need to be transformed to do so" (Cotter, 2001: 8).

What is needed now is a dialectical linkage between praxis and theory. A collective feminist democratic project requires a historical materialist critique of all structures, institutions, and practices and exposition of the ontology of fear, violence, exploitation, and lack of safety, and requires struggles in a movement that encompasses groups worldwide. Only in this way could a global justice movement emerge.

Marianna, a sex worker from Moldavia, raised the following question during a focus-group interview:

> Marianna (a sex worker from Moldavia): Why do you want to write a book about us? Why don't we write the book together?
>
> Author: Why don't we?
>
> Marianna: Writing a book will change my life. It'll make me a writer and not just a prostitute. I will not be just desired for sex—my sexy body, my long legs, my blue eyes, by long blond hair—but also for my mind. But you are the professor [laughing]. Perhaps, next year when I receive my citizenship and I will not depend on [my pimp] any longer. I could make time to become famous by helping other women who find themselves in prostitution. Now, I have to focus on my papers otherwise I will be kicked out and find myself nowhere.

Her approach of saying "let's write the book together" questioned the educational/professional academic boundaries and alienation between interviewer and interviewee, inviting the possibility of collective action albeit within the capitalist–patriarchal framework of success, fame and security. She challenges us to move beyond coping mechanisms and defenses and to consider the kind of world in which we want to live.

Elena also pushes the arbitrary boundaries between the state and citizenship and political action.

Elena (sex worker from Bulgaria): I love being a truck driver. After I received my citizenship papers in Cyprus, I no longer had to sell my body for money. I was determined to change that because every time I went back to Bulgaria everybody in the neighborhood looked at me as being a whore. I was not. I needed to work to change my life and my son's life. And I did!

Anna (sex worker from Bulgaria): I am working on myself now with the support of Elena. I have my papers and Cyprus now is my country. This country is ours and will stay ours. We do not want to migrate again. We do not want to leave from Cyprus. I married this Greek man whom I met at one of the cabarets. He was twenty years older than me. I did not care. I just wanted to get out of the business and I did. After four years of being together I asked him for a divorce. He was very kind to me and he gave it to me. Now I have to get rid of this habit. While working in the cabarets for year after year I ended up using alcohol to numb the pain and frustration. I now work in collecting resources from different NGOs such as the International Prostitutes Collective, and the Center for Inspirational Living to create a center with Marianna. We are now citizens and nobody can prevent us from creating this local support center.

Bourgeois democracy remains "an unfulfilled promise of liberal capitalism" (Rupert, 2000: 5). As citizens now of Cyprus, Elena and Anna are making connections with NGOs to loosen the grip of private property in their lives and to support other women from having to experience the exploitation, violence, and violation daily in their lives and their bodies.

Marianna finished the interview by stating:

Imagine yourself a butterfly. Unfortunately, you get caught and put in a box so that a child can enjoy you. A few days later, the child demands that you be put in a smaller box for him to be able to carry you in his pocket and to see you more closely. Finally, he forces you into a matchbox so that he can have you on his table to enjoy all of the time. What happens to you? You lose your ability to fly—learning to fly requires you to get out of the box—it takes time to learn to fly and teach others like you to do the same. We are all butterflies, everywhere.

In Marianna's story, the box represents the constraints imposed on migrant workers at the local, state, and transnational levels. Transforming our world through revolutionary praxis where true freedom from necessity exists, requires knowledges and praxes that challenge the pimps and the employers who command women's labor for their own benefit and private powers. She reminds us that we need connections that traditionally are unimaginable and incarcerate us in boxes. Similarly to Marianna, Kollontai reminds us that we need to struggle toward building free and equal relations of love, sexuality, and comradeship in which there are multiple and collective connections and relations with others. Notes from Nowhere captures a similar idea and practice.

> "We are everywhere? We're not, you know-but we could be. And if we're going to be, then we have to acknowledge what a scary thought that really is: for once 'we' are everywhere then there will be nothing to define ourselves against.... If we really want to make the world a better place then that's what we have to want. But learning to want it will take courage, the courage to accept the risk of our identities which real change always poses." So let's have the courage, let's have the heart that lies in the root of the word courage, le coeur-the heart to build a rebellion that embraces, the heart to insist on an insurrection that listens, the heart to create revolution that when it looks in the mirror understands that it's not just about rage, but that it begins with the word 'lover'. Let's have the courage to demand... the courage to keep the spaces that this movement of movement has created, radically open, rebelliously inviting, and profoundly popular... For when we are truly everywhere, we will be nowhere -for we will be everyone. (Notes from Nowhere, 2003: 510-511)

Building a rebellion that critiques and changes the capitalist ontology (that is, prioritizing private property's desires, interests and security, divisions, and violences at all times at the expense of the majority of the world's peoples) requires alternative methods for building an alternative ontology where democracy is substantively accountable to the needs of the majority and their safety (e.g., basic daily food, physical, psychological and other needs are met; human rights are not violated, communities and social life is demilitarized; the environment is not poisoned; terrorism subsides; resources are socialized to meet the needs of all and not the select few). Artificial boundaries such as national/international, high-income/lower income generating nation-states, licit and illicit have so far divided the "movement in progress" and the racialized sexed workers in it. However, in Cyprus, Greece, and Turkey as many other parts of the world, people are beginning to see these mirages for what they are and recognize their effect on their lives. For the first time, many peoples are recognizing that racialized gendered working-class and not the nation is the basis for collective solidarity. For the first time, many people are recognizing that the safety of their communities and their livelihood and not the nation are the basis for a collective movement.

What is needed now more than ever is a dialectical linkage between praxis and theory. Reconceptualizing and integrating into theory building the many struggles of the different groups worldwide toward a "global movement in progress" becomes significant for a collective feminist democratic project. Feminist participation in collective racialized, sexual, class struggles is crucial in establishing the material conditions to emancipate all people from such a wage-labor regime, insecurities, and the lack of safety generated within the capitalist structures.

NOTES

1   SEX AND DOMESTIC WORK IN THE PERIPHERY: FENCED-OFF ECONOMIES OF DESIRE

1. Ehrenreich and Hochschild (2002) focus on the "global chain care" as women's work worldwide resulting from globalization. The exploitation of women's work is not a result of globalization. Rather, globalization has intensified exploitation. Their presentation of the "global chain care" presumes an essentialization of women, as if all women are the same and occupy the same location in the global division of labor. This assumption makes invisible the complicity of women in the "First World" in hiring and exploiting women's labor in the "Third World". As my book indicates, women of upper and owning-classes in the peripheries or Third World sites are able to hire and exploit working-class women of other peripheral sites both within their countries and outside them. Their theorization, though, silences the reasons behind the class differences among women. Moreover, it diverts attention away from the production relations that enable some women as well as their desires (e.g., to experience care as emotion) to be prioritized in the process of exploiting and displacing the needs of women who end up being assigned their drudgery or "care as labor."

2. See video by Ursula Biemann, *Writing Desire* on Filipina, Russian, and Colombian Internet matchmaking clients and sex workers.

3. See also Ebert (2001), Cotter (2001) for a similar approach to understanding sex, desire, and their dialectical relation to material relations of production. Ebert calls this theory *red feminism* following Kollontai's incisive analysis of the relations of bourgeois notions of sexuality and love in early twentieth-century Russia. This theory makes it possible for us to move beyond the historical limits of our current social formations and to "envision the fundamentals of an egalitarian, non-exploitative and post-gender future." (Ebert, 2001: 5)

4. Rubin (1975) was the first to coin the term political economy of sex.

5. According to Ferguson (2002: 130–131) sex/affective production is "a way of understanding the social organization of labor and the exchange of services that occur between men and women in the production of children, affection, and sexuality....[both] sexuality and affection are bodily as well as social energies." Ferguson's definition does not link production and reproduction; she sees these sites as independent.

6. Many times these romantic relations are also used as a point of reference to dissolving "traditional" family relations. Again, this decision is based on sexual relations: it is my privilege and right to move to a new relationship that offers me a more "human" connection.

7. Fanon wrote about the "naked truth of decolonization": "For if the last shall be first, this will only come to pass after a murderous and decisive struggle between the two protagonists" (37). Fanon stressed that Marxist analysts need to rethink class struggle in the colonized areas of the world to account for the role of race in the colonies (40) since the "cause is the consequence, you are rich because you are white, you are white because you are rich." For Fanon, the "colonial world is a Manichean world" with rigidities around race that imbue all with its values. The colonial society portrayed non-whites as completely lacking in values, knowledge, beauty, dignity, and humanity and whites as the fount of all knowledge and all that is good in the world. Non-whites are "the corrosive element, destroying all that comes" close (41). Based on this mystification of the social relation of exploitation, the colonial society treated non-whites as "less than" economically, socially, and politically. However, during decolonization "the colonized masses mock[ed] at these values, insult[ed] them, and vomit[ed] them up" (43).

8. Pateman focuses on prostitution to explain the sexual contract. She states "the story of the sexual contract also supplies the answer; prostitution is part of the exercise of the law of male sex-right, one of the ways in which men are ensured access to women's bodies.... Feminist criticism of prostitution is now sometimes rejected on the grounds that prostitutes exploit or cheat their male clients; men are presented as the injured parties, not women. To be sure, prostitutes are often able to obtain control over the transaction with their customers by various stratagems and tricks of the trade...[these] particular instances of the prostitution contract, in which a prostitute exploits a male customer, should be distinguished from prostitution as a social institution. Within the institution of prostitution, 'prostitutes' are subject to 'clients', just as 'wives' [and domestic workers] are subordinate to 'husbands' [and madams] within the structure of marriage [and the contract of domestic and sex work]" (1988:194).

9. Ibid., 259.

2   PERIPHERAL ECONOMIES WORKING AND PLAYING HARD: SOCIAL REPRODUCTION AND RACIAL AND SEXUAL DESIRE IN THE MEDITERRANEAN

1. Several feminists critiqued this separation. (Anderson, 2000; Ebert, 1996; Aguilar, 2004)

2. "Crisis tendencies" refers to the historical developments that call into question the properties of a gender regime in the family, the state, the labor market, and other institutions. (Connell, 1988: 158)

3. It should be noted here that many feminist groups in Greece organized against this Article, including ACT UP, Network of Social Support of Refugees and Migrants, Movement of Democratic Women, Social Aid of Greece, Union of Greek Women Lawyers, Groups of Feminist Center of Women, Feminist Priority Against the Forced Prostitution of Migrant women. The Human Rights Watch on Greek Immigration Law sent the following statement to the parliament on January 31, 2001: "Chapter VIII of the bill, although couched in language related to 'artists' and their employment in 'entertainment centres,' includes within its scope the employment of migrant women in bars, nightclubs, and other venues. This chapter, however, makes no mention at all of an increasingly serious problem of trafficking of women and children into Greece for forced prostitution and other forms of forced labor. In our view, the entire chapter should be reconstructed taking into particular consideration the phenomenon of trafficking. Trafficking in women for forced prostitution in Greece has increased sharply in recent years, yet Greece has no laws specifically criminalizing trafficking in persons." (HRW, January 31, 2002)

4. Interestingly enough, the state collapsed the migration of sex and domestic workers under one Article (19) after serious critiques from feminists, migrant NGOs, and the Human Rights Committee, which declared through correspondence with the Greek state the "illegality of the migration bill."

5. Many North American feminists have focused on womens's choice in prostitution and have advocated for this "choice." See Deborah Nord, *Walking the Victorian Streets: Women, Representation, and the City.* (London: Cornell University Press, 1995); Kempadoo (1998).

6. The exploitation and a series of marginalizations begin long before sex and domestic workers enter the transnational market.

7. Razack (1998) argues that prostitution secures them their bourgeois hegemony and subjectivity. She argues that their move into the spaces of prostitution strengthens their position in the dominant group. "Their abandonment of societal norms does not weaken these men's claims of respectability, but, rather, it puts the mark of degeneracy on the women in prostitution ... That is, once men leave the space of degeneracy, having survived it unscathed, they return to respectablity. In this way prostitution reaffirms not only the hierarchies of gender but also of class, race, and sexual orientation" (Razack, 1998: 357).

8. Sexual relations have been an important part of the formation of class relations and struggles and class relations shape sexual relations and struggles.

9. A similar language was used in Politis, a Greek Cypriot newspaper. The article used the same word "excite" to justify the behaviors of young men who were throwing stones on a house that female artists were renting in Limassol. (Politis, by Kalatzis, August 23, 2001: 16)

3   REPRODUCTIVE LABOR: SEX AND DOMESTIC WORK IN CYPRUS, GREECE, AND TURKEY

1. I agree with Kempadoo that the eroticization processes are part and parcel of the desire industries; however, I disagree with her point that work is not exploitation, i.e., the production of surplus-value. For Kempadoo (1998: 226), sex work is a "'necessary sexual labor' or 'emotional labor' and not inherently exploitative. Whether it would be exploitative or not depends on the capacity of the sex workers to assert their agency by developing strategies of resistance. 'Sex work' is exploitative when the state imposes particular moral and legal restrictions and makes it impossible for women to 'freely choose' sex work" (Kempadoo, 1998). For an excellent critique of transnational feminists who follow a similar logic on sex work see Jennifer M. Cotter (2001).

2. It should be noted here that sex and domestic workers' countries of origin participate in generating profits for their own owning-class by turning whole sectors of their economy into desire industries.

3. See (1998) Razack for an excellent analysis of the constitution of spaces and securing of privileges.

4. Ibid., 398.

5. See Alexander (1998: 287) for a similar argument.

6. We still see this refusal in the debates around the joining of Turkey and Cyprus into the EU. In the case of Cyprus, the debate is linked to the militarization of the North by Turkey, and, thus, debates around Cyprus joining the EU bring to the fore that its entry will be contingent upon resolving the "ethnic conflict" between Greek and Turkish Cypriots. Müftüler-Bac argues, "Turkey's failure to uphold democracy justifies the EU's rejection but at the same time conceals an aspect of the EU's reservations about Turkey: its perception of Turkey as the other of Europe" (240).

7. Alexander uses this logic to explain the interdependence and competition between heterosexual and homosexual capital. This logic applies to the relation between metropole and peripheral capital.

8. Within the economies of desire there exist multiple racial constructions. The "white but not quite" identification refers to both men and women in the peripheries who through the purchase of cheap reproductive labor assume that they have the possibility of becoming part and parcel of the "white" race. Conversely, the local male population in the Mediterranean, who is "white but not quite," is drawn to Eastern bloc women as a way to become "whiter," and therefore acquire a higher status, both locally and globally. Similarly, the women in the Mediterranean also hire "darker" women to raise their status. (Laura Parisi, personal communication, October 23, 2003)

9. Despite their professional power and status in a social context that makes it possible for them to access the formal market, many women feel the pressure of capitalist-patriarchy to sustain intact reproductive relations.

4 DESIRING POWER IN THE EUROPEAN UNION: PERIPHERAL ECONOMIC STATES' PARTICIPATION IN CAPITAL ACCUMULATION

1. See Agathangelou and Ling (2004) for a discussion of knowledge production in International Relations.
2. F. Webster, *Theories of Information Society, supra*, chapter 7 "Information and Restructuring: Beyond Fordism," p. 135 ff.
3. See also (Yilmaz, 2003; http://europa.eu.int/comm/economy_ finance/about/activities/activities_thirdcountrieseconomic_pep_ en.htm).
4. The membership of Greece in the EU and its participation in the multilateral trading system have played a major role in shaping the general policy environment toward international market openness and bringing momentum and commitment to reform. Multilateral trade agreements have resulted in historically low tariffs for products, and set the trade in services on the path of progressive liberalisation.

   The development of the Single Market has led to the removal of regulatory barriers to trade among EU countries....The implementation of internal market directives is progressively opening key sectors, such as the telecommunications or energy sectors, to competition. However, Greece has frequently sought derogations that have delayed major reforms. (OECD, 2001: 9)

5. The welcoming mat was used by M. Jacqui Alexander (1998: 287) who cites Reed Abelson, "Welcome Mat is Out for Gay Investors— They Have Cash, and Distinct Needs," *New York Times* (September 1, 1996), 1, 7. It is a metaphor for capital inviting anyone to participate in its generation and reaping of riches, however, on its own terms.
6. Ling (2002: 116) argues that the ideology of formal mimicry's is "conventional, [and an] externally-borrowed one."
7. Now this is dramatically changing. Many of the core countries of the EU like Germany are having discussions about importing skilled labor from countries like India, Pakistan, and other Asian countries (from personal discussions with German parliamentarians). This import of skilled labor will change the demands for social provisions.
8. This is the case in many other countries including the United States, Canada, and Japan. (Hanochi, 2003; Chang 2004)
9. In Greece the National Action Plan published in May 1999, by the Ministry of Labour reflects the ideology that Tricia's madame expressed. This ideology is about global flexibility of the worker. "The lack of job opportunities which continues and has become a structural element in our time as well as the market deregulation for the employed and the unemployed has been a decisive factor in order

for flexibility of the job market to appear as a means to the effective balance between these two groups of the work force (employed and unemployed) with the redistribution of job opportunities to a wider number of employed people. The reduction of working time is also a way to get more jobs in times of crisis.... our goal is to promote the functional needs of business but also the personal needs and wishes of the employed so as to give them the opportunity to combine professional and family life...." (National Action Plan, 1999: 36–37)

10. Chang and Ling focus on the globalized service economy and more specifically on domestic work. In my work here, I combine domestic with sex work—i.e., reproductive labor—as part of a larger regime of the desire industries.

11. The transformation of the state into a neoliberal institution in the world economy is a contestable process. Situated agents such as women in the desire industries contest the state and its agents, and institutions such as nongovernmental organizations challenge and confront the politics of this changing state, both importing and exporting.

5   NATIONAL DESIRES FOR SECURITY

1. I am thankful to Sonita Sarker for this point.

2. For a genealogy of the competition between the church and state about the management of security see Jean Delumeau (1989) *Rassurer et proteger: Le sentiment de securite dans l'Occident d'autrefois*. Paris: Fayard.

3. "Smuggling is clearly concerned with the manner in which a person enters a country, and the involvement of third parties to assist the migrant to cross illegally into a foreign country. Trafficking is a more complicated concept, in that it requires consideration not only of the manner in which a migrant entered the country but also his/her working conditions, and whether he/she consented to the irregular entry and/or working conditions." (Salt, 2000: 37)

4. The parliament made an amendment to the citizenship law that was enacted on June 4, 2003 to make sure that Turkish citizenship through marriage was not as easy as it has been previously.

5. It should be noted here that these discourses are part of a larger debate in Turkey regarding the factors that change the security agenda. During the 1990s, the National Security Policy Document or the "Red Book" was changed twice to address security concerns. In 1992 "internal threats" such as separatism and terrorism were prioritized on the security agenda list. In 1997 the "Red Book" was amended to respond further to internal threats. "Internal threats against the territorial integrity of the country and the founding

principles of the republic became more grave than external threats" (Milliyet, 1997 cited in Bilgin, 2004: 10). By the end of 1990s, in Turkey it has become "difficult to find a political and societal topic that does not concern national security" (Ožcan, 1998: 90). In 1998 Ismail Hakki Karadayi (then Chief of Staff) presented a speech entitled "Factors that Cause Change and Their Impact upon Conceptualizations of Security" at a seminar organized by the Organization for Security and Cooperation in Europe (OSCE) in January of 1998. This is what he had to say about the new risks and threats of Turkey:

> The first category includes illegal trafficking of arms and drugs, international terrorism and condoning of terrorism in cases where it is considered as war of independence, the proliferation of weapons of mass destruction and environmental damage. The second category includes ethnic conflicts, intolerance, radical nationalisms and all kinds of separatism, and human trade in the form of migration. (Cited in Bilgin, 2004: 13)

6. Governmentability here refers to the dialectic relationship of real, effective social structures, and active interpretive social agents. It specifically refers to all the practices that constitute, organize, and define how historically situated social agents whose actions are enabled or constrained by their social self-understandings relate with each other either through routine interactions or political struggles. (Isaac, 1987: 78)

7. Weiner argues that there are two major paradigms of security: an international political economy framework that focuses on global forces to explain the politics of migration, and a security stability framework that focuses on the importance of the state's decision-making capacity with regard to migration and security. I argue that these approaches are not independent of each other. Epistemically and politically, the organization of the global economy comprises social relations generating the conditions that effect and are effected by the state, a social relation itself.

8. It should be noted that the upper class economic and political elites in Turkey are divided regarding the issue of security. For an excellent review of these divisions and contestations, see Pinar Bilgin (2004).

9. Discourses among pro-EU actors and EU-skeptics in Turkey around security reveal the existence of different stakes elites have in the restructuring of the EU regional powers and the role of Turkey within that. However, the discourses remain within a fundamentalist nationalism (or inter-state with a dash of multilateralism) and cosmopolitan frameworks, which in the end support (by making invisible) the neo-imperialism of corporate globalization.

6   A GLOBAL POLITICAL ECONOMY OF SEX: FEMINIST POSSIBILITIES FOR TRANSBORDER DEMOCRACY AND SAFETY

1. The WSF was set up by grassroots organizations, NGOs, and dissidents as an alternative to the WEF that assembles annually the world's leading industrialists, high-profile academics/advisors, and many state leaders for one week of "informal consultations." The WSF has met since 2000 in Porto Alegre, Brazil. The WSF met in India in January of 2004.
2. These assumptions are: (1) "the state as the unit of analysis, rather than either humanity as a whole or the individual," (2) "distinction between the inside and the outside of the state," (3) "distinction between economics and politics," (4) "the notion of a common progression of humanity towards one end-state as exemplified in most accounts of globalization," (5) "absence of considerations of gender and ethnicity from the main theories," (6) "definition of violence [as] war," (7) "stress on structure over agency," (8) "the idea of one, universal rationality," (9) "underplaying of the importance of issues of identity in theories of international relations," and (10) "the search for explanation rather than understanding" (Smith, 2004).

BIBLIOGRAPHY

Agathangelou, A.M. (2002) "Sexing 'Democracy' in International Relations: Migrant Sex and Domestic Workers in Cyprus, Greece, and Turkey." In G. Chowdhry and S. Nair (eds.), *Power, Postcolonialism and International Relations: Reading Race, Gender and Class*, pp. 142–169. New York: Routledge.

———(2003) "Envisioning a Feminist Global Society: Cypriot Women, Civil Society and Social Change." *International Feminist Journal of Politics* 5(2): 290–299.

Agathangelou, A.M. and L.H.M. Ling (2003) "Desire Industries: Sex Trafficking, UN Peacekeeping, and the Neo-Liberal World Order." *Brown Journal of World Affairs* X (1): 133–148.

———(2004) "Power, Borders, Security, Wealth: Lessons of Violence and Desire From September 11." *International Studies Quarterly* 48: 517–538.

———(2004) "The House of IR: From Family Power Politics to the Poisies of Worldism." *International Studies Review*. Vol. 6 (4).

Aguilar, D. (2002) "Imperialism, Female Diaspora, and Feminism." *The Red Critique: Marxist Theory and Critique of the Contemporary* 6 (September/October): 1–23.

Aguilar, D.D. (2004) "Questionable Claims: Colonialism Redux, Feminist Style." In D.D. Aguilar and Anne Lacsamana (eds.), *Women and Globalization*, pp. 404–423. New York: Humanity Books.

Alexander, J.M. and Chandra Talpade Mohanty (1997) *Feminist Genealogies, Colonial Legacies, Democratic Futures*. New York and London: Routledge.

Alexander, J.M. (1998) "Imperial Desire/Sexual Utopias: White Gay Capital and Transnational Tourism." In E. Shohat (ed.), *Talking Visions: Multicultural Feminism in a Transnational Age*. New York and Massachusetts: The MIT Press.

Allen, T. (2000) "Turkey and the EU" Statistics in Focus: External Trade, Theme 6-5/2000. *Eurostat, Luxembourg*. European Communities, 1–4.

Altink, S. (1995) *Stolen Lives: Trading Women into Sex and Slavery*. London: Scarlet Press/New York: Harrington Park Press.

Altman, D. (2001) *Global Sex*. Australia: Allen & Unwin Pvt. Ltd.

Amin, S. (1989) *Eurocentrism*. Trans. Russell Moore. New York: Monthly Review Press.

Amitsis, G. and G. Lazaridis (2001) *Legal and Socio-Political of Migration in Greece*. Athens: Papazisis.

Anderson, B. (2000) *Doing the Dirty Work? The Global Politics of Domestic Labour.* London: Zed Books.

Anderson, B. (2004) "Who Needs Yehudi Menuhin? Costs and Impact of Migration." In D.D. Aguilar and Anne E. Lacsamana (eds.), *Women and Globalization*, pp. 262–277. New York: Humanity Books.

Angouras, V. (1998) "Greece's Northern Frontier." In E. Bort (ed.), *Borders and Borderlands in Europe*, pp. 121–130. Edinburgh: International Social Sciences Institute.

Antoniou, T. (1993) "Issues and Problems in the Greek Law of Aliens." In H. Schermers et al. (eds.), *Free Movement of Persons in Europe*, p. 125. The Hague: T.M.C. Asser Institute, Martinus Nijhoff Publishers.

Apap, J. (2002) *The Rights of Immigrant Workers in the European Union: An Evaluation of the EU Public Policy Process and the Legal Status of Labour Immigrants from the Maghreb Countries in the New Receiving States.* The Hague/London/New York: Kluwer Law International.

Appadurai, A. (1991) "Global Ethnoscapes: Notes and Queries for a Transnational Anthropology." In R. Fox (ed.), *Recapturing Anthropology: Working in the Present.* Santa Fe: School of American Research Press.

Avgi, 2002; 2001; 2000; 1999, http://193.218.80.70/cgi-bin/hwebpress-rem.exe?-A = 61575&-w = PORNEIA_&-V = hpress_int&. Accessed June 2002.

Bakker, I. And Stephen Gill (eds.), *Power, Production and Social Reproduction: Human In/Security in the Global Political Economy.* Basingstoke, Hampshire; New York: Palgrave.

Baldwin-Edwards, M. (1998) "The Greek Regularization: A Comparative Analysis with the Spanish, Portuguese and Italian Experiences." University of Reading, Centre for Euro-Mediterranean Studies, Working Paper 98/2, April. http://www.rdg.ac.uk/EIS/research.

———(2002) "Immigration and the Welfare State: A European Challenge to American Mythology." MMO, Working Paper, 4, November. http://www.antigone.gr./southern, European Labour Markets and Immigration.

———(2002) "Semi-Reluctant Hosts: Southern Europe's Ambivalent Response to Immigration." *Brown Journal of World Affairs*, Fall; revised version published in *Studi Emigrazione*, 145 (July): 27–48.

Baldwin-Edwards, M. and J. Arango (eds.) (1998) "Immigrants and the Informal Economy in Southern Europe," Special Issue of *South European Society & Politics* 3(3) (Winter).

Bertsch, C. (2002) "An Interview with Wendy Brown." In J. Schalit (ed.), *The Anticapitalism Reader: Imagining a Geography of Opposition.* New York: Akashic Books.

Bhabha, H. (1986) "The Other Question: Difference, Discrimination and the Discourse of Colonialism." In F. Barker, P. Hulmer, M. Iverson, and D. Loxley (eds.), *Literature, Politics, and Theory*, pp. 148–172. London: Methuen.

———(1987) "What does the Black Man Want?" *New Formations* 1:118–123.

———(1994) *The Location of Culture.* London: Routledge.

————(1995) "Cultural Diversity and Cultural Differences." In B. Ashcroft, B. Gareth Griffiths, and Helen Tiffin (eds.), *The Post-Colonial Studies Reader*. London: Routledge, 1995. 206–210.

Bhattacharjee, A. (1997) "The Public/Private Mirage: Mapping Homes and Undomesticating Violence Work in the South Asian Immigrant Community." In M.J. Alexander and Chandra Talpade Mohanty (eds.), *Feminist Genealogies, Colonial Legacies, Democratic Futures*. New York and London: Routledge.

Bigo, D. (2002) "Security and Immigration: Toward a Critique of the Governmentality of Unease." *Alternatives* 27(1): 63–92.

Bilgin, Pinar (2004) "Turkey's Changing Security Discourses: A Critical Security Studies Perspective." Paper presented at the annual meeting of the International Studies Association, Montréal, Canada, March 17–20, 2004.

Brenner, J. and B. Lasslett (1989) "Gender and Social Reproduction: Historical Perspectives." *Annual Review of Sociology* (15): 381–404.

Bridger, S., R. Kay and K. Pinnick (1996) *No More Heroines? Russia, Women and the Market*. London and New York: Routledge.

Broyelle, C. (1998) *Women's Liberation in China*, http://www.blythe. org.mlm/misc/women/wom_toc.htm.

Bulbeck, C. (1998) *Re-Orienting Western Feminisms: Women's Diversity in a Postcolonial World*. United Kingdom: Cambridge University Press.

Bureau of Democracy, *Human Rights and Labor* (1999) *Reports on Human Rights Practices of Greece, Turkey, and Cyprus*. Bureau of Democracy, Human Rights and Labor U.S. Department of State, http://www. state.gov/g/drl/rls/hrrpt/1999/c30.htm. Accessed January 2004.

Bush, K.D. and E.F. Keyman (1997) "Identity-Based Conflict—Rethinking Security in a Post-Cold-War World." *Global Governance* 3(3): 311–328.

Campani, G. (2000) "Immigrant Women in Southern Europe: Social Exclusion, Domestic Work and Prostitution in Italy." In R. King, G. Lazaridis, and Charalambos Tsardanidis (eds.), *Eldorado or Fortress? Migration in Southern Europe*, pp. 145–169. Great Britain: MacMillan Press Ltd.

————(2001) "Immigrant women in Southern Europe: Social Exclusion and Gender." Paper presented at the Conference "Migration in S. Europe" organized by IIER and Regional Network on Southern European Societies, September 19–21, Santorini, Greece.

Campbell, D. (1992) *Writing Security, Revised Edition United States Foreign Policy and the Politics of Identity*. Minneapolis: University of Minnesota Press.

Cavounidis, J. (2002) "Migration in Southern Europe and the case of Greece." *International Migration* 40(1): 45–70.

Chair of Labor Ministry Committee on Migration (2001) Conference on "Irregular Migration and Dignity of Migrants: Co-operation in the Mediterranean Region." Athens, October 3–4, 2001. Council of Europe.

Chang, G. (2004) "Globalization in Living Color: Women of Color Living under and over the 'New World Order.'" In D.D. Aguilar and Anne Lacsamana (eds.), *Women and Globalization*, pp. 230–231. New York: Humanity Books.

Chang, K.A. and L.H.M. Ling (2000) "Globalization and Its Intimate Other: Filipina Domestic Workers in Hong Kong." In H.M. Marchard, and Anne Sisson Runyan (eds.), *Gender and Global Restructuring Sightings, Sites and Resistances.* London and New York: Routledge.

Chekuri, C. and H. Muppidi (2003) "Diasporas Before and After the Nation." *Journal of Postcolonial Studies* 5(1): 45–57.

Chin, C.B.N. (1998) *Service and Servitude: Foreign Domestic Workers and the Malaysian "Modernity" Project.* New York: Columbia University Press.

Chin, C.B.N. and J. Mittleman (2000) "Conceptualizing Resistance to Globalization." In B.K. Gills (ed.), *Globalization and the Politics of Resistance.* Great Britain: St. Martin's Press.

Choucri, N. (2002) "Migration and Security: Some Key Linkages." *Journal of International Affairs* 56(1): 97–122.

Chow, R. (1990) *Women and Chinese Modernity.* Minneapolis: University of Minnesota Press.

———(1993) *Writing Diaspora: Tactics of Intervention in Contemporary Cultural Studies.* Bloomington: Indiana Univerisity Press.

———(1995) *Primitive Passions.* New York: Columbia University Press.

Chronas, G. (1989) *The Woman of Patras.* Athens: Sigareta (in Greek).

Cixous, H. (1998) *The Third Body.* Massachussetts: Northwestern University Press.

Clifford, J. (1986) "Introduction: Partial Truths." In J. Clifford and G.E. Marcus (eds.), *Writing Culture: The Poetics and Politics of Ethnography.* Berkeley: University of California Press.

Coalition Against Trafficking (2004). Houston, Texas.

Commission of the European Communities (1993) *PUBLAW 2: Draft Final Report Europe.* A Report to the Commission of the European Communities on an Evaluation of the Implementation of the Commission's Guidelines for Improving the Synergy between the Public and Private Sectors of the Information Market. Luxembourg: CEC Legal Advisory Board.

Connell, R.W. (1987) *Gender and Power.* Cambridge: Polity Press.

———(1988) *Gender and Power: Society, the Person and Sexual Politics.* Stanford Press.

Constanble, N. (1997) *Maid to Order in Hong Kong: Stories of Filipina Workers.* New York: Cornell University Press.

Cooper, F. and A.L. Stoler (eds.) (1997) *Tensions of Empire: Colonial Cultures in a Bourgeois World.* Berkeley: University of California Press.

Cothran, H. (ed.) (2001) *Illegal Immigration.* San Diego: Greenhaven Press.

Cotter, J. (2001) "Eclipsing Exploitation: Transnational Feminism, Sex Work, and the State." *The Red Critique: Marxist Theory and Critique of the Contemporary* 1(Spring): 1–27.

———(2002) "Feminism Now." *The Red Critique: Marxist Theory and Critique of the Contemporary* 3(March/April): 1–23.

——— (2003) "The Class Regimen of Contemporary Feminism." *The Red Critique: Marxist Theory and Critique of the Contemporary* 8(Spring): 1–23.

"Country Report on Trafficking in human beings: Turkey." Paper distributed at the conference on Prevention of and Fighting Against Trafficking in Human Beings, organized by IOM and EU, Brussels, September 2002.

Cox, R. (1987) *Production, Power, and World-Order.* New York: Columbia University Press.

——— (1993) "Structural Issues of Global Governance: Implications for Europe." In S. Gill (ed.), *Gramsci, Historical Materialism and International Relations*, pp. 259–289. Cambridge, MA: Cambridge University Press.

Danaher, K. and R. Burbach (eds.) (2000) *Globalize This, Monroe.* ME: Common Courage Press.

Davis, A. (1984) *Women, Race, and Class.* London: The Women's Press.

Debord, G. (1988) *Comments on the Society of the Spectacle.* London: Verso, 1991.

Delaunay, D. and Georges Tapinos (1998) *The Extent of Illegal Migration in Europe. Volume 1: Summary Report.* [La measure de la migration clandestine en Europe. Volume 1: rapport de synthèse.] EUROSTAT Working Paper, Vol. 3, No. 7, March 1998, 104 pp. European Communities, Statistical Office [EUROSTAT]: Luxembourg.

Deleuze, G. and Felix Guattari (1983) *Anti-Oedipus: Capitalism and Schizophrenia.* Trans. R. Hurley et al. Minneapolis: University of Minnesota Press.

Demetriou, A. (2000) *Strictly Akatallilon. Greek: From Omonia to Alkazar.* Athens: Oxi.

Demleitner, N.V. (2001) "The Law at Crossroads: The Construction of Migrant Trafficked into Prostitution." In D. Kyle and R. Koslowski (eds.), *Global Human Smuggling.* Baltimore: The John Hopkins University Press.

Di Nicola, A. (1999) "Trafficking in immigrants, A European Perspective." Paper Presented at the Colloquium on Cross-border crime in Europe, Prague, September 27–28, 1999, Transcrime Research Centre on Transnational Crime, University of Trento, Trento, Italia (mimeo).

Droukas, E. (1998) "Albanians in the Greek informal economy." *Journal of Ethnic and Migration Studies* 24(2) (April): 347–365.

Ebert, T.M. (1995) "Subalternity and Feminism in the Moment of the (Post) Modern: The Materialist Return." In K. Myrsiades and J. McGuire (eds.), *Order Partialities: Theory, Pedagogy, and the "Postcolonial."* Albany, NY: SUNY Press.

——— (1996) *Ludic Feminism and After: Postmodernism, Desire, and Labor in Late Capitalism.* Ann Arbor: University of Michigan Press.

——— (2001a) "Globalization, Internationalism, and the Class Politics of Cynical Reason." *Nature, Society, and Thought* 12(4): 389–410.

——— (2001b) "Left of Desire." *Cultural Logic: An Electronic Journal of Marxist Theory and Practice* 3 (1): 1–23.

Economist (1998) "Vivid Imagination: Technology and Entertainment Survey." November 21, p. 15.
——— (1999) "Plenty of Muck, Not Much Money." May 8, p. 58.
Ehrenreich, B. and A.R. Hochschild (2002) *Global Woman: Nannies, Maids, and Sex Workers in the New Economy.* New York: Henry Holt Company, Metropolitan Books.
Elson, D. (1998) "The Economic, the Political and the Domestic: Businesses, States and Households in the Organisation of Production." *New Political Economy* 3(2): 189–208.
Emke-Papadopoulou, I. (2001) "Trafficking in Women and Children: Greece a Country of Destination and Transit." MMO, Working Paper 2, August. http://www.uehr.panteion.gr/data en/3541.htm. Accessed October 2003.
Engels, F. (1884) *The Origin of the Family, Private Property and the State.* 1978 edition. Peking: Foreign Languages Press.
Enloe, C. (1989) *Bananas, Beaches, and Bases.* Berkeley: University of California Press.
——— (1993) *The Morning After: Sexual Politics at the End of the Cold War.* Berkeley: University of California Press.
Erder, S. (2000) "New Tendencies in International Migration: Is Turkey Becoming a Receiving Country?" In F. Atacan, F. Ercan, H. Kurtulus, and M. Turkay (eds.), *Mubeccel Kiray icin Yazilar*, Baglam Yayinlari. Baglam Yayinlari: Istanbul.
Erder, S. and Selmin Kaska (2003) *Irregular Migration and Trafficking in Women: The Case of Turkey.* IOM International Organization for Migration.
Eremicheva, G. (1996) "Articulating a Catastrophic Sense of Life." In A. Rotkirch and Elina Haavio-Mannila (eds.), *Women's Voices in Russia Today*, pp. 153–163. Aldershot, GB, and Brookfield, VT: Darmouth Press.
Erginsoy, F.G. (2000) "Female Child Sex Workers in Istanbul Metropolitan Area, Turkey: Gendered and Informal Child Labour in the City." Paper presented at International Association for Feminist Economics, Bosphorus University, Istanbul, August 15–17, 2000.
Ergüvenç, Ş. (1998). Turkey's Security Perceptions, *Perceptions* 3(3): 32–42.
——— (1999). Milli Güvenliğin Yeni Öncelikleri [New Priorities for National Security], *Ulusal Strateji* 2(9): 46–49.
——— (2000). Türkiye-ABD-AD Uçgeninde Askeri İşlerin Gidişati [Trends in Military Affairs in the Turkey-US-EU Triangle], *Ulusal Strateji* 2(11): 44–48.
Escobar, A. (2001) A Bottom Line of Sorts. http://www.ucolick.org/~de/WTChit/Escobar.html.
Eviota, E.U. (1992) *The Political Economy of Gender: Women and the Sexual Division of Labor in the Philippines.* London: Zed Books.
Fakiolas, R. (1999) "Socio-Economic Effects of Immigration in Greece." *Journal of European Social Policy* 9(3): 211–229.
Fakiolas, R. and Laura Maratou-Alipranti (2000) "Foreign Female Immigrants in Greece." National Centre for Social Research, Papers 60: 101–117.
Fanon, F. (1963) *The Wretched of the Earth.* New York: Grove Press.

Farley, P.A. (1997) "The Black Body as Fetish Object." *Oregon Law Review*, 76(3): 457–535.

Ferguson, A. (2002) "On Conceiving Motherhood and Sexuality: A Feminist-Materialist Approach." In N. Holstrom (ed.), *The Socialist Feminist Project: A Contemporary Theory and Politics*. New York: Monthly Review Press.

Firat, A.F. and N. Dholakia (1998) *Consuming People: From Political Economy to Theaters of Consumption* (Routledge Studies in Consumer Research).

Frelick, B. (1997) "Barriers to Protection: Turkey's Asylum Regulations." *International Journal of Refugee Law* 9(1): 8–34.

Fuentes, A. and Barbara Ehrenreich (1983) *Women in the Global Factory*. New York: Institute for New Communications; Boston, MA: South End Press.

Gallop, J. (1988) *Thinking Through the Body*. New York: Columbia University Press.

General Directorate of Turkey. (2001).

General Secretary of Public Order Ministry (2001). Athens: Greece.

Gershuny, J. and S. Jones (1986) "Time Budgets: Preliminary Analysis of a National Survey." *Quarterly Journal of Social Affairs* 2(1).

Ghosh, M. (ed.) (2000) *Managing Migration: Time for a New International Regime?* Oxford: Oxford University Press.

Ghosh, B. (1998) *Huddled Masses and Uncertain Shores: Insights into Irregular Migration*. The Hague: IOM: Martinus Nijhoff Publishers.

Gill, S. (1993). Gramsci and Global Politics: Toward a Post-Hegemonic Research Agenda. In Stephen Gill (ed.) *Gramsci, Historical Materialism and International Relations*. Cambridge: Cambridge University Press.

——— (2003) "Social Reproduction of Affluence and Human In/Security." In Bakker, I. And Stephen Gill (eds.), *Power, Production and Social Reproduction: Human In/Security in the Global Political Economy*. Palgrave.

——— (2003) "National In/Security on a Universal Scale." In Bakker, I. And Stephen Gill (eds.), *Power, Production and Social Reproduction: Human In/Security in the Global Political Economy*. Basingstoke, Hampshire; New York: Palgrave.

Glenn, E.N. (1992) "From Servitude to Service Work: Historical Continuities in the Racial Division of Paid Reproductive Labor." *Signs: Journal of Women in Culture and Society* 18 (Spring): 1–43.

——— (2002) *Unequal Freedom: How Race and Gender Shaped American Citizenship and Labor*. Cambridge, MA: Harvard University Press.

Global Alliance Against Traffick in Women (GAATW) Canada (1998). *Whores, Maids & Wives: Making Links*. Victoria: GAATW Canada.

Graburn, N.H.H. (ed.) (1983) *The Anthropology of Tourism*. New York: Pergammon Press.

Graham-Gibson, J.K. (1996) *The End of Capitalism (as we Knew it): A Feminist Critique of Political Economy*. London: Blackwell Publishers.

Gray, F.D.P. (1990) *Soviet Women: Walking the Tightrope*. New York: Anchor-Doubleday.

Greek Helsinki Monitor (2002) "Violence against Women in Greece." A report prepared by Greek Helsinki Monitor and the World Organization Against Torture for the Committee on the Elimination of Discrimination

194   BIBLIOGRAPHY

against Women at its Exceptional Session, August 5–23, 2002, http://www.greekhelsinki.gr. Accessed October 2003.

Greek Helsinki Monitor and Minority Rights Group-Greece Background Materials to Amnesty International & International Helsinki Federation Report (2002) "Greece: In the Shadow of Impunity – Ill-Treatment and the Misuse of Firearms." September. http://www.greekhelsinki. gr/bhr/english/special_issues/ai-ihf-torture-background.html. Accessed January 2004.

Greek Helsinki Monitor and Minority Rights Group-Greece Background Materials to Amnesty International & International Helsinki Federation Report (2000) Report and Releases (AI/IHF, 24/09/2002) IHF-HR: "*A Form of Slavery: Trafficking in Women in OSCE Member States*" Greece Report. http://www.greekhelsinki.gr/english/reports/ihf-wit-july-2000.html. Accessed January 2004.

Grewal, I. (1994) *Scattered Hegemonies: Postmodernity and Trans-national Feminist Practices.* Minneapolis, MN: University of Minnesota Press.

Griffiths and H. Tiffin (eds.), *The Post-Colonial Studies Reader*, pp. 206–209. London: Routledge.

Gülçür L. and P. İlkkaracan (2002) "The 'Natasha' Experience: Migrant Sex Workers From the Former Soviet Union and Eastern Europe in Turkey." *Women's Studies International Forum* 25(4): 411–421.

Günçikan, B. (1995) *Haraşo'dan Nataşa'ya (From Haraso to Natasa).* Istanbul: Arion.

Hanochi, S. (2003) "Constitutionalism in a Modern Patriarchal State: Japan, the Sex Sector and Social Reproduction." In Isabella Baker and Stephen Gill (eds.), *Power, Production and Social Reproduction.* Palgrave Macmillan.

Hare-Mustin, R.T. (1994) "Discourses in the Mirrored Room: A Postmodern Analysis of Therapy." *Family Process* 33: 19–35.

Harisopoulou, V. "They all know," *Ta Nea* (October 22).

Hatton, T.J. and Jeffrey G. Williamson (1998) *The Age of Mass Migration.* New York: Routledge.

Hatty, S.E. (2000) *Masculinities, Violence, and Culture.* United Kingdom and California: Sage Publications, Inc.

Hatzi, T. (1993) *Poutana: Dekatria Hronia Meta. (Whore: Thirteen Years Later).* Athens: Odysseas (in Greek).

Hatzikosta, A. (1998) "Foreign Workers and Employment in Cyprus." Paper Presented at the Fifth Mediterranean Conference, Hilton, Nicosia, Cyprus.

Hennessy, R. (2000) *Profit and Pleasure: Sexual Identities in Late Capitalism.* London and New York: Routledge.

Holmstrom, N. and Smith (2000) "The Necessity of Gangster Capitalism: Primitive Accumulation in Russia and China" Monthly Review, 51:9. http:/www.monthlyreview.org/200holm.htm. Accessed June 2003.

hooks, B. (1995). *Killing Rage: Ending Racism.* New York: H. Holt and Co.

Hughes, D.M. (2000) "The 'Natasha' Trade: The Transnational Shadow Market of Trafficking in Women." *Journal of International Affairs* (Spring).

Human Rights Watch (2000) *Memorandum of Concern Trafficking of Migrant Women for Forced Prostitution into Greece, Country of Transit and Destination for Human Trafficking.* Member of European Forum for Left Feminists, Athens, November 14.

Hyde-Price, A., H. Gärtner, and E. Reiter and Reiter (2001) *Europe's New Security Agenda.* Boulder: Lynne Rienner.

Içduygu, A. (2003) "Turkey." In Forced Labour Outcomes of Irregular Migration and Human Trafficking in Europe, Special Action Programme to Combat Forced Labour, January 8–9. Work in Freedom, International Labour Office.

——— (2003) "Irregular Migration in Turkey." Prepared for International Organization for Migration. Geneva.

——— (2004) "Transborder Crime between Turkey and Greece and Regional Consequences." *Journal of Southeast European and Black Sea Studies* 4(2).

Içdyugu, A. and Keyman E. Fuat (2000) "Globalization, Security, and Migration: The Case of Turkey." *Global Governance* 6(3) (July–September): 383–399.

Içduygu, A., İ. Sirkeci and Gülnur Muradoğlu (2001) "Socio-Economic Development and International Migration: A Turkish Study." *International Migration* 39(4): 39–62.

İlhan, S. (2000) *Avrupa Birliğine Neden Hayir: Jeopolitic Yaklasim* (Why 'No' to the European Union: The Geopolitical Approach). İstanbul: Ötüken.

——— (2002) *Avrupa Birliğine Neden Hayir.* 2 (Why 'No' to the European Union: 2) İstanbul: Ötüken.

Immigration Office (2002) *Contract of Employment.* Nicosia: Republic of Cyprus.

International Helsinki Federation for Human Rights, *A Form of Slavery: Trafficking Women in OSCE Member States,* June, pp. 21–24.

International Organization for Migration (IMO) (1995) *Trafficking and Prostitution: The Growing Exploitation of Migrant Women from Central and Eastern Europe.* IOM: Geneva.

International Organization for Migration (IMO) (1995) *Transit Migration in Turkey.* Study completed in December 1995. Migration Information Programme: Geneva.

International Organization for Migration (IMO) (1996a) *Trafficking in Women to Austria for Sexual Exploitation.* IOM: Geneva.

——— (1996b) *Trafficking in Women to Italy for Sexual Exploitation.* IOM: Geneva.

——— (2001) *New IOM Figures on the Global Scale of Trafficking.* Trafficking in Migrants Quarterly Bulletin, no. 23, April, Special Issue.

Irigaray, L. (1985) *Speculum of the Other Woman.* Trans. G. Gill. Ithaca, NY: Cornell University Press.

——— (1985) *This Sex Which Is Not One.* Trans. Catherine Porter and Carolyn Burke. Ithaca, NY: Cornell University Press.

Irek, M. (1998) *Der Schmugglerzug. Warschau-Berlin-Warschau*. Berlin: Das Arabische Buch.

Isaac, J. (1987) *Power and Marxist Theory: A Realist View*. Ithaca: Cornell University Press.

Jacobs, H. (1988) *Incidents in the Life of a Slavegirl*. New York: Oxford University Press.

Joffe, G. (1996) "The Economic Factor in Mediterranean Security." *International Spectator* 31(4): 75–87.

Kadir, N. (2001) A Preliminary Report: *Labor Conditions of Asian Domestic Workers and Cypriot Government Migration Policy*. For Cyprus Fullbright Commission.

Kalatzis, G. (2001) "Attacks on Female Artists in Limassol" *Politis* August 23, 2001: 16:5.

Kandaraki, M. (2000) "Refugee and Migrant Women Forced Victims into Prostitutions." In E. Daskalaki, P. Papadopoulou, P. Tsambarli, I. Tsinganou, and E. Fronimou (eds.), *Criminals and Victims in the 21st Century*, pp. 581–588. Athens: EKKE (in Greek).

Kaur Puar, J. (2001) "Transnational Configurations of Desire: The Nation and its White Closets" In B. Brander Rasmussen, Eric Klineberg, Irene J. Nexica, and Matt Wray (eds.), *The Making and Unmaking of Whiteness*, pp. 167–183. Durham & London: Duke University.

Karaduman-Taş, (2001) Personal communication, State Institute of Statistics, Turkey.

Karasavvoglou, A. et al. (1998) *Foreign Workers in Kavala*. School of Social Administration/TEI Kavala.

Katsoridas, K. (1994) "Foreign Workers in Greece." Information Bulletin of Labour Institute (INE).

Kemp, G. (1991) *The Control Of The Middle East Arms Race*. Washington: Carnegie Endowment for International Peace.

Kempadoo, K. (1994) "Prostitution, Marginality, and Empowerment: Caribbean Women in the Sex Trade." *Beyond Law* 5(14): 69–84.

———(1999) "Continuities and Change: Five Centuries of Prostitution in the Caribbean." In Kamala Kempadoo (ed.), *Sun, Sex and Gold: Tourism and Sex Work in the Caribbean*, pp. 3–36. Boulder: Rowman and Littlefield.

Kempadoo, K. and Jo Doezema (eds.) (1998) *Global Sex Workers: Rights, Resistance, and Redefinition*. New York: Routledge.

Kethi, Research Center for Equality (2002) Human Resources Information. http://www.kethi.gr/greek/meletes/index.htm

Klein, N. (2002) *Fences and Windows: Dispatches from the Front Lines of the Globalization Debate*. New York: Picador USA.

Kofman, E. and Gillian Youngs (eds.) (1996) *Globalization: Theory and Practice*. London: Pinter.

Kollontai, A. (1977) *Selected Writings of Alexandra Kollontai*. Ed. and Trans. Alix Holt. New York: Norton.

Kontis, A. (2000) "Greece as a Receiving Country of Foreign Migrants." In S. Kostandinidis and Th. Pelagidis (eds.), *Greece in the 21st Century*, pp. 293–324. Athens: Papazisis (in Greek).

Kranidiotis, G. (1996) "Cypriot Economy in the European Context." In P. Pasiardis (ed.), *The Harmonization of the Cypriot Economy with the European Unification*, pp. 88–99. Nicosia, Cyprus: University of Cyprus.

Krause, K. and Williams, M.C. (1997) *Critical Security Studies: Concepts and Cases.* Minneapolis, Minnesota: University of Minnesota Press.

Kristeva, J. (1986) *The Kristeva Reader.* Ed. Toril Moi. New York: Columbia University Press.

Krugman, P. R. and Anthony J. Venables. (1995) Globalization and the Inequality of Nations. NBER Working Paper #5098. Cambridge, MA: NBER.

Krugman, P.R. and Maurice Obstfeld (1997) *International Economics.* Reading: Addison-Wesley.

Kuniholm, B. (2001). "Turkey's Accession to the European Union: Differences in European and American Attitudes, and the Challenges for Turkey." Working Papers Series SAN01-24, January 2001, pp. 1–26. Terry Sanford Institute of Public Policy, Duke.

Kupchan, C. (1994) *The Vulnerability of Empire.* Ithaca: Cornell University Press.

Lacsamana, A. (2004) "Sex Worker or Prostituted Woman? An Examination of the Sex Work Debates in Western Feminist Theory." In D.D. Aguilar and Anne Lacsamana (eds.), *Women and Globalization*, pp. 404–423. New York: Humanity Books.

Latza, B. (1987) *Sextourismus in Suedostasien.* Frankfurt am Main: Fischer Taschenbuch Verlag.

Lazari, D. and I. Laliotou (2001) *Sex Trafficking, Prostitution, and Sexual Exploitation.* Center of Research for Gender Equality (K.E.TH.I). Athens.

Lazaridis, G. (1995) "Sexuality and Its Cultural Construction in Rural Greece." *Journal of Gender Studies* 4(3): 281–295.

——— (2001) "Trafficking and Prostitution: The Growing Exploitation of Migrant Women in Greece." *The European Journal of Women's Studies* 8: 67–102.

Lazaridis, G. and K. Romaniszyn (1996) "Albanian and Polish Undocumented Workers in Greece: A Comparative Analysis." *European Social Policy Journal* 8(1): 42–56.

Lazos, G. (1997) *Sexuality as a Value in Modern Greece.* Athens: Delfini.

——— (1998) *The Problem of Qualitative Research in the Social Sciences: Theory and Praxis.* Athens: Papazisis (in Greek).

——— (2002) *Pornia ke Diethniki Somatemporia sti Sighroni Ellada: H Ekdidomeni (Prostitution and International Sex Trafficking in Modern Greece): The Issued.* Athens: Kastanioti.

——— (2002) "Trafficking in Greece in 2002: Stop Now, Stop Trafficking of People." Athens, Greece: STOPNOW-KEDE.

Lenin, V.I. (1939) *Imperialism: The Highest Stage of Capitalism.* New York: International Publishers.

Lepp, A. (2003) "Trafficking in Woman and the feminization of migration: The Canadian context" *Canadian Woman Studies*, 22: (3/4) Spring/Summer: 90–99.

Lianos, T. (1993) "Greece: Waning of Labor Migration." In D. Kubat (ed.), *The Politics of Migration Policies.* New York: Center for Migration Studies.

Lianos, T. (2001) "Illegal immigrants in Greece and Their Choice of Destination." *International Migration* 39(2): 3–28.

Lim, L.L. (1998) *The Sex Sector: The Economic and Social Bases of Prostitution in Southeast Asia.* Geneva: International Labour Office.

Ling, L.H.M. (2000) *Postcolonial International Relations Conquest and Desire between Asia and the West.* London and New York: Palgrave MacMillan.

Ling, L.H. (2002) "Cultural chauvinism and the Liberal International Order: 'West versus Rest' in Asia's Financial Crisis." In G. Chowdhry, Sheila, and N. Power (eds.), *Postcolonialism and International Relations: Reading Race, Gender and Class,* pp. 115–141. London and New York: Routledge.

Loizos, P. and E. Papataxiarchis (1991) *Contested Identities: Gender and Kinship in Modern Greece.* Princeton University Press.

Lutz, H. (2002) At Your Service Madam! The Globalization of Domestic Service. *Feminist Review* 70: 89–103.

Magganas, A. (ed.) (1994) *Ta Ekdidomena Atoma. Pornia: Parekklisi h Paravasi (The Issued Persons: Prostitution: Deviation or Infringement?)* Athens: Papazisis.

Malaos, A. (2000) "Cyprus Economy and EU Accession Process." Speech Summer School, 4th September, 2000. http://www.eic.ac.cy/EN/PaperMalaosE10.htm. Accessed June 2002.

Manderson, L. (1996) *Sickness and the State: Health and Illness in Colonial Malaya, 1870–1940.* Cambridge and Melbourne: Cambridge University Press.

Manderville, B. (1970) *Fable of the Bees.* Harmondsworth: Penguin.

Manisali, E. (2001) *Yirmibirinci Yüzyilda Küresel Kiskaç: Küreselleşme, Ulus Devlet Ve Türkiye* (Global Jam in the Twenty-first Century: Globalization, Nation-state and Turkey). Istanbul: Otopsi.

Manisali, E. (2002) *Türkiye-Avrupa Ilişkilerinde "Sessiz Darbe"* ("Silent Coup" in Turkey–Europe Relations). İstanbul: Derin Yayinlari.

Marx, K. (1972) *On Colonialism.* New York: International Publishers.

Marx, K. (1973) Grundrisse. Trans. Martin Nicolaus. New York: Vintage.

———(1976) *Capital, Vol. 1.* Trans. Ben Fowkes. London: Penguin Books.

———(1977) *Capital: A Critique of Political Economy.* Ed. Maurice Dobb. Trans. S.W. Ryazanskaya. New York: International Publishers.

———(1988) *Economic and Philosophic Manuscripts of 1844.* In Quintinh Hoare (ed.), *Early Writings,* Trans. R. Livingstone and G. Benton. London: Penguin.

———(1991) *Capital, Vol. 3.* Harmondsworth, Middlesex: Penguin.

———Economic Manuscripts of 1861–63. http://www.marxists.org/archive/marx/works/1861/economic/ch15.htm. Accessed May 21, 2004.

Marx, K. and F. Engels (1976) *The German Ideology.* Moscow: Progress Publishers.

Menegou, N. (2000) "Oi xenoi ergates ke oi dihasmenes sinidisis" ("Foreign Workers and Divided Consciousness"), *Spartacus* 55: 22–34.

Mies, M. (1986) *Patriarchy and Accumulation on a World Scale Women in the International Division of Labour.* London and New York: Zed Press.

——— (1998) *Patriarchy and Accumulation on a World Scale Women in the International Division of Labour.* London and New York: Zed Press.

Mies, M., Bennholdt-Thomsen, V.A and C. von Werlhof (1988) *Women, the Last Colony.* London: Atlantic Highlands, NJ, USA: Zed Books.

Miles, A. (2003) "Prostitution, Trafficking and the Global Sex Industry: A Conversation with Janice Raymond." *Canadian Woman Studies* 22:3(4): 26–37.

Miliband, R. and L. Panitch (eds.) (1992) *New World Order? Socialist Register.* New York: Monthly Review Press.

Mills, C. (1997) *The Racial Contract.* Ithaca: Cornell University Press.

Ministry of National Economy (1998). Athens: Greece.

——— (1999). Athens: Greece.

——— July (2002). Athens. Greece.

Mittleman, J.H. (2000) *The Globalization Syndrome.* Princeton, NJ: Princeton University Press.

Moghadam, V. (1999) "Gender and Globalization: Female Labor and Women's Mobilization." *Journal of World-Systems Research* 5(2): 367–388.

——— (2001) *Conflict, Peace, and Feminist Alternatives.* Talk delivered at the Institute of Social Studies, The Hague, May 30.

Mohanty, C.T. (1997) "Women Workers and Capitalist Scripts: Ideologies of Domination, Common Interests, and the Politics of Solidarity." In M.J. Alexander and M.C. Talpade (eds.), *Feminist Genealogies, Colonial Legacies, Democratic Futures.* London and New York: Routledge.

——— (2003) *Feminism Without Borders: Decolonizing Theory, Practicing Solidarity.* Durham and London: Duke University Press.

Morokvasic, M. and A. de Tinguy (1993) "Between East and West: A New Migratory Space." In Hedwig Rudolph and Mirjana Morkvasic (eds.), *Bridging States and Markets: International Migration in the Early 1990s.* Berlin: WZB.

Mueller, J. (1989) *Retreat from Doomsday: The Obsolescence of Major War.* New York: Basic Books.

Müftüler-Bac, M. (1998) "The Never-Ending Story: Turkey and the European Union." *Middle Eastern Studies* 34(4): 240–258.

———, "Turkey's Candidacy to the European Union, The Role of Security Considerations," *Security Dialogue,* vol. 32, pp. 379–382 (2001).

Munoz, A. and A. Woods (2000) "Marxism and the Emancipation of Women." In *Defence of Marxism,* March 3, http://www.marxist.com/Theory/marxism_and_women.html.

Murray, Alison (1998) "Debt-Bondage and Trafficking: Don't Believe the Hype." In Kempadoo and Doezema (eds.), *Global Sex Workers,* pp. 51–64.

Nagle, J. (ed.) (1997) *Whores and Other Feminists.* New York: Routledge.

Narli, N.A. (2002) "Human Smuggling and Migration of Illegal Labour To Turkey." Istanbul: Marmara University.

National Action Plan for Employment (1999) Athens, Greece: Ministry of Labor.

Niblock, T. (1996) "North-South Socio Economic Relations within the Mediterranean." In R. Aliboni, G. Joffee, and T. Niblock (eds.), *Security Challenges in the Mediterranean Region*, pp. 115–136. London: Franck Cass.

Nilüfern, N., A. Türkmen, S. Ekrem, and M. Çoban (2002) "Transit Migration and Human Smuggling in Turkey: Preliminary Findings from the Field Work." http://www.ucansupurge.org/newhtml/english/links/movementarchive/transitmigration.php. Accessed January 2003.

Non-Aligned Women's Movement (1995) "Forced Prostitution of Immigrant and Refugees Women." In *Europoean Forum of Left Feminists, Greek Branch, Nationalism, Racism, and Social Sex*. Thessaloniki: Paratiritis.

———(1999a) "Silence is a Partnership to the Crime of Sexual Exploitation of Women." June. Thessaloniki: Paratiritis.

Non-Aligned Women's Movement (1999b) "Survey on the Forced Prostitution of Foreign Women." Athens.

O'Brien, M. (1981) *The Politics of Reproduction*. New York: Routledge & Kegan Paul.

O'Connell Davidson, J. (2001) "The Sex Tourist, the Expatriate, His Ex-Wife and Her "Other": The Politics of Loss, Difference, and Desire." *Sexualities* 4(1): 5–24.

———(2002) "The Rights and Wrongs of Prostitution." *Hypatia* 17(2): 84–98.

O'Connell Davidson, J. and Jacqueline Sanchez Taylor (1999) "Fantasy Islands: Exploring the Demand for Sex Tourism." In Kamala Kempadoo (ed.), *Sun, Sex and Gold: Tourism and Sex Work in the Caribbean*, pp. 37–54. Boulder: Rowman and Littlefield.

OECD (2001) "Enhancing Regulatory Reform: Regulatory Reform in Greece: Enhancing Market Openness through Regulatory Reform" *Organization for Economic Co-operation and Development*, OECD, 2001. http://www.oecd.org/dataoecd/23/02756295.pdf. Accessed June 10, 2003.

O'Grady, R. (1992) *The Child and the Tourist*. Bangkok: ECPAT.

O'Neill, M. (2001) *Prostitution and Feminism: Towards a Politics of Feeling*. Cambridge: Polity.

Opperman, M. (ed.) (1997) *Pacific Rim Tourism*. New York: CAB International.

Organization of Development of Human Resources (1998). Athens: Greece.

Organisation for Economic Co-operation and Development, Economic Outlook (2001) *Developments in Individual OECD Countries: Greece – Statistical Data Included*. Paris. http://www.oecd.org/home/ (Accessed January 2004).

Organization for Security and Co-operation in Europe (2001) *Annual Report on OSCE Activities*. Europe. http://www.osce.org/docs/english/misc/anrep01e_activ.htm#00063

Özcan, G. (1998) *Doksanlarda Türkiye'nin Ulusal Güvenlik ve Dış Politikasinda Askeri Yapinin Artan Etkisi* (The Increasing Influence of the Military Structure on Turkey's National Security and Foreign Policies During the 1990s), in G. Özcan and Ş. Kut (eds.), *En Uzun Onyil: Türk*

Diş Politikasinda Doksanli Yillar (The Longest Decade: The Nineties in Turkish Foreign Policy), pp. 67–100. Istanbul: Boyut.

Pahl, R. (1984) *Divisions of Labour*. Oxford: Basil Blackwell.

Paolini, A.J. (1999) *Navigating Modernity: Postcolonialism, Identity, and International Relations*. Critical Perspectives on World Politics. Boulder London: Lynne Rienner Publishers.

Papandreou, V., July 29, 1999. Athens: Greece.

Paraskevopoulos, N. (2000a) "Neo-Conservatism, Sexual Life and Prostitution." *Eleftherotypia* 15 (March): 15.

———(2000b) "Prostitution's Protectors." *Eleftherotypia* 6 (December): 6.

Parrenas, R. (2001) *Servants of Globalization: Women, Migration, and Domestic Work*. CA: Stanford University Press.

Patel, G. "Sleight(s) of Hand in Mirror Houses." Paper delivered at conference Queer Theory on Location, New York University, April 1996.

Pateman, C. (1988) *The Sexual Contract*. Stanford, CA: Stanford University Press.

———(1996) "A Comment on Johnson's Does Capitalism Really Need Patriarchy?" *Women's Studies International Forum* 19 (1996): 203–205.

Perni, O. (2001) "Migration Flows, Societal Security and EU's Integration Process. The Spanish Case." Paper prepared for the International Conference "European Security in the XXI Century," Granada, November 5–9, pp. 1–39. Workshop 7. Europe Facing Migration Flows. http://www.ugr.es/-ceas. Accessed January 2004.

Persaud, R. (2002) "Situating Race in International Relations: the Dialectics of Civilizational Security in American Immigration." In G. Chowdhry and Sheila N. Power (eds.), *Postcolonialism and International Relations: Reading Race, Gender and Class*, pp. 56–81. London and New York: Routledge.

Peterson, V.S. (1996) "Shifting Ground(s): Epistemological and Territorial Remapping in the Context of Globalization(s)." In E. Kofman and G. Youngs (eds.), *Globalization*, pp. 11–28. London: Pinter.

———(2002) "Rewriting (Global) Political Economy as Reproductive, Productive, and Virtual (Foucauldian) Economies." *International Feminist Journal of Politics* 4(1): 1–30.

———(2003) *A Critical Rewriting of Global Political Economy: Integrating Reproductive, Productive, and Virtual Economies*. London and New York: Routledge (RIPE Series in Global Political Economy).

Petras, J. (1987) "Political Economy of State Terror: Chile, El Salvador, and Brazil" *Crime and Social Justice*, Nos. 27–28: 88–109.

Pettman, J. (1996) "An International Political Economy of Sex" in *Worlding Women*. Sydney: Allen & Unwin, pp. 185–207.

Picchio, A. (1992) *Social Reproduction: The Political Economy of the Labour Market*. Great Britain: Cambridge University Press.

Picchio, A. (1998) "Wages as a Reflection of Socially Embedded Production and Reproduction Processes." In L. Clarke, P.D. Gijsel, and J. Janssen (eds.), *The Dynamics of Wage Relations in the New Europe*, pp. 195–214. London: Kluwer.

Pigem, J. (2003) "The Altered Landscape" in *We Are Everywhere: the irresistible rise of global anticapitalism*. Notes From Nowhere (eds.) London and New York: Verso, pp. 408–412.

Poulatzas, N. (1973) *Political Power and Social Classes*. Trans. T. O'Hagan. London: New Left Books.

———(1980) *Fascism and Dictatorship*. London: Verso.

Pre-Accession Economic Programme of the Republic of Cyprus (2001).

Pre-Accession Economic Programme of the Republic of Cyprus (2002).

Pre-Accession Economic Programme Turkey (2001).

Psimmenos, I. (2000) "The Making of Periphractic Spaces: The Case of Albanian Undocumented Female Migrants in the Sex Industry in Athens." In F. Anthias and G. Lazaridis (eds.), *Gender and Migration in Southern Europe: Women on the Move*. London: Oxford University Press.

Rajalakshmi (2003) "Delinking prostitution from trafficking: A Look at India's Immoral Traffic Prevention Act, 1956" *Canadian Women Studies*, 22: (3/4) Spring/Summer: 110–113.

Razack, S. (1998) "Race, Space, and Prostitution: The Making of the Bourgeois Subject." *Canadian Journal of Women and the Law* 10(2): 338–376.

———(2000) "Gendered Racial Violence and Spatialized Justice: The Murder of Pamela George" *Canadian Journal of Law and Society/Revue canadienne droit et societe*, 15, 2: 91–130.

Reanda, L. (1991) "Prostitution as a Human Rights Question: Problems and Prospects of United Nations Action" *Human Rights Quarterly*, 13: 2–22

Reinhardt, J., Shamleh, O. and Christian Uhlig (1989) *Der Dienstleistungssektor ausgenwahlter Entiwicklungslander: entwicklungs-und handelspolitische Aspekte: Fallstudien Malaysia, Jordanien, Zimbabwe*. Munchen: Weltforum.

Ricardo, D. (1951) "On the Principles of Political Economy and Taxation." In P. Sraffa (ed.), *Works and Correspondence, Vol. I*. Cambridge: Cambridge University Press.

———(1951) "Absolute Value and Exchangeable Value." In P. Sraffa (ed.), *Works and Correspondence, Vol. I*. Cambridge: Cambridge University Press.

Ricardo, D. (1955) *Works*. Cambridge: Cambridge University Press.

Robertson, R. (1992) *Globalization: Social Theory and Global Culture*. London and Thousand Oaks, California: Sage.

Robinson, W.I. (1998) "Capitalist Globalization and the Transnationalization of the State." For Presentation at the Transatlantic Workshop, "Historical Materialism and Globalization," University of Warwick, April 15–17, 1998.

———(2002) "Capitalist Globalization and the Transnationalization of the State" in M. Rupert and H. Smith (eds.), *Historical Materialism and Globalization*. London: Routledge.

Rogowski, R. (1998) *Commerce and Coalitions*. Princeton: Princeton University Press.

———(1998) "Commentary on Migration as International Trade." In Christopher Rudolph (ed.), *Reconsidering Immigration in an Integrating World, UCLA Journal of International Law and Foreign Affairs* 3(2): 415–418, special issue.

RohatynskyJ, M.A. "Individual agency, the traffic in women and layered hegemonies in Ukraine" *Canadian Woman Studies,* 22(3/4): 160–165.

Rosca, N. (1995) "The Philippines' Shameful Export." *The Nation* 17 (April): 522–527.

Roubani, N., Rena Mihalitsis, and Laura Loli (2000) A Perspective on the Women's Status in Greece. Report: The European Network of Women-Greece prepared this report for Greek Helsinki Monitor in the framework of IHF Royaumont Project. Athens.

Roumeliotou, A. and H. Kornarou (1996) *Country Report of Greece.* Athens School of Public Health Department of Epidemiology and Medical Statistics.

Roumeliotou, A. and H. Kornarou (1997) "HIV Infection and Mobility. The Problem of Prostitution in Greece." Athens: Greece.

Rousseau, G.S. and Roy Porter (eds.) (1990) *Exoticism in the Enlightenment.* Manchester: Manchester University Press.

Rubin, G. (1975). "The Traffic in Women: Notes on the 'Political Economy' of Sex." In R. Reiter (ed.), *Toward an Anthropology of Women.* New York: Monthly Review.

Rudolph, C. (2002) "Security and the Political Economy of International Migration." University of Southern California.

——(2002) "Globalization and Security: Migration and Evolving Conceptions of Security in Statecraft and Scholarship." Center for International Studies, University of Southern California, Los Angeles.

Rupert, M. (1995) *Producing Hegemony.* London: Cambridge University Press.

——(2000) *Ideologies of Globalization Contending Visions of a New World Order.* New York and London: Routledge.

——(2002) "Class Powers and Politics of Global Governance." Paper presented for conference on *Power and Global Governance,* Madison, Wisconsin, April 19–21, 2002.

Sahay, A. (2001) "(Corporate) Transnationalism and *Red* Internationalism: Globality and Class Struggle Today." *Red Critique* (Spring, 2001): 1–9.

Salazar, P.R. (2001) *Servants of Globalization: Women, Migration, and Domestic Work.* Stanford, California: Stanford University Press.

Salt, J. (2000) "Trafficking and human smuggling: a European perspective," *International Migration,* 38 (3), 31–56.

Sassen, S. (1996) *Losing Control? Sovereignty in an Age of Globalization.* New York: Columbia University Press.

Savigliano, M.E. (1995) *Tango and the Political Economy of Passion.* Boulder, SanFrancisco, Oxford: Westview Press.

Scholte, J.A. (2001) "Civil Society and Democracy in Global Governance." CSGR Working Paper No. 65/01. Centre for the Study of Globalization and Regionalisation. United Kingdom: University of Warwick.

Scott, J. (1995) "Sexual and National Boundaries in Tourism." *Annals of Tourism Research* 22(Fall): 385–403.

Shrage, L. (1994) *Moral Dilemmas of Feminism.* London: Routledge.

Singh, J. (2001) "India, the WTO and Capitalist Globalization." *Alternative Press Review* 5(1), http://www.altpr.org/apr12/india.html. Accessed October 2002.

Sitaropoulos, N. (1992) "The New Legal Framework of Alien Immigration in Greece: A Draconian Contribution to Europe's Unification." *Immigration and Nationality Law & Practice*, 6: 89–96.

———. (2003) *Immigration Law and Management in Greece*. Athens, Ant. N. Sakkoulas Publishers.

Smith, A. (2002) "Better Dead than Pregnant: The Colonization of Native Women's Reproductive Health." In J. Silliman and A. Bhattacharjee (eds.), *Policing the National Body: Race, Gender, and Criminalization*. Cambridge, Massachusetts: South End Press.

Smith, S. (2004) "Singing Our World into Existence: International Relations Theory and September 11: Presidential Address to the International Studies Association, February 27, 2003, Portland, OR" *International Studies Quarterly*, September 2004, vol. 48 (3): 499–515.

Snyder, J. (1991) *Myths of Empire*. Ithaca: Cornell University Press.

Solow, R.M. (1990) *The Labour Market as a Social Institution*. Oxford: Basil Blackwell.

Standing, G. (1989) "Global Feminization through Flexible Labor." *World Development* 17(7): 1077–1095.

Stoler, A.L. (1995) *Race and the Education of Desire: Foucault's History of Sexuality and the Colonial Order of Things*. Durham: Duke University Press. *Sun-Star Daily*, August 26, 1993.

Stoler, A.L. (2002) *Carnal Knowledge and Imperial Power:Race and the Intimate in Colonial Rule*. Berkeley: University of California Press.

Strange, S. (1994) "Wake Up, Krasner! The World has Changed." *Review of International Political Economy* 1(2): 209–219.

Straubhaar, J. (1997) Distinguishing the Global, Regional and National Levels of World Television. In A. Sreberny-Mohammadi, D. Winseck, J. McKenna, and O. Boyd-Barrett (eds.), *Media in Global Context: A Reader,* pp. 284–298. New York: St. Martin's.

Straubhaar, T. Klaus, F. Zimmermann (1992) *Towards a European Migration Policy*. Great Britain: Centre for Economic Policy Research.

Tocci, N. J. H., Barkey, N. Houltchenko, H. Baggi, and Saban Kardas (2003) "Turkey's Strategic Future." *The International Institute for Strategic Studies*, United Kingdom: Centre for European Policy Studies, ESF Working Paper, 13, May, pp. 1–48.

Trends in International Migration, SOPEMI, 2001.

Trepanier, M. (2003) "Trafficking in women for purposes of sexual exploitation: a matter of consent?" *Canadian Woman Studies*, 22 (3/4): 48–54

Trimikliniotis, N. (1999) "Racism and New Migration to Cyprus: The Racialisation of Migrant Workers." In Floya Anthias and Gabriella Lazaridis (eds.) *Into the Margins: Migration and Exclusion in Southern Europe*. UK and United States: Ashgate.

Tsardanidis, C. and Stefano Guerra (2000) "The EU Mediterranean States, the Migration Issue and the 'Threat' from the South." In R. King, G. Lazaridis, and Charalambos Tsardanidis (eds.), *Eldorado or Fortress? Migration in Southern Europe*, pp. 321–344. Great Britain: MacMillan Press Ltd.

Tsingris, A.A. (1997) *Female Trade and Sexual Exploitation: The Results of a Research.* Athens: Sakkoula (in Greek).

Tsoukalas, S. (1992) *Exartisi ke anaparagogi.* (Dependence and Reproduction) Athens: Themelio.

Tumino, S. (2002) "Contesting the Empire-al Imaginary: The Truth of Democracy as Class." In *Red Critique*, 4 (May and June). http://www.geocities.com/redtheory/redcritique/MayJune02/contestingtheempire-alimaginary.htm. Accessed July 2002.

Turkey Country Report (2002) *Country Report on Human Rights Practices.* Released by the Bureau of Democracy, Human Rights, and Labor. U.S. Department of State. http://www.state.gov/g/drl/rls/hrrpt/2002/18396.htm. Accessed January 2003.

Valencia, D. (1995) "The Situation of Filippinas in Greece—a Woman from the Philippines Tells," In S. Vovou, L. Mpompolou, and E. Pambouki (eds.), *Nationalism, Racism, Social Gender, and Papers of a Two Day Meeting of Women* in 11-12-/11/94, European Forum of Left Feminists-Greek Branch. pp. 79–83. Thesalonika: Paratiritis.

Ventura, L. (1993) "Female Migration: Birth and Development of the Scientific Interest." *Dini*, 6, May (in Greek).

Ucarer, E.M. (1999) *Trafficking in Women, the European Union, and Nongovernmental Organizations.* Paper Presented at the International Studies Association, Washington, DC, February 16–20.

U.S. Department of State to the U.S. Congress (1999) *Human Rights and Labor: The Country Reports on Human Rights Practices.* Cyprus, Greece, and Turkey. http://www.state.gov/g/drl/rls/hrrpt/1999/ (Accessed February 2003).

U.S. Department of State Publication 11057, Office of the Under Secretary For Global Affairs (June 2003) *Trafficking in Persons Report, Trafficking Victims Protection Act of 2000.* http://www.state.gov/g/tip/rls/tiprpt/2003/. Accessed May 2003.

U.S. Department of State Publication 11057, Office of the Under Secretary For Global Affairs (2004) *Victims of Trafficking and Violence Protection Act of 2000: Trafficking in Persons Report* (2004). http://www.state.gov/g/tip/rls/tiprpt/2004/. Accessed May 2004.

U.S. Department of State (2001) *Country Reports on Human Rights Practices.* http://www.state.gov/g/drl/rls/hrrpt/2001/ (Accessed January 2003).

Ugur, M. (2003) *AB Hangi Kosullarda Yararli Olabilir?* (Under What Conditions Could the EU be Beneficial?) Gorus, January 42–51.

Walkowitz, J. (1980) *Prostitution and Victorian Society: Women, Class, and the State.* Cambridge: Cambridge University Press.

206   Bibliography

Wallerstein, I. (1979) "Class Conflict in the Capitalist World-Economy," In *The Capitalist World-Economy*, pp. 283–293. Cambridge: Cambridge University Press.

Webster, F. (1995) *Theories of Information Society*. London and New York: Routledge.

Weiner, M. and Sharon Stanton Russell (eds.) (2001) *Demography and National Security*. New York: Berghahn Books.

Werlhof, C. (1988) "Investment in the Poor: An Analysis of World Bank Policy." In M. Mies, V. Bennholdt-Thomsen, and C. von Werlhof (eds.), *Women, the Last Colony*. London: Atlantic Highlands, NJ, USA: Zed Books.

Wong, K. (2001) "The Showdown before Seattle: Race, Class and the Framing of a Movement." In E. Yuen, G. Katsiaficas, and D. Rose (eds.), *The Battle for Seattle: The New Challenge to Capitalist Globalization*. New York: Soft Skull Press.

Wood, C.H. (1982) *International Migration and International Trade*. World Bank Discussion Papers/160, Washington: World Bank.

Xletsos, M. (2001) "I Politiki Economia tis Metanastefsis (The Political Economy of Migration)." In X. Naxakis and M. Xletsos (eds.), *Metanastes ke Metanastefsi: Economikes, Politikes Ptyhes (Migrants and Migration: Economic, Political Aspects)*, pp. 17–42. Athens: Patakis.

Yilmaz, B. (2003) "Turkey's Competitiveness in the European Union: A Comparison with Five Candidate Countries-Bulgaria, the Czech Republic, Hungary, Poland, Romania-and the EU15" Ezoneplus Working Paper No. 12: The Eastward Enlargement of the Eurozone Research Project HPSE-CT-2001-00084 Fifth Framework Programme 2001–2004 European Commission, pp. 2–20. www.ezoneplus.org. Accessed January 2004.

Young, R. (1995) *White Mythologies*. London: Routledge.

———(1995) *Colonial Desire*. London: Routledge.

Youngs, G. (1996) "Dangers of Discourse: The Case of Globalization," In E. Kofman and Gillian Youngs (eds.), pp. 58–71. London: Pinter.

Yuen, E., G. Katsiaficas, and D. Rose (eds.) (2001) *The Battle for Seattle: The New Challenge to Capitalist Globalization*. New York: Soft Skull Press.

Zapatistas (1998) *Documents from the 1996 Encounter for Humanity and Against Neoliberalism*. New York: Seven Stories Press.

Zatz, Noah D. (1997). Sex Work/Sex Act: Law, Labor, and Desire in Constructions of Prostitution. Signs: *Journal of Women in Culture and Society*, 22(2):276–308.

Zenios, K. (2002) "The Cypriot Society on the Divan." *Man to Man*. pp. 63–67.

Zissi, M. (2001) "Prostitution and the client. Accomplices, Participants in Violence." *Eleftherotypia*, 106, April 3.

Zographos, A. (1991) "I katastasi ton tritokosmikon ergaton stin Ellada (The Condition of Third World Workers in Greece)" *Kinoniki Ergasia*, 23: 165–184.

INDEX

Printed in the United States
96627LV00001BA/178-183/A

9 780312 294663